2016

ALMANAC

FOR kids

SCHOLASTIC INC.

Scholastic Almanac for Kids 2016 is produced by J.A. Ball Associates, LLC, 4815 California Ave. SW, Suite 603, Seattle, WA 98116.

President: Jacqueline A. Ball
Design Director: Ron Leighton
Writers: Jacqueline A. Ball, Delia Greve, Mark Sparacio
Editor: Lelia W. Mander

Library of Congress Cataloging-in-Publication Data available

ISBN 978-0-545-82625-9

10 9 8 7 6 5 4 3 2 1   15 16 17 18 19

Printed in the U.S.A.   40
First edition, September 2015

Cover design by David DeWitt

Due to the publication date, statistics are current as of May 2015.

CONTENTS

POP CULTURE PAGE 8

CELEBRATE! PAGE 38

OUR WORLD 2016 PAGE 56

SCIENCE & TECHNOLOGY

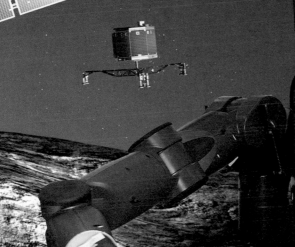

NATURE

PAGE 144

HISTORY

GEOGRAPHY

POP CULTURE

The best songs and top performers of the year. Taylor, Beyoncé and Jay Z, Pharrell, and more. See page 10.

Emmys and Kids' and Teen Choice Award Winners. Zombies. *The Voice*! See page 16.

Oscars, Golden Globes. Cool stuff about Star Wars. See page 22.

Award winners and top-selling books. Which ones have you read? Plus, books being made into movies in 2016. See page 28.

Minecraft and other video games. The best free app games of 2014. See page 32.

Pharrell Williams

Top 10 Songs of 2014

Song	Artist
"Happy"	Pharrell Williams
"Dark Horse"	Katy Perry featuring Juicy J
"All of Me"	John Legend
"Fancy"	Iggy Azalea featuring Charli XCX
"Counting Stars"	OneRepublic
"Talk Dirty"	Jason Derulo featuring 2 Chainz
"Rude"	MAGIC!
"All About That Bass"	Meghan Trainor
"Problem"	Ariana Grande featuring Iggy Azalea
"Stay with Me"	Sam Smith

Taylor Swift is as generous as she is talented. In 2014 she donated $50,000 to the public schools in New York City, where she is a global welcome ambassador. She also donated almost $2,000 to help a fan pay her student loans.

Taylor Swift

Top 10 Albums of 2014

Album	Artist
Frozen Soundtrack	(Various)
Beyoncé	Beyoncé
1989	Taylor Swift
Midnight Memories	One Direction
The Marshall Mathers LP 2	Eminem
Pure Heroine	Lorde
Crash My Party	Luke Bryan
Prism	Katy Perry
Blame It All on My Roots: Five Decades of Influences	Garth Brooks
Here's to the Good Times	Florida Georgia Line

2015 Grammy Award Winners

Sam Smith's "Stay with Me" was a big winner at the 2015 Grammy Awards.

Record of the Year: "Stay with Me (Darkchild Version)," Sam Smith

Album of the Year: *Morning Phase,* Beck

Song of the Year: "Stay With Me," Sam Smith

Best New Artist: Sam Smith

Best Rap Album: *The Marshall Mathers LP 2,* Eminem

Best Rap Song: "I," K. Duckworth & C. Smith, songwriters (Kendrick Lamar)

Best R & B Album: *Love, Marriage & Divorce,* Toni Braxton & Babyface

Best Rock Album: *Morning Phase,* Beck

Best Rock Song: "Ain't It Fun," Hayley Williams & Taylor York, songwriters (Paramore)

Beck won for Album of the Year over Beyoncé, Pharrell Williams, Ed Sheeran, and Sam Smith. With a total of 52 Grammy nominations, Beyoncé is the most nominated woman in Grammy history.

Beyoncé Jay Z & Blue Ivy

Best R & B Song: "Drunk in Love," Shawn Carter, Rasool Diaz, Noel Fisher, Jerome Harmon, Beyoncé Knowles, Timothy Mosely, Andre Eric Proctor, Brian Soko, songwriters (Beyoncé featuring Jay Z)

Best Alternative Music Album: *St. Vincent*, St. Vincent

Best Pop Vocal Album: *In the Lonely Hour,* Sam Smith

Best Country Song: "I'm Not Gonna Miss You," Glen Campbell & Julian Raymond, songwriters (Glen Campbell)

Music

Dan Reynolds shows why Imagine Dragons was voted the year's Best Rock Group.

2014 Teen Choice Awards

Rock Song: "Pompeii," Bastille

Rock Group: Imagine Dragons

R & B/Hip-Hop Song: "Fancy," Iggy Azalea featuring Charli XCX

R & B/Hip-Hop Artist: Iggy Azalea

Love Song: "You & I," One Direction

Breakout Artist: Austin Mahone

Female Artist: Ariana Grande

Male Artist: Ed Sheeran

Group: One Direction

Single, Female: "Problem," Ariana Grande featuring Iggy Azalea

Single, Male: "Sing," Ed Sheeran

Can you guess the music stars behind these real names?
(Answers below)

- Ella Yelich-O'Connor
- Alecia Moore
- Paul Hewson
- Katheryn Elizabeth Hudson
- Stefani Germanotta
- Amethyst Amelia Kelly

Lorde, Pink, Bono, Katy Perry, Lady Gaga, Iggy Azalea

All-female favorite new group Fifth Harmony performed at the White House on April 6, 2015, for the annual Easter Egg Roll. The group sang a special version of "Happy Birthday" to the First Lady's five-year-old Let's Move! program.

2015 Nickelodeon Kids' Choice Awards Music Winners

Favorite Music Group: One Direction
Favorite Song: "Bang Bang," Jessie J, Ariana Grande, Nicki Minaj
Favorite Male Singer: Nick Jonas
Favorite Female Singer: Selena Gomez
Favorite New Artist: Fifth Harmony

Television

Most Watched Broadcast Entertainment Shows of 2014

NCIS
The Big Bang Theory
NCIS: New Orleans
NCIS: Los Angeles
The Walking Dead
Dancing with the Stars
Madam Secretary
The Voice
Blue Bloods

THE WALK

Zombies have become so popular that there is a World Zombie Day, where people dress up and walk—or lurch—like the dead. A zombie "crawl" in October 2014 brought 30,000 participants staggering to the Twin Cities of Minneapolis–Saint Paul, MN.

2014 Emmy Award Winners

Outstanding Series, Drama: *Breaking Bad*

Outstanding Series, Comedy: *Modern Family*

Outstanding Reality Program, Competition: *The Amazing Race*

Outstanding Actor, Drama: Bryan Cranston, *Breaking Bad*

Outstanding Actress, Drama: Julianna Margulies, *The Good Wife*

Outstanding Actor, Comedy: Jim Parsons, *The Big Bang Theory*

Outstanding Actress, Comedy: Julia Louis-Dreyfus, *Veep*

Outstanding Supporting Actor, Drama: Aaron Paul, *Breaking Bad*

Outstanding Supporting Actress, Drama: Anna Gunn, *Breaking Bad*

Outstanding Supporting Actor, Comedy: Ty Burrell, *Modern Family*

Outstanding Supporting Actress, Comedy: Allison Janney, *Mom*

A living woman is transformed into the living dead by a makeup artist at Walker Stalker Con, a convention based on *The Walking Dead*. A tip: Use red and yellow powdered food coloring and mix it with corn syrup to create fake blood. Liquid food coloring stains.

Television

The Nickelodeon Kids' Choice Awards give out balloons and blimps to favorite personalities in TV, Movies, Music, and other categories, and cover hosts and guests with green slime. Vote for 2016 winners at Nickelodeon.com.

2015 Nickelodeon Kids' Choice Awards TV Winners

Favorite TV Show: *Austin & Ally*

Favorite Family Show: *Modern Family*

Favorite Reality Show: *Dance Moms*

Favorite Talent Competition Show: *The Voice*

Favorite TV Actor: Ross Lynch, *Austin & Ally*

Favorite TV Actress: Laura Marano, *Austin & Ally*

Favorite Cartoon: *SpongeBob SquarePants*

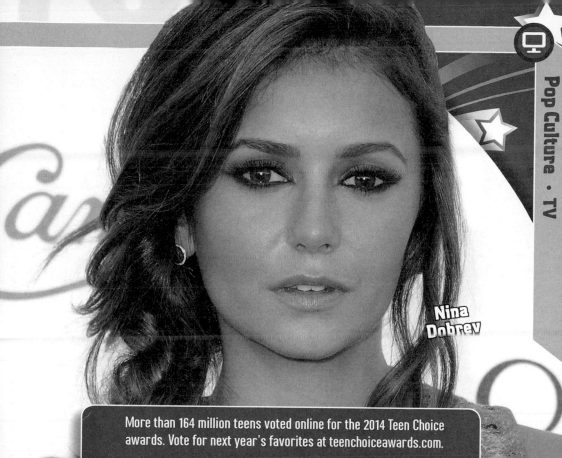

Nina Dobrev

More than 164 million teens voted online for the 2014 Teen Choice awards. Vote for next year's favorites at teenchoiceawards.com.

2014 Teen Choice Awards TV Winners

Animated Show: *The Simpsons*

Comedy: *The Big Bang Theory*

Actor, Comedy: Ross Lynch, *Austin & Ally*

Actress, Comedy: Lea Michele, *Glee*

Drama: *Pretty Little Liars*

Actor, Drama: Ian Harding, *Pretty Little Liars*

Actress, Drama: Lucy Hale, *Pretty Little Liars*

Fantasy/Sci-Fi: *The Vampire Diaries*

Actor, Sci-Fi/Fantasy: Ian Somerhalder, *The Vampire Diaries*

Actress, Sci-Fi/Fantasy: Nina Dobrev, *The Vampire Diaries*

Reality Show: *Keeping Up with the Kardashians*

Reality Competition: *The Voice*

Male, Reality: Adam Levine, *The Voice*

Female, Reality: Shakira, *The Voice*

Villain: Dylan O'Brien, *Teen Wolf*

the Voice

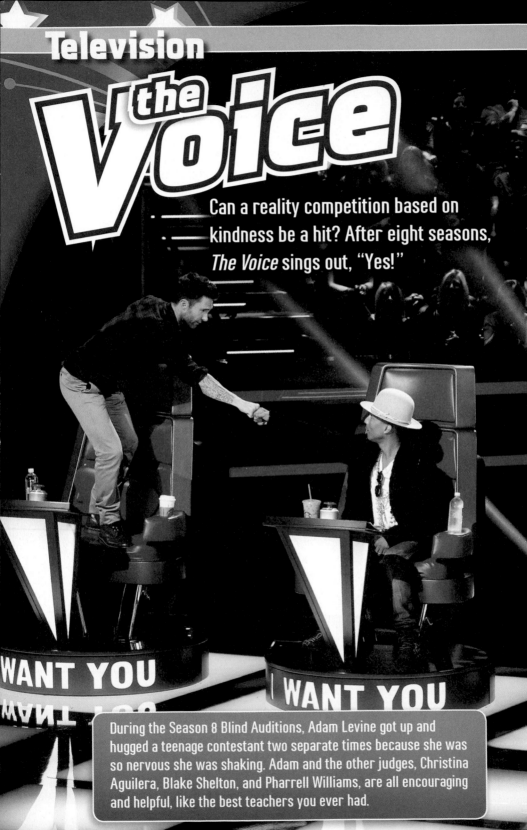

Can a reality competition based on kindness be a hit? After eight seasons, *The Voice* sings out, "Yes!"

WANT YOU

WANT YOU

During the Season 8 Blind Auditions, Adam Levine got up and hugged a teenage contestant two separate times because she was so nervous she was shaking. Adam and the other judges, Christina Aguilera, Blake Shelton, and Pharrell Williams, are all encouraging and helpful, like the best teachers you ever had.

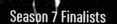

Season 7 Finalists

Runner-up: Matt McAndrew	4th: Damien Lawson	3rd: Chris Jamison	Winner: Craig Wayne Boyd
Team Adam	Team Adam	Team Adam	Team Blake

Carson Daly is great at being a host. He should be! He's had lots of practice. He had his own late-night show and has hosted *New Year's Eve with Carson Daly* since 2003. His kids and Christina's daughter, Summer Rain, sometimes share a nursery on the set.

10 Top-Grossing Movies of 2014

Movie	Box-Office Receipts
1. The Hunger Games: Mockingjay—Part I	$336,410,376
2. Guardians of the Galaxy	336,176,600
3. American Sniper	320,009,625
4. Captain America: The Winter Soldier	259,766,572
5. The LEGO Movie	257,760,692
6. The Hobbit: The Battle of the Five Armies	253,949,155
7. Transformers: Age of Extinction	245,439,076
8. Maleficent	241,410,378
9. X-Men: Days of Future Past	233,921,534
10. Big Hero 6	220,212,093

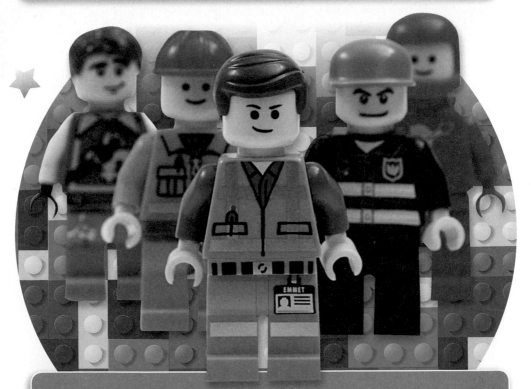

According to the producer of *The LEGO Movie*, there were 3,863,484 different LEGO bricks used in the film. But it would take 15,080,330 LEGO bricks to recreate the scenes in real life. Filmmakers used computer software to make virtual bricks.

2015 Teen Choice Awards Movie Winners

Action: *Divergent*

Actor, Action: Theo James, *Divergent*

Actress, Action: Shailene Woodley, *Divergent*

Comedy: *The Other Woman*

Actor, Comedy: Kevin Hart, *Ride Along*

Actress, Comedy: Emma Roberts, *We're the Millers*

Drama: *The Fault in Our Stars*

Actor, Drama: Ansel Elgort, *The Fault in Our Stars*

Actress, Drama: Shailene Woodley, *The Fault in Our Stars*

Sci-Fi/Fantasy: *The Hunger Games: Catching Fire*

Actor, Sci-Fi/Fantasy: Josh Hutcherson, *The Hunger Games: Catching Fire*

Actress, Sci-Fi/Fantasy: Jennifer Lawrence, *The Hunger Games: Catching Fire*
and *X-Men: Days of Future Past*

Breakout Star: Ansel Elgort, *Divergent* and *The Fault in Our Stars*

Villain: Donald Sutherland, *The Hunger Games: Catching Fire*

Shailene
Woodley

Theo
James

2014 Golden Globe Winners

Best Picture, Drama: *Boyhood*

Best Actor, Drama: Eddie Redmayne, *The Theory of Everything*

Best Actress, Drama: Julianne Moore, *Still Alice*

Best Picture, Comedy or Musical: *The Grand Budapest Hotel*

Best Actor, Comedy or Musical: Michael Keaton, *Birdman: Or (The Unexpected Virtue of Ignorance)*

Best Actress, Comedy or Musical: Amy Adams, *Big Eyes*

Best Director: Richard Linklater, *Boyhood*

Best Supporting Actor: J.K. Simmons, *Whiplash*

Best Supporting Actress: Patricia Arquette, *Boyhood*

Best Animated Film: *How to Train Your Dragon 2*

Best Foreign Film: *Leviathan* (Russia)

Best Screenplay: Alejandro G. Iñárritu, Nicolás Giacobone, Alexander Dinelaris, Jr. & Armando Bo: *Birdman: Or (The Unexpected Virtue of Ignorance)*

2015 Nickelodeon Kids' Choice Awards Movie Winners

Favorite Movie: *The Hunger Games: Mockingjay—Part 1*

Favorite Movie Actor: Ben Stiller

Favorite Movie Actress: Emma Stone

Favorite Male Action Star: Liam Hemsworth

Favorite Female Action Star: Jennifer Lawrence

Favorite Movie Villain: Angelina Jolie, *Maleficent*

Favorite Animated Movie: *Big Hero 6*

Angelina Jolie brought daughters Zahara (l) and Shiloh (r) to the show to help celebrate her win as Favorite Villain for her role in *Maleficent*. Zahara had a part in the movie, too.

2015 Oscar Winners

Best Picture: *Birdman: Or (The Unexpected Virtue of Ignorance)*

Best Director: Alejandro G. Iñárritu, *Birdman: Or (The Unexpected Virtue of Ignorance)*

Best Actor: Eddie Redmayne, *The Theory of Everything*

Best Supporting Actor: J.K. Simmons, *Whiplash*

Best Actress: Julianne Moore, *Still Alice*

Best Supporting Actress: Patricia Arquette, *Boyhood*

Best Animated Film: *Big Hero 6*

Best Foreign Film: *Ida* (Poland)

Best Original Screenplay: Alejandro G. Iñárritu, Nicolás Giacobone, Alexander Dinelaris, Jr. & Armando Bo: *Birdman: Or (the Unexpected Virtue of Ignorance)*

Best Adapted Screenplay: Graham Moore, *The Imitation Game*

Best Original Song: "Glory," from *Selma*

J.K. Simmons

Patricia Arquette

Julianne Moore

Eddie Redmayne

The Force Awakens

When the first Star Wars movie came out in 1977, one director called it "the worst movie ever." Even its creator, George Lucas, thought it would be a huge flop. Wrong! That movie, and the next five, have earned close to $5 billion. Now *Star Wars: Episode VII—The Force Awakens* is scheduled to be in theaters December 18, 2015. Another will come out in 2017 and a third in 2019. Meanwhile, the early movies are available for purchase online. If you watch, be aware of the behind-the-scenes secrets revealed here.

Ten Star Wars Secrets

1 Luke Skywalker was originally named Luke Starkiller.

2 Most of the Storm Troopers are left-handed, because of the way the weapons are made.

3 In *The Empire Strikes Back*, the third asteroid Han Solo dodges in the *Millennium Falcon* is actually a potato.

4 "Yoda" is the Sanskrit word for "warrior." The puppet's looks were partly modeled on Albert Einstein.

5 Yoda has a first name! It's Minch. George Lucas decided not to use the name in the films to keep the character mysterious.

Star Wars Movies

▷ *Episode IV: A New Hope,* 1977

▷ *Episode V: The Empire Strikes Back,* 1980

▷ *Episode VI: Return of the Jedi,* 1983

▷ *Episode I: The Phantom Menace,* 1999

▷ *Episode II: Attack of the Clones,* 2002

▷ *Episode III: Revenge of the Sith,* 2005

In *A New Hope:*

6 The sound of Darth Vader crushing the neck of Captain Antilles in the first movie was made by cracking walnut shells.

7 Mark Hamill held his breath for so long during the trash compactor scene that he broke a blood vessel in his face. In later scenes, only one side of his face is showing.

8 The escape pod for C-3PO and R2-D2 was made from two paint buckets.

9 The C-3PO costume was so stiff that actor Anthony Daniels couldn't bend at the waist in it. He had to sit down without the costume and let the crew build it around him.

10 A sound effects team banged ice cube trays together to make the rattling sound of C-3PO moving.

Academy Award-winning actress Lupita Nyong'o will play Maz Kanata, a pirate, in *The Force Awakens.* Her character was a closely guarded secret until May 2015.

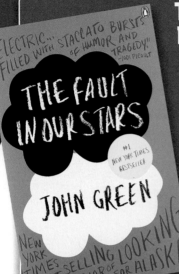

Top-Selling Kids and Young Adult Books of 2014

(Adapted from Nielsen BookScan)

Title	Author
The Fault in Our Stars	John Green
The Long Haul (Diary of a Wimpy Kid #9)	Jeff Kinney
Divergent	Veronica Roth
Insurgent	Veronica Roth
Allegiant	Veronica Roth
Frozen	Victoria Saxon
If I Stay	Gayle Forman
Looking for Alaska	John Green
The Maze Runner	James Dashner
Frozen: Journey to the Ice Palace	Frank Berrios
Minecraft: Redstone Handbook	Scholastic
Minecraft: Essential Handbook	Scholastic
Four	Veronica Roth
Frozen: Big Snowman	Tish Rabe
Hard Luck (Diary of a Wimpy Kid #7)	Jeff Kinney
Paper Towns	John Green
Frozen: A Tale of Two Sisters	Melissa Lagonegro
Frozen: Troll Magic	Courtney Carbone

FUN FACT

The book *Frozen* sold more than 780,000 copies in 2014. Four other books based on the movie, including *Frozen: Journey to the Ice Palace*, were best sellers, too. The movie was the highest grossing animated film of all time and the movie soundtrack was the most downloaded album of 2014 on iTunes. Cool!

A Bookstore, not a "*Wimpy* World"

Jeff Kinney, author of the Wimpy Kid books, loves books. That's no surprise, but he loves them so much that he's opening a bookstore in Plainville, MA, the small town where he lives. He says people shouldn't expect his store to be a "*Wimpy* world." It will sell great books of all kinds, by lots of different authors. Jeff wants the store to be a place where kids and adults can come together as a community as well as find books.

FUN FACT

Wimpy Kid #10, *Old School*, will be published November 3, 2015. Catch up on all the Wimpy news at WimpyKid.com

Teens
Prefer Print

A survey of 13–17-year-olds in December 2014 by the Nielsen company says only 20% of teens buy ebooks. That surprised some experts, because teens are so tech savvy. However, even if teens prefer to read print, many hear about new books online, through reviews or friends' posts on Facebook and Twitter. The biggest reason to read a book: Liking other books by the same author.

Books

2015 Children's Book Award Winners

Caldecott Medal: : *The Adventures of Beekle: The Unimaginary Friend*, Dan Santat

Newbery Medal: *The Crossover*, Kwame Alexander

National Book Award, Young People's Literature:
Brown Girl Dreaming, Jacqueline Woodson

Printz Award: *I'll Give You the Sun*, Jandy Nelson

Coretta Scott King Book Award (Author):
Brown Girl Dreaming, Jacqueline Woodson

Coretta Scott King Book Award (Illustrator):
Firebird, Christopher Myers

Scott O'Dell Award for Historical Fiction:
Dash, Kirby Larson

Teen Choice Book of the Year: *Allegiant*, Veronica Roth

2015 Nickelodeon Kids' Choice Awards Book Winner

Favorite Book: Diary of a Wimpy Kid series

Harper Lee then and now

A sequel to the modern classic *To Kill a Mockingbird*, by Harper Lee, was scheduled for publication in July 2015. Ms. Lee wrote the manuscript around 60 years ago, but it was never published. The book is called *Go Set a Watchman*, and it shows Scout, the young heroine of *Mockingbird*, as an adult looking back. *To Kill a Mockingbird* won the Pulitzer Prize in 1961 and is one of the most popular books ever written. It has sold about 30 million copies.

YA Books Star on Screen

Some great movies have come from books young adults love, such as *The Hobbit* and *The Fault in Our Stars*. Four movies coming out in late 2015 and 2016 are also based on favorite YA books and stories, old and new. Release dates may change, so stay on the lookout.

Animator and filmmaker Tim Burton is directing the film adaptation of the book *Miss Peregrine's Home for Peculiar Children*. He has worked on over 30 films. Catch up on some of his other fantastic movies, *James and the Giant Peach*, *The Nightmare Before Christmas*, and *Alice in Wonderland*.

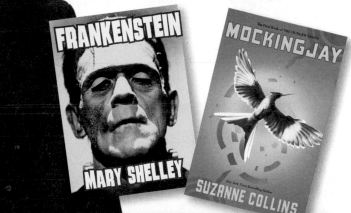

Movie	Book	Author	Release Date
Victor Frankenstein	Frankenstein	Mary Shelley	October 2, 2015 Starring Daniel Radcliffe
Mockingjay Part 2	Mockingjay	Suzanne Collins	November 20, 2015
Miss Peregrine's Home for Peculiar Children	Miss Peregrine's Home for Peculiar Children	Ransom Riggs	March 4, 2016 Directed by Tim Burton
Allegiant: Part 1	Allegiant	Veronica Roth	March 18, 2016

Top Paid iPhone Game Apps of 2014

The top paid iPhone app in 2014 was *Heads Up!*, in which players guess a word based on clues given by other players.

Heads Up!

Minecraft—Pocket Edition

Plague Inc.

Cut the Rope 2

Bloons Tower Defense 5

A Dark Room

ıll Carrier

1:37 PM

Top Paid iPad Game Apps for 2014

The most popular paid iPad app was *Minecraft—Pocket Edition*, which was also on the top iPhone app list. Since Minecraft came out in 2011 it has been updated more than 20 times.

Minecraft — Pocket Edition

Cut the Rope 2

Heads Up!

The Room Two

Survivalcraft

Notability

Terraria

Plants vs. Zombies HD

Hide N Seek: Mini Game With Worldwide Multiplayer

Card Wars—Adventure Time

10 Top Social Games Played on Facebook*

Candy Crush Saga	Trivia Crack
Candy Crush Soda Saga	Pet Rescue Saga
Farm Heroes Saga	Bubble Witch 2 Saga
Clash of Clans	Subway Surfers
Hay Day	8 Ball Pool

*(As of February 2015)

FUN FACT

The only game in iPhone's top ten free apps was *2048*. Top Free iPad Game Apps 2014 had two games: *Candy Crush Saga* and *Clash of Clans*.

Games

10 Top-Selling Video Games of All Time*

Game	Copies Sold
Wii Sports	82.9 million
Minecraft	60 million
Grand Theft Auto V	45 million
Mario Kart Wii	34.3 million
Wii Sports Resort	32.6 million
New Super Brothers	30.7 million
Call of Duty: Modern Warfare 2	28.5 million
Wii Play	28.2 million
Super Mario Bros. Wii	27.8 million
Grand Theft Auto: San Andreas	27.5 million
Call of Duty: Black Ops	24.8 million
Mario Kart DS	23.3 million
The Elder Scrolls V: Skyrim	20 million

*(As of February 2015)

10 Top-Selling Video Games of 2014*

Call of Duty: Advanced Warfare

Madden NFL 15

Destiny

Grand Theft Auto 5

Minecraft

Super Smash Bros. (for 3DS and Wii U)

NBA 2K15

Watch Dogs

FIFA 15

Call of Duty: Ghosts

*(US Only)

FUN FACT

Super Mario games have sold a combined 297.9 million copies since the first one came out in September 1985. Pokemon games have sold 270.8 million copies since February 1996.

History's Game Changer

Do you like Monopoly? You're one in a billion. More than a billion people have played the game since its official release date of March 19, 1935. Some people like to play Monopoly so much they can't stop! The longest game on record lasted 70 straight days.

Historians say the inspiration for Monopoly was The Landlord's Game, patented by Elizabeth Magie in 1904. Magie's game rewarded players who broke up the real estate holdings of wealthy individuals. In today's game, the goal is the opposite: to buy the most houses and hotels.

Monopoly was inspired by The Landlord's Game, which was patented in 1904.

There are versions of Monopoly that feature SpongeBob SquarePants, Marvel Avengers, and the state of Rhode Island. Neiman Marcus, a luxury store in Dallas, TX, marketed a solid chocolate Monopoly game in 1978. A San Francisco jeweler named Sidney Mobell created the most expensive Monopoly game ever. It was made of gold, with diamond-studded dice, and cost $2 million.

Over 10 million Monopoly fans voted on Facebook to replace a game piece shaped like an old-fashioned iron with this cat game piece.

Monopoly was much more than fun and games to British servicemen held in Nazi prison camps during World War II. The British secret service created escape kits containing real money, maps, and tools such as files and compasses. They disguised the kits as Monopoly sets and smuggled them in as part of care packages. Historians say these Monopoly games could have helped thousands of captured soldiers escape.

Mr. Monopoly is the mascot for the Monopoly board game. He is also know as Rich Uncle Pennybags.

Gold Mine

According to the LEGO company, more than 85 million kids around the world played with LEGOs during 2014. Not too many years ago, one of those kids would have been Markus "Notch" Persson of Sweden. During the hours Markus spent building things with LEGO bricks, he came up with the idea of a game that used textured 3D blocks to create structures and landscapes for virtual worlds. Today that game is *Minecraft*.

More than 54 million copies have been sold since the game came out in 2011. It was the best-selling video game of 2014 and is the third most popular video game ever. *Minecraft* mobile apps topped the 2014 charts for iPad and iPhone. *Minecraft* has been a gold mine for Persson, who sold it to Microsoft for $2.5 billion.

One big reason players love *Minecraft* is that there are no rules or "right" outcomes. You can build anything you want, and you can keep building forever. *Minecraft* is so popular that there are international competitions such as the one pictured below, which took place August 9, 2014, in Ascot, England.

Catherine Brunzos— at the Top of Her Game

Thanks to the American Library Association (ALA), gamers now have their own special day. In 2008, the ALA chose November 15 as International Game Day (IGD), dedicated to showing and sharing library gaming programs and services around the world.

On November 15, 2014, 70 libraries from North America, 11 from Europe, and 14 from Australia sent their best players to compete in the two-day *Minecraft Hunger Games* tournament. In the competition, teams of one boy and one girl fight teams from other "districts" until one champion remains. Thirteen-year-old Catherine Brunzos of Providence, RI, was the 2014 worldwide winner. Catherine is a member of an after-school *Minecraft* club who says she wants to be a computer programmer.

CELEBRATE!

Happy birthday, Mark Foster! In 2016, Foster the People's lead singer will be . . . eight?

Mark was born in 1984, so he will have lived 32 years. But he was born on Leap Day, February 29, which only appears on the calendar every four years.

Having a birthday every four years makes for some pretty weird math. You can't vote until you are 72. You can't rent a car from most companies until you are 100! And what day do you get your birthday cake and presents when it's not a leap year?

Many choose March 1, since they are not officially a year older until after midnight on February 28, whatever day the calendar says that is. Others pick February 28. After waiting four years, they want to get the party started already!

Birthdays

January

1. Paul Revere, American patriot, 1735
2. Kate Bosworth, actor, 1983
3. J. R. R. Tolkien, author, 1892
4. Doris Kearns Goodwin, historian, 1943
5. Bradley Cooper, actor, 1975
6. Joan of Arc, military leader and saint, around 1412
7. Blue Ivy Carter, daughter of Beyoncé and Jay Z, 2012
8. Stephen Hawking, physicist, 1942
9. Nina Dobrev, actor, 1989
10. George Foreman, boxer, 1949
11. Alice Paul, suffragist, 1885
12. Zayn Malik, musician (One Direction), 1993
13. Orlando Bloom, actor, 1977
14. Albert Schweitzer, scientist and humanitarian, 1875
15. Drew Brees, football player, 1979
16. Kate Moss, model, 1974
17. Michelle Obama, US First Lady, 1964
18. Kevin Costner, actor, 1955
19. Edgar Allan Poe, author, 1809
20. Edwin "Buzz" Aldrin, astronaut, 1930
21. Plácido Domingo, operatic tenor, 1941
22. Sir Francis Bacon, explorer, 1561
23. Edouard Manet, painter, 1832
24. Maria Tallchief, ballerina, 1925
25. Alicia Keys, musician, 1981
26. Ellen DeGeneres, TV personality, 1958
27. Wolfgang Amadeus Mozart, composer, 1756
28. Jackson Pollock, artist, 1912
29. Oprah Winfrey, media personality, 1954
30. Christian Bale, actor, 1974
31. Justin Timberlake, entertainer, 1981

February

1. Harry Styles, musician (One Direction), 1994
2. Christie Brinkley, model, 1954
3. Norman Rockwell, painter, 1894
4. Rosa Parks, civil rights activist, 1913
5. Cristiano Ronaldo, soccer player, 1985
6. Babe Ruth, baseball player, 1895
7. Ashton Kutcher, actor, 1978
8. Jules Verne, author, 1828
9. Alice Walker, author, 1944
10. George Stephanopoulos, TV journalist and former political advisor, 1961
11. Thomas Edison, inventor, 1847
12. Judy Blume, author, 1938
13. Chuck Yeager, test pilot, 1923
14. Jack Benny, radio and TV entertainer, 1894
15. Susan B. Anthony, suffragist and civil rights leader, 1820
16. Ice-T, rap musician and actor, 1958
17. Ed Sheeran, singer, 1991
18. John Travolta, actor, 1954
19. Jeff Kinney, author of Diary of a Wimpy Kid series, 1971
20. Gloria Vanderbilt, fashion designer, 1924
21. W. H. Auden, poet, 1907
22. Edward Kennedy, US senator, 1932
23. Dakota Fanning, actor, 1994
24. Steve Jobs, cofounder of Apple Computer, 1955
25. Sean Astin, actor, 1971
26. Johnny Cash, singer and songwriter, 1932
27. Chelsea Clinton, US presidential daughter, 1980
28. Daniel Handler (Lemony Snicket), author, 1970
29. Mark Foster, musician, 1984

March

1. Lupita Nyong'o, actor, 1983
2. Theodor Geisel (Dr. Seuss), author, 1904
3. Julie Bowen, actor, 1970
4. Knute Rockne, football star, 1888
5. Eva Mendes, actor, 1974
6. Michelangelo, painter, 1475
7. Rachel Weisz, actor, 1970
8. Freddie Prinze Jr., actor, 1976
9. Juliette Binoche, actor, 1964
10. Shannon Miller, gymnast, 1977
11. Terrence Howard, actor, 1969
12. Jack Kerouac, poet, 1922
13. Abigail Fillmore, US First Lady, 1798
14. Billy Crystal, actor, 1948
15. Ruth Bader Ginsburg, US Supreme Court justice, 1933
16. Jerry Lewis, entertainer, 1926
17. Mia Hamm, soccer player, 1972
18. Adam Levine, singer, 1979
19. Wyatt Earp, US western lawman, 1848
20. Spike Lee, director, 1957
21. Matthew Broderick, actor, 1962
22. Bob Costas, sportscaster, 1952
23. Wernher von Braun, rocket scientist, 1912
24. Peyton Manning, football player, 1976
25. Danica Patrick, race car driver, 1982
26. Sandra Day O'Connor, US Supreme Court justice, 1930
27. Fergie, singer, 1975
28. Lady Gaga, singer, 1986
29. Elle Macpherson, model, 1964
30. Vincent van Gogh, painter, 1853
31. René Descartes, philosopher, 1596

April

1 Lon Chaney, Sr., horror movie star, 1883
2 Dana Carvey, entertainer, 1955
3 Jane Goodall, primatologist and conservationist, 1934
4 Austin Mahone, singer, 1996
5 Pharrell Williams, singer, 1973
6 Zach Braff, actor, 1975
7 Jackie Chan, actor, 1954
8 Kofi Atta Annan, UN secretary-general, 1938
9 Elle Fanning, actor, 1998
10 Frances Perkins, first female member of US presidential cabinet (secretary of labor), 1880
11 Viola Liuzzo, US civil rights activist, 1925
12 Tom Clancy, author, 1947
13 Samuel Beckett, playwright, 1906
14 Adrien Brody, actor, 1973
15 Emma Watson, actor, 1990
16 Wilbur Wright, aviator, 1867
17 John Pierpont Morgan, industrialist, 1837
18 Conan O'Brien, TV personality, 1963
19 Kate Hudson, actor, 1979
20 Don Mattingly, baseball player, 1961
21 John Muir, conservationist, 1838
22 Jack Nicholson, actor, 1937
23 William Shakespeare, poet and playwright, 1564
24 Kelly Clarkson, singer, 1982
25 Renée Zellweger, actor, 1969
26 John James Audubon, naturalist, 1785
27 Samuel Morse, inventor, 1791
28 Jay Leno, TV personality, 1950
29 Duke Ellington, jazz musician, 1899
30 Kirsten Dunst, actor, 1982

May

1 Tim McGraw, country singer, 1967
2 David Beckham, soccer player, 1975
3 James Brown, singer and songwriter, 1933
4 Will Arnett, actor, 1970
5 Adele, singer and songwriter, 1988
6 George Clooney, actor, 1961
7 Tim Russert, TV news personality, 1950
8 Adrian Gonzalez, baseball player, 1982
9 Howard Carter, archaeologist, 1873
10 Fred Astaire, actor, 1899
11 Salvador Dalí, painter, 1904
12 Yogi Berra, baseball player, 1925
13 Robert Pattinson, actor, 1986
14 Mark Zuckerberg, Facebook founder, 1984
15 Madeleine Albright, US secretary of state, 1937
16 Adrienne Rich, poet, 1929
17 Craig Ferguson, TV personality, 1962
18 Tina Fey, actor and writer, 1970
19 Sam Smith, singer, 1992
20 Cher, singer and actress, 1946
21 Al Franken, entertainer and US senator, 1951
22 Apolo Anton Ohno, speed skater, 1982
23 Jewel, singer and songwriter, 1974
24 Bob Dylan, musician, 1941
25 Mike Myers, actor, 1963
26 Sally Ride, astronaut, 1951
27 Henry Kissinger, US diplomat, 1923
28 Kylie Minogue, singer, 1968
29 Carmelo Anthony, basketball player, 1984
30 Wynonna Judd, country singer and songwriter, 1964
31 Clint Eastwood, actor and director, 1930

June

1 Heidi Klum, model and TV host, 1973
2 Martha Washington, first US First Lady, 1731
3 Rafael Nadal, tennis player, 1986
4 Pal, "Lassie" in *Lassie Come Home*, 1940
5 Mark Wahlberg, actor, 1971
6 Alexander Pushkin, author, 1799
7 Iggy Azalea, singer, 1990
8 Frank Lloyd Wright, architect, 1867
9 Natalie Portman, actor, 1981
10 Maurice Sendak, author, 1928
11 Shia LaBeouf, actor, 1986
12 Anne Frank, Holocaust diarist, 1929
13 Ashley and Mary-Kate Olsen, actors, 1986
14 Lucy Hale, actor, 1989
15 Courteney Cox, actor, 1964
16 Joyce Carol Oates, author, 1938
17 Venus Williams, tennis player, 1980
18 Paul McCartney, musician, 1942
19 Guy Lombardo, band leader, 1902
20 Shefali Chowdhury, actor, 1988
21 Prince William of Wales, British royal, 1982
22 John Dillinger, bank robber, 1903
23 Randy Jackson, TV personality, 1956
24 Mick Fleetwood, musician, 1947
25 Sonia Sotomayor, US Supreme Court justice, 1954
26 Babe Didrikson Zaharias, athlete, 1911
27 Helen Keller, deaf-blind author and activist, 1880
28 John Cusack, actor, 1966
29 George Washington Goethals, chief engineer of the Panama Canal, 1858
30 Michael Phelps, swimmer, 1985

July

1 Benjamin Oliver Davis, first African American general in the US Army, 1877
2 Lindsay Lohan, actor, 1986
3 Tom Cruise, actor, 1962
4 George Steinbrenner, New York Yankees owner, 1930
5 P. T. Barnum, showman and entertainer, 1810
6 Kevin Hart, actor, 1979
7 Michelle Kwan, ice skater, 1980
8 Anna Quindlen, author, 1952
9 Tom Hanks, actor, 1956
10 Jessica Simpson, actor and singer, 1980
11 Sela Ward, actor, 1956
12 Malala Yousafzai, activist and Nobel Peace Prize winner, 1997
13 Harrison Ford, actor, 1942
14 Crown Princess Victoria, Swedish monarch, 1977
15 Rembrandt, painter, 1606
16 Will Ferrell, actor, 1967
17 Erle Stanley Gardner, mystery writer, 1889
18 Nelson Mandela, South African political leader, 1918
19 Edgar Degas, painter, 1834
20 Gisele Bündchen, model, 1980
21 Brandi Chastain, soccer player, 1968
22 Prince George Alexander Louis of Cambridge, British royal, 2013
23 Daniel Radcliffe, actor, 1989
24 Jennifer Lopez, actor and singer, 1969
25 Matt LeBlanc, actor, 1967
26 Sandra Bullock, actor, 1964
27 Alex Rodriguez, baseball player, 1975
28 Beatrix Potter, author, 1866
29 Martina McBride, country singer, 1966
30 Emily Brontë, author, 1818
31 J. K. Rowling, author, 1965

August

1 Francis Scott Key, writer of "The Star-Spangled Banner," 1779
2 James Baldwin, author, 1924
3 Martha Stewart, lifestyle spokesperson and TV personality, 1941
4 Meg Whitman, CEO of eBay, 1956
5 Neil Armstrong, astronaut, 1930
6 Lucille Ball, actor, 1911
7 Ralph Bunche, Nobel Peace Prize winner, 1904
8 Roger Federer, tennis player, 1981
9 John Dryden, poet, 1631
10 Betsey Johnson, fashion designer, 1942
11 Viola Davis, actor, 1965
12 Pete Sampras, tennis player, 1971
13 Annie Oakley, Wild West entertainer, 1860
14 Tim Tebow, football player, 1987
15 Jennifer Lawrence, actor, 1990
16 Steve Carell, actor, 1962
17 Davy Crockett, frontiersman, 1786
18 Roberto Clemente, baseball player, 1934
19 Veronica Roth, author of the Divergent trilogy, 1988
20 Amy Adams, actor, 1974
21 Wilt Chamberlain, basketball player, 1936
22 Tori Amos, musician, 1963
23 Kobe Bryant, basketball player, 1978
24 Anna Lee Fisher, chemist and astronaut, 1949
25 Leonard Bernstein, conductor and composer, 1918
26 Liam Payne, musician (One Direction), 1993
27 Mother Teresa, nun and humanitarian, 1910
28 Shania Twain, country singer, 1965
29 Michael Jackson, entertainer, 1958
30 Mary Shelley, author of *Frankenstein*, 1797
31 Richard Gere, actor, 1949

September

1 Gloria Estefan, singer, 1957
2 Keanu Reeves, actor, 1964
3 Shaun White, snowboarder, 1986
4 Beyoncé, singer and actress, 1981
5 John Cage, composer, 1912
6 Jane Addams, Nobel Peace Prize winner, 1860
7 Michael DeBakey, pioneer heart surgeon, 1908
8 Pink, singer, 1979
9 Adam Sandler, actor, 1966
10 Colin Firth, actor, 1960
11 William Sydney Porter (O. Henry), short story writer, 1862
12 Yao Ming, basketball player, 1980
13 Milton Hershey, chocolate magnate, 1857
14 Amy Winehouse, singer and songwriter, 1983
15 Prince Henry ("Harry") of Wales, British royal, 1984
16 Nick Jonas, singer, 1992
17 William Carlos Williams, poet, 1883
18 Agnes de Mille, choreographer, 1905
19 Trisha Yearwood, country singer, 1964
20 Sophia Loren, actor, 1934
21 Stephen King, author, 1947
22 Joan Jett, singer, 1958
23 Bruce Springsteen, musician, 1949
24 Jim Henson, creator of the Muppets, 1936
25 Will Smith, actor, 1968
26 Serena Williams, tennis player, 1981
27 Avril Lavigne, singer, 1984
28 Ed Sullivan, entertainer, 1901
29 Enrico Fermi, physicist and atom bomb developer, 1901
30 Elie Wiesel, author and Holocaust survivor, 1928

October

1 Vladimir Horowitz, pianist, 1903
2 Groucho Marx, comedian, 1890
3 Gwen Stefani, singer, 1969
4 Alicia Silverstone, actor, 1976
5 Maya Lin, architect, 1959
6 George Westinghouse, inventor, 1846
7 Yo-Yo Ma, cellist, 1955
8 Bruno Mars, musician, 1985
9 John Lennon, singer and songwriter, 1940
10 Brett Favre, football player, 1969
11 Eleanor Roosevelt, US First Lady and diplomat, 1884
12 Josh Hutcherson, actor, 1992
13 Margaret Thatcher, British prime minister, 1925
14 Usher, rap singer, 1978
15 Emeril Lagasse, chef, 1959
16 John Mayer, singer, 1977
17 Eminem, singer, 1972
18 Lindsey Vonn, skier, 1984
19 Peter Max, artist, 1937
20 Bela Lugosi, actor who played Dracula, 1882
21 Alfred Nobel, scientist, 1883
22 Deepak Chopra, self-help writer, 1946
23 Pelé, soccer player, 1940
24 Kevin Kline, actor, 1947
25 Katy Perry, singer, 1984
26 Hillary Rodham Clinton, US First Lady, US senator, and secretary of state, 1947
27 Captain James Cook, explorer, 1728
28 Bill Gates, founder of Microsoft, 1955
29 Gabrielle Union, actor, 1972
30 Nastia Liukin, gymnast, 1989
31 Chiang Kai-shek, Nationalist Chinese leader, 1887

November

1 Toni Collette, actor, 1972
2 Daniel Boone, frontiersman, 1734
3 Vincenzo Bellini, composer, 1801
4 Sean Combs, musician, 1969
5 Roy Rogers, TV cowboy, 1911
6 Ethan Hawke, actor, 1970
7 Lorde, musician, 1996
8 Margaret Mitchell, author, 1900
9 Carl Sagan, scientist, 1934
10 Miranda Lambert, singer and songwriter, 1983
11 Leonardo DiCaprio, actor, 1974
12 Elizabeth Cady Stanton, suffragist, 1815
13 Louis Brandeis, US Supreme Court justice, 1856
14 Claude Monet, painter, 1840
15 Shailene Woodley, actor, 1991
16 Shigeru Miyamoto, video game designer, 1952
17 Danny DeVito, actor, 1944
18 Owen Wilson, actor, 1968
19 Calvin Klein, fashion designer, 1942
20 Edwin Hubble, scientist, 1889
21 Ken Griffey Jr., baseball player, 1969
22 Mark Ruffalo, actor, 1967
23 Miley Cyrus, singer and actor, 1992
24 Scott Joplin, composer, 1868
25 Andrew Carnegie, industrialist, 1835
26 Charles Schulz, cartoonist, 1922
27 Anders Celsius, scientist, 1701
28 Jon Stewart, TV personality, 1962
29 Russell Wilson, football player, 1988
30 Samuel Clemens (Mark Twain), author, 1835

December

1 Woody Allen, actor and director, 1935
2 Britney Spears, singer, 1981
3 Ozzy Osbourne, musician and performer, 1948
4 Jay Z, rap singer and songwriter, 1969
5 Walt Disney, producer and animator, 1901
6 Ira Gershwin, lyricist, 1896
7 Willa Cather, author, 1873
8 Noelle Pikus-Pace, Olympic skeleton medalist, 1982
9 Clarence Birdseye, frozen food pioneer, 1886
10 Emily Dickinson, poet, 1830
11 Mo'Nique, actor, 1967
12 Frank Sinatra, singer and actor, 1915
13 Taylor Swift, singer, 1989
14 Vanessa Hudgens, actor, 1988
15 Gustave Eiffel, designer of the Eiffel Tower, 1832
16 Theo James, actor, 1984
17 Milla Jovovich, actor, 1975
18 Christina Aguilera, musician, 1980
19 Edith Piaf, singer, 1915
20 Harvey Samuel Firestone, tire manufacturer, 1868
21 Kiefer Sutherland, actor, 1966
22 Diane Sawyer, TV news personality, 1945
23 Madame C. J. Walker, inventor and businesswoman, 1867
24 Louis Tomlinson, musician (One Direction), 1991
25 Clara Barton, founder, American Red Cross, 1821
26 Chris Daughtry, musician, 1979
27 Louis Pasteur, chemist, 1822
28 Denzel Washington, actor, 1954
29 Charles Goodyear, inventor, 1800
30 LeBron James, basketball player, 1984
31 Henri Matisse, painter, 1869

Time never stands still. Earth is constantly moving, rotating counterclockwise on its axis as it orbits the sun. It takes about 24 hours—one day—to make one rotation. It takes 365 ¼ days to make one revolution around the sun. Nearly every four years, we add an extra day in February to keep the calendar in synch with Earth's revolutions. Why "nearly"? Dating back to an old rule, the first year of a century is only a leap year if it's exactly divisible by 400. So 1900 was not a leap year, but 2000 was.

The next leap day is February 29, 2016. Leap day activities often celebrate our favorite leapers: frogs. And they deserve some cheers! Average US bullfrogs can leap up to 6 feet (1.8 m), or ten times their body length. The US record belongs to Rosie the Ribiter, a bullfrog that jumped 7.16 feet (2.2 m) in a contest in 1986.

CALENDARS & HOLIDAYS

This European green frog, also called an edible frog, may be leaping away from someone's dinner plate. It is highly prized for food in France and other countries. Read about holidays and traditions around the world in this chapter.

Periods of Time

annual	yearly
biannual	twice a year
bicentennial	marking a period of 200 years
biennial	marking a period of 2 years
bimonthly	every 2 months; twice a month
biweekly	every 2 weeks; twice a week
centennial	marking a period of 100 years
decennial	marking a period of 10 years
diurnal	daily; of a day
duodecennial	marking a period of 12 years
millennial	marking a period of 1,000 years
novennial	marking a period of 9 years
octennial	marking a period of 8 years
perennial	occurring year after year
quadrennial	marking a period of 4 years
quadricentennial	marking a period of 400 years
quincentennial	marking a period of 500 years
quindecennial	marking a period of 15 years
quinquennial	marking a period of 5 years
semiannual	twice a year
semicentennial	marking a period of 50 years
semidiurnal	twice a day
semiweekly	twice a week
septennial	marking a period of 7 years
sesquicentennial	marking a period of 150 years
sexennial	marking a period of 6 years
thrice weekly	3 times a week
tricennial	marking a period of 30 years
triennial	marking a period of 3 years
trimonthly	every 3 months
triweekly	every 3 weeks; 3 times a week
undecennial	marking a period of 11 years
vicennial	marking a period of 20 years

Months of the Year in Different Calendars

Gregorian	Jewish	Hindu	Muslim
January	Shevat	Magha	Muharram
February	Adar	Phalguda	Safar
March	Nisan	Chaitra	Rabi' al awwal
April	Iyar	Vaisakha	Rabi' al thani
May	Sivan	Jyaistha	Jumada al-awwal
June	Tammuz	Asadha	Jumada al-Thani
July	Av	Shravana	Rajab
August	Elul	Bhadra	Sha'ban
September	Tishrei	Asvina	Ramadan
October	Cheshvan	Kartika	Shawwal
November	Kislev	Agrahayana	Dhul-Qa'dah
December	Tevet	Pausa	Dhul-Hijjah

Wedding Anniversary Gift Chart

Anniversary	Traditional	Modern
1st	paper	clocks
2nd	cotton	china
3rd	leather	crystal
4th	fruit/flowers	linen/silk
5th	wood	silverware
6th	iron	wood
7th	wool	desk sets
8th	bronze	linen
9th	pottery	leather
10th	tin	diamond jewelry
11th	steel	fashion jewelry
12th	silk/linen	pearls
13th	lace	textiles
14th	ivory	gold jewelry
15th	crystal	watches
20th	china	platinum
25th	silver	silver
30th	pearls	diamonds
35th	coral	jade
40th	rubies	rubies
45th	sapphires	sapphires
50th	gold	gold
55th	emeralds	emeralds
60th	diamonds	diamonds

Holidays in the United States and Canada

Fixed Dates

These events are celebrated on the same date every year, regardless of where the date falls in the week.

Event	Date
New Year's Day[1]	January 1
Groundhog Day	February 2
Abraham Lincoln's Birthday	February 12
Valentine's Day	February 14
Susan B. Anthony Day	February 15
George Washington's Birthday	February 22
St. Patrick's Day	March 17
April Fools' Day	April 1
Earth Day	April 22
National Maritime Day	May 22
Flag Day	June 14
Canada Day[2]	July 1
Independence Day[1]	July 4
Citizenship Day	September 17
United Nations Day	October 24
Halloween	October 31
Veterans Day[1,3]	November 11
Remembrance Day[2]	November 11
Christmas	December 25
Boxing Day[2]	December 26
New Year's Eve	December 31

Changing Dates

These events are celebrated on different dates every year, but are always on a certain day of a certain week of a certain month.

Event	Day
Martin Luther King Jr. Day[1]	third Monday in January
Presidents' Day[1]	third Monday in February
Daylight saving time begins	second Sunday in March
Arbor Day	last Friday in April
National Teacher Day	Tuesday of the first full week in May
Mother's Day	second Sunday in May
Armed Forces Day	third Saturday in May
Victoria Day[2]	Monday on or before May 24
Memorial Day[1]	last Monday in May
Father's Day	third Sunday in June
Labor Day[1,2]	first Monday in September
Columbus Day[1]	second Monday in October
Thanksgiving Day (Canada)[2]	second Monday in October
Daylight saving time ends	first Sunday in November
Thanksgiving Day (United States)[1]	fourth Thursday in November

1. Federal holiday in United States   2. Federal holiday in Canada   3. Also known as Armistice Day

Why we celebrate...

New Year's Day

The first record of a new year festival is from about 2000 BCE in Mesopotamia. The festival took place not in January but in mid-March, with the new moon after the spring equinox.

Martin Luther King Jr. Day

This holiday honors the birthday of the slain civil rights leader who preached nonviolence and led the March on Washington in 1963. Dr. King's most famous speech is entitled "I Have a Dream."

Groundhog Day

According to legend, if a groundhog in Punxsutawney, Pennsylvania, peeks his head out of his burrow and sees his shadow, he'll return to his hole and there will be six more weeks of winter.

Lincoln's Birthday

This holiday honors the 16th president of the United States, who led the nation through the Civil War (1861—1865) and was then assassinated. It was first formally observed in Washington, DC, in 1866, when both houses of Congress gathered to pay tribute to the slain president.

Valentine's Day

This holiday of love originated as a festival for several martyrs from the third century, all named St. Valentine. The holiday's association with romance may have come from an ancient belief that birds mate on this day.

Presidents' Day

This official government holiday was created in observance of both Washington's and Lincoln's birthdays.

Washington's Birthday

This holiday honors the first president of the United States, known as the Father of Our Country. It was first officially observed in America in 1879.

St. Patrick's Day

This holiday honors the patron saint of Ireland. Most often celebrated in the United States with parties and special dinners, the most famous event is the annual St. Patrick's Day parade on Fifth Avenue in New York City.

Mother's Day

First proposed by Anna Jarvis of Philadelphia in 1907, this holiday has become a national time for family gatherings and showing appreciation for mothers.

Memorial Day

Also known as Decoration Day, this legal holiday was created in 1868 by order of General John A. Logan as a day on which the graves of Civil War soldiers would be decorated. Since that time, the day has been set aside to honor all American soldiers who have given their lives for their country.

Flag Day

This holiday was set aside to commemorate the adoption of the Stars and Stripes by the Continental Congress on June 14, 1777. It is a legal holiday only in Pennsylvania but is generally acknowledged and observed in many states each year.

Father's Day

This holiday honors the role of the father in the American family, as Mother's Day honors the role of the mother.

Independence Day

This holiday celebrates the signing of the Declaration of Independence, on July 4, 1776. It has been celebrated nationwide since 1777, the first anniversary of the signing.

Labor Day

First proposed by Peter J. McGuire in New York in 1882, this holiday was created to honor the labor unions and workers who built the nation.

Columbus Day

This holiday commemorates the discovery of the New World by Italian explorer Christopher Columbus in 1492. Even though the land was already populated by Native Americans when Columbus arrived, this discovery marks the beginning of European influence in America.

United Nations Day

This holiday marks the founding of the United Nations, which began in its present capacity in 1945 but had already been in operation as the League of Nations.

Halloween

Also known as All Hallows' Eve, this holiday has its origins in ancient Celtic rituals that marked the beginning of winter with bonfires, masquerades, and dressing in costume to frighten away spirits.

Election Day

Since Congress declared it an official holiday in 1845, this has been the day for presidential elections every four years. Most statewide elections are also held on this day, but election years vary according to state.

Veterans Day

Originally called Armistice Day, this holiday was created to celebrate the end of World War I in 1918. In June 1954, Congress changed the name of the holiday to Veterans Day and declared that the day would honor all men and women who have served in America's armed forces.

Thanksgiving

President Lincoln proclaimed Thanksgiving a national holiday in 1863. Most people believe the tradition of reserving a day of thanks began with a 1621 order by Governor Bradford of Plymouth Colony.

Major World Holidays

January 1 New Year's Day throughout the Western world and in India, Indonesia, Japan, Korea, the Philippines, Singapore, Taiwan, and Thailand; Founding Day of Republic of China (Taiwan)

January 2 Berchtoldstag in Switzerland

January 3 Genshi-Sai (First Beginning) in Japan

January 5 Twelfth Night (Wassail Eve or Eve of Epiphany) in England

January 6 Epiphany, observed by Catholics throughout Europe and Latin America

Third Monday in January Martin Luther King Jr.'s Birthday in the United States and the Virgin Islands

Second Monday in January Adults' Day in Japan

January 20 St. Agnes Eve in Great Britain

January 26 Republic Day in India; Australia Day in Australia

January–February Chinese New Year and Vietnamese New Year (Tet)

February 3 Setsubun (Bean-throwing Festival) in Japan

First Monday in February Constitution Day in Mexico

February 11 National Foundation Day in Japan

February 27 Independence Day in the Dominican Republic

March 1 Independence Movement Day in Korea

March 8 International Women's Day in China, Russia, Great Britain, and the United States

March 17 St. Patrick's Day in Ireland and Northern Ireland

March 19 St. Joseph's Day in Colombia, Costa Rica, Italy, and Spain

Third Monday in March Benito Juarez's Birthday in Mexico

March 22 Arab League Day in Arab League countries

March 23 Pakistan Day in Pakistan

March 25 Independence Day in Greece; Lady Day (Quarter Day) in Great Britain

March 26 Fiesta del Arbol (Arbor Day) in Spain

March 29 Youth and Martyr's Day in Taiwan

March–April Carnival/Lent/Easter: The pre-Lenten celebration of Carnival (Mardi Gras) and the post-Lenten celebration of Easter are movable feasts widely observed in Christian countries

April 1 April Fools' Day (All Fools' Day) in Great Britain and the United States

April 5 Arbor Day in Korea

April 7 World Health Day in UN member nations

April 8 Buddha's Birthday in Korea and Japan; Hana Matsuri (Flower Festival) in Japan

April 14 Pan American Day in the Americas

April 19 Declaration of Independence Day in Venezuela

April 23 St. George's Day in England

April 25 Liberation Day in Italy; ANZAC Day in Australia and New Zealand

April 30 Queen's Birthday in the Netherlands; Walpurgis Night in Germany and Scandinavia

May 3 Constitution Day in Japan

May 1 May Day (Labor Day) in Russia and most of Europe and Latin America

May 5 Children's Day in Japan and Korea; Cinco de Mayo in Mexico; Liberation Day in the Netherlands

May 8 V-E Day in Europe

May 9 Victory over Fascism Day in Russia

Late May Victoria Day on Monday before May 25 in Canada

June 2 Founding of the Republic Day in Italy

June 5 Constitution Day in Denmark

June 6 Memorial Day in Korea; National Day in Sweden

June 10 Portugal Day in Portugal

June 12 Independence Day in the Philippines

Mid-June Queen's Official Birthday on second Saturday in Great Britain

June 16 Soweto Day in UN member nations

June 20 Flag Day in Argentina

June 24 Midsummer's Day in Great Britain

June 29 Feasts of Saints Peter and Paul in Chile, Colombia, Italy, Peru, Spain, and Venezuela

July 1 Canada Day in Canada; Half-year Holiday in Hong Kong; Bank Holiday in Taiwan

July 5 Independence Day in Venezuela

July 9 Independence Day in Argentina

July 12 Orangemen's Day in Northern Ireland

July 14 Bastille Day in France

Mid-July Feria de San Fermin during second week in Spain

July 17 Constitution Day in Korea

July 20 Independence Day in Colombia

July 21 National Holiday in Belgium

July 22 National Liberation Day in Poland

July 24 Simón Bolivar's Birthday in Ecuador and Venezuela

July 25 St. James Day in Spain

July 28 Independence Day in Peru

First Monday in August August Bank Holiday in Ireland; Emancipation Day in Grenada and Guyana

August 1 Lammas Day in England; National Day in Switzerland

August 6 Independence Day in Jamaica

August 9 National Day in Singapore

August 10 Independence Day in Ecuador

August 12 Queen's Birthday in Thailand

August 14 Independence Day in Pakistan

August 15 Independence Day in India; Liberation Day in South Korea; Assumption Day in Catholic countries

August 16 National Restoration Day in the Dominican Republic

August 17 Independence Day in Indonesia

August 31 Independence Day in Trinidad and Tobago

September Respect for the Aged Day in Japan on third Monday

September 7 Independence Day in Brazil

September 9 Choyo-no-Sekku (Chrysanthemum Day) in Japan

September 14 Battle of San Jacinto Day in Nicaragua

Mid-September Sherry Wine Harvest in Spain

September 15 Independence Day in Costa Rica, Guatemala, and Nicaragua

September 16 Independence Day in Mexico and Papua New Guinea

September 18–19 Independence Day in Chile; St. Gennaro Day in Italy

September 28 Confucius's Birthday in Taiwan

October 1 National Day in People's Republic of China; Armed Forces Day in Korea; National Holiday in Nigeria

October 2 Mahatma Gandhi's Birthday in India

October 3 National Foundation Day in Korea; Day of German Unity in Germany

October 5 Proclamation of the Portuguese Republic Day in Portugal

October 9 Korean Alphabet Day in Korea

October 10 Kruger Day in South Africa; Founding Day of the Republic of China in Taiwan

October 12 Columbus Day in Spain and widely throughout Mexico, and Central and South America

October 20 Revolution Day in Guatemala; Kenyatta Day in Kenya

October 24 United Nations Day in UN member nations

October 26 National Holiday in Austria

October 28 Greek National Day in Greece

November 1 All Saints' Day, observed by Catholics in most countries

November 2 All Souls' Day in Ecuador, El Salvador, Luxembourg, Macao, Mexico (Day of the Dead), San Marino, Uruguay, and Vatican City

November 4 National Unity Day in Italy

November 5 Guy Fawkes Day in Great Britain

November 7–8 October Revolution Day in Russia

November 11 Armistice Day in Belgium, France, French Guiana, and Tahiti; Remembrance Day in Canada

November 12 Sun Yat-sen's Birthday in Taiwan

November 15 Proclamation of the Republic Day in Brazil

November 19 National Holiday in Monaco

November 20 Anniversary of the Revolution in Mexico

November 23 Kinro-Kansha-no-Hi (Labor Thanksgiving Day) in Japan

November 30 Bonifacio Day in the Philippines

December 5 Discovery by Columbus Day in Haiti; Constitution Day in Russia

December 6 Independence Day in Finland

December 8 Feast of the Immaculate Conception, widely observed in Catholic countries

December 10 Constitution Day in Thailand; Human Rights Day in UN member nations

December 12 Jamhuri Day in Kenya; Guadalupe Day in Mexico

Mid-December Nine Days of Posada during third week in Mexico

December 25 Christmas Day, widely observed in all Christian countries

December 26 St. Stephen's Day in Christian countries; Boxing Day in Canada, Australia, and Great Britain

December 26–January 1 Kwanzaa in the United States

December 31 New Year's Eve throughout the world; Omisoka (Grand Last Day) in Japan; Hogmanay Day in Scotland

WHAT'S YOUR SIGN?

The original zodiac signs are thought to have originated in Mesopotamia as far back as 2000 BCE. The Greeks later picked up some of the symbols from the Babylonians and then passed them on to other ancient cultures. Some other societies that developed their own zodiac charts based on the constellations include the Egyptians, the Chinese, and the Aztecs.

The positions of celestial objects such as the Sun, Moon, and planets in the zodiac on the day you are born determine your astrological sign. **What's yours?**

Aries, the Ram

March 21–April 19

Planet: Mars
Element: Fire
Personality Traits: Independent, enthusiastic, bold, impulsive, confident

Taurus, the Bull

April 20–May 20

Planet: Venus
Element: Earth
Personality Traits: Decisive, determined, stubborn, stable

Gemini, the Twins

May 21–June 21

Planet: Mercury
Element: Air
Personality Traits: Curious, sociable, ambitious, alert, intelligent, temperamental

Cancer, the Crab

June 22–July 22

Planet (Celestial Object): Moon
Element: Water
Personality Traits: Organized, busy, moody, sensitive, supportive

Leo, the Lion

July 23—August 22

Planet (Celestial Object): Sun
Element: Fire
Personality Traits: Born leader, bold, noble, generous, enthusiastic, sympathetic

Virgo, the Virgin

August 23—September 22

Planet: Mercury
Element: Earth
Personality Traits: Analytical, critical, intellectual, clever

Libra, the Scales

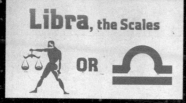

September 23—October 23

Planet: Venus
Element: Air
Personality Traits: Affectionate, thoughtful, sympathetic, orderly, persuasive

Scorpio, the Scorpion

October 24—November 21

Planet (Celestial Object): Pluto
Element: Water
Personality Traits: Intense, fearless, loyal, willful

Sagittarius, the Archer

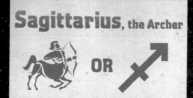

November 22—December 21

Planet: Jupiter
Element: Fire
Personality Traits: Energetic, good-natured, practical, clever

Capricorn, the Goat

December 22—January 19

Planet: Saturn
Element: Earth
Personality Traits: Serious, domineering, ambitious, blunt, loyal, persistent

Aquarius, the Water Bearer

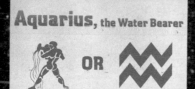

January 20—February 18

Planet: Uranus
Element: Air
Personality Traits: Independent, unselfish, generous, idealistic

Pisces, the Fishes

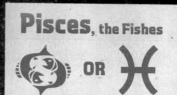

February 19—March 20

Planet: Neptune
Element: Water
Personality Traits: Compassionate, sympathetic, sensitive, timid, creative

What Animal Are You?

The ancient Chinese lunar calendar is based on cycles of the moon and names each year for one of 12 animals. In February 2015, Chinese New Year celebrations marked the beginning of a Year of the Sheep. This animal symbolizes beauty and style.

Find the year you were born and the animal that matches it at right. Then read all about your special animal below.

NEW YEAR SHEEP 2015

Rat

- Sincere, generous
- Likes Dragon and Monkey
- Opposite: Horse

Dragon

- Strong, interesting
- Likes Monkey and Rat
- Opposite: Dog

Monkey

- Smart, skillful
- Likes Dragon and Rat
- Opposite: Tiger

Ox

- Intelligent, patient
- Likes Snake and Rooster
- Opposite: Sheep

Snake

- Wise, strong-minded
- Likes Rooster and Ox
- Opposite: Pig

Rooster

- Adventuresome, spirited
- Likes Snake and Ox
- Opposite: Rabbit

Tiger

- Kind, brave
- Likes Horse and Dog
- Opposite: Monkey

Horse

- Popular, social
- Likes Tiger and Dog
- Opposite: Rat

Dog

- Loyal, friendly
- Likes Horse and Tiger
- Opposite: Dragon

Rabbit

- Talented, affectionate
- Likes: Sheep and Pig
- Opposite: Rooster

Sheep
(Goat)

- Stylish, loves beauty
- Likes Pig and Rabbit
- Opposite: Ox

Pig

- Noble, brave
- Likes Rabbit and Sheep
- Opposite: Snake

Chinese Years, 1900–2019

Rat	Ox	Tiger	Rabbit	Dragon	Snake
1900	1901	1902	1903	1904	1905
1912	1913	1914	1915	1916	1917
1924	1925	1926	1927	1928	1929
1936	1937	1938	1939	1940	1941
1948	1949	1950	1951	1952	1953
1960	1961	1962	1963	1964	1965
1972	1973	1974	1975	1976	1977
1984	1985	1986	1987	1988	1989
1996	1997	1998	1999	2000	2001
2008	2009	2010	2011	2012	2013

Horse	Sheep	Monkey	Rooster	Dog	Pig
1906	1907	1908	1909	1910	1911
1918	1919	1920	1921	1922	1923
1930	1931	1932	1933	1934	1935
1942	1943	1944	1945	1946	1947
1954	1955	1956	1957	1958	1959
1966	1967	1968	1969	1970	1971
1978	1979	1980	1981	1982	1983
1990	1991	1992	1993	1994	1995
2002	2003	2004	2005	2006	2007
2014	2015	2016	2017	2018	2019

OUR WORLD
2016

In July 2014, New York passed a law replacing the International Symbol of Access, used all over the country and around the world. The symbol of a figure in a wheelchair appears on elevators, parking spaces, emergency exits, restrooms, and many other public places. Created for a contest in 1968 by a Danish designer, the original figure was headless. (A head was added later.)

The new sign depicts a figure with its head forward and arms back, showing forward motion and a take-charge attitude. It also replaces the word "handicapped" with "accessible." The new symbol was created by a group called the Accessible Icon Project, who wanted people to start thinking in new ways about the rights of disabled persons. Some companies and cities are using it, but New York is the first state to make it official.

Ali Stroker, an actress and activist for disabled people, helped paint one of the first new signs. New ways to think, new names and faces to know: Change is everywhere in today's world. See for yourself in this section.

OLD TO NEW
The Accessible Icon

Signs & Symbols

Basic Signs

Fire extinguisher

Women's room

Men's room

First aid

Elevator

Information

Disabled (parking, restrooms, access)

Bus

Recycle

Fallout shelter

No smoking

No admittance

No parking

Danger

Poison

Stop

Yield

Do not enter

No left turn

Falling rock

Stop ahead

Bicycle path

Traffic light ahead

Railroad crossing

Pedestrian crossing

Intersection ahead

Left turn

Right turn

Two-way traffic

Slippery when wet

American Sign Language

In the manual alphabet of the hearing impaired, the fingers of the hand are moved to positions that represent the letters of the alphabet. Whole words and ideas are also expressed in sign language.

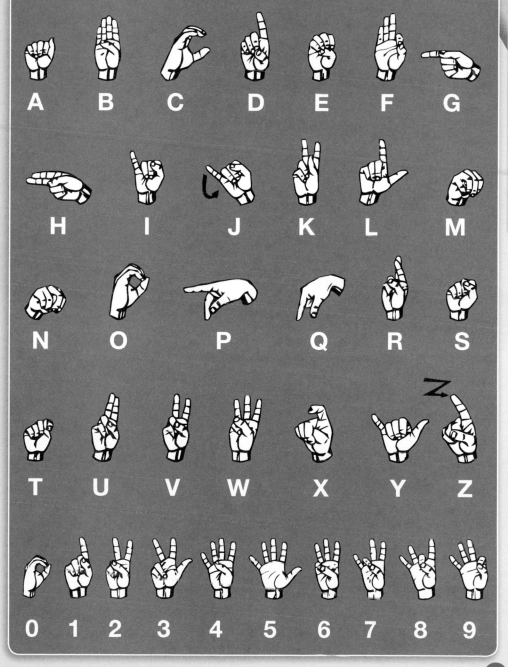

In 2014, archaeologists carefully removed pieces of heavy but delicate plaster sphinxes buried on a California beach for more than 90 years.

BUILDINGS & LANDMARKS

The half-human, half-lion Great Sphinx of Giza is one of the largest stone statues in the world. Its mammoth head towers higher than a 6-story building in front of the Great Pyramid of Giza near Cairo, Egypt (see p. 64). Historians believe the Sphinx was built to honor Pharaoh Khufu between 2558 and 2531 BCE. They also say the Sphinx originally had a beard, but it crumbled off. Its nose was broken off on purpose, but no one knows who did it, or why.

4,500 years later, archaeologists dug up another sphinx, not in the Egyptian desert but on the California coast. This statue was made of plaster, not limestone. It was one of 21 model sphinxes built in Hollywood for a 1923 movie, *The Ten Commandments*, and shipped in pieces to the movie set on the coast. When production was over, the producer buried the whole set in the sand to avoid paying shipping costs back to Hollywood.

Milestones in Modern Architecture

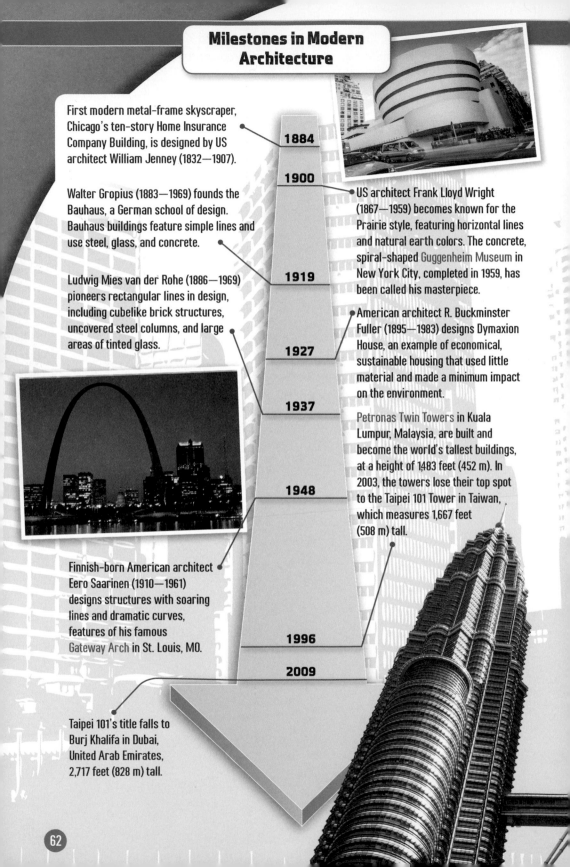

First modern metal-frame skyscraper, Chicago's ten-story Home Insurance Company Building, is designed by US architect William Jenney (1832—1907).

Walter Gropius (1883—1969) founds the Bauhaus, a German school of design. Bauhaus buildings feature simple lines and use steel, glass, and concrete.

Ludwig Mies van der Rohe (1886—1969) pioneers rectangular lines in design, including cubelike brick structures, uncovered steel columns, and large areas of tinted glass.

1884

1900

US architect Frank Lloyd Wright (1867—1959) becomes known for the Prairie style, featuring horizontal lines and natural earth colors. The concrete, spiral-shaped Guggenheim Museum in New York City, completed in 1959, has been called his masterpiece.

1919

American architect R. Buckminster Fuller (1895—1983) designs Dymaxion House, an example of economical, sustainable housing that used little material and made a minimum impact on the environment.

1927

1937

Petronas Twin Towers in Kuala Lumpur, Malaysia, are built and become the world's tallest buildings, at a height of 1,483 feet (452 m). In 2003, the towers lose their top spot to the Taipei 101 Tower in Taiwan, which measures 1,667 feet (508 m) tall.

1948

Finnish-born American architect Eero Saarinen (1910—1961) designs structures with soaring lines and dramatic curves, features of his famous Gateway Arch in St. Louis, MO.

1996

2009

Taipei 101's title falls to Burj Khalifa in Dubai, United Arab Emirates, 2,717 feet (828 m) tall.

Important Earthworks, Dams, and Canals

Elaborate system of earthen levees is built along the Mississippi River at New Orleans, Louisiana, to control floodwaters.

1718

United States opens New York's Erie Canal, linking the Great Lakes with New York City by way of the Hudson River.

Suez Canal, 101 miles (163 km) long, is completed, built by French engineer Ferdinand de Lesseps (1805-1894) to connect the Mediterranean and Red Seas. It is enlarged in 1980 to enable passage of supertankers.

1825

1869

Aswan Dam is built on the Nile River in Egypt. It has a record-setting length of 6,400 feet (1,951 m).

Panama Canal, dug across the Isthmus of Panama, connects the Atlantic and Pacific Oceans. It is built by US military engineers on land leased from the Republic of Panama.

1902

1904–1914

Grand Coulee Dam, built for electric generation and irrigation, is completed on the Columbia River in Washington State. At 550 feet (168 m) high and 5,223 feet (1,592 m) long, it is the largest concrete structure in the US.

World's longest tunnel, Delaware Aqueduct, is completed. It is 105 miles (169 km) long and supplies water to New York City.

1942

1944

Aswan High Dam, on the Nile River in Egypt, is completed. The dam is 364 feet (111 m) high and 12,562 feet (3,829 m) long.

United States and Canada complete construction of the Saint Lawrence Seaway. It provides access to Lake Ontario for oceangoing traffic by way of the Saint Lawrence River.

1959

1970

Japan's Seikan Tunnel, connecting the islands of Hokkaido and Honshu, becomes the longest railroad tunnel in the world. It is almost 334 miles (54 km) long.

1988

2000

Lærdal-Aurland Tunnel, the world's longest road tunnel, opens in Norway. This 15.2-mile (24.5 km) tunnel connects Oslo to the port of Bergen

Seven Wonders of the Ancient World

Wonder/Location	Description
Colossus of Rhodes Harbor of Rhodes, in Aegean Sea, off coast of Turkey	This huge bronze statue of the sun god, Helios, took 12 years to build and stood about 105 feet (32 m) tall. It was destroyed by an earthquake in 225 BCE.
Hanging Gardens of Babylon Ancient city of Babylon (now near Baghdad, Iraq)	The hanging gardens were a series of landscaped terraces along the banks of the Euphrates River, planted with trees, flowers, and shrubs. The gardens were probably built by King Nebuchadnezzar II for his wife.
Pharos (lighthouse) Pharos Island, off coast of Alexandria, Egypt	Built around 270 BCE, this was the world's first important lighthouse. It stood in the harbor for 1,000 years until it was destroyed by an earthquake. It served as a prototype for all other lighthouses built during the Roman Empire.
Mausoleum of Halicarnassus Ancient city of Halicarnassus, now Turkish town of Bodrum	This monumental marble tomb was built by the widow of Mausolus, king of Anatolia, in 353 BCE.
Statue of Zeus Olympia, Greece	This huge, ornate statue of the god on his throne was almost 60 feet (18 m) tall.
Pyramids of Egypt Giza, Egypt	The oldest pyramid was built with more than two million limestone blocks and stands more than 480 feet (146 m) high. This is the only one of the ancient wonders still in existence.
Temple of Artemis Ancient Greek city of Ephesus, now in Turkey near Selçuk	Built in the sixth century BCE to honor the goddess Artemis, this was one of the largest Greek temples ever built. It was famous for the artistic decoration and use of marble.

Seven Wonders of the Modern World

Wonder/Location

Channel Tunnel
England and France

The 31-mile (50-km) Channel Tunnel (Chunnel) is actually three concrete tubes, each 5 feet (2 m) thick, which burrow under the English Channel. They enter the earth at Coquelles, France, and reemerge at Folkestone, England, behind the White Cliffs of Dover.

CN Tower
Toronto

The world's third-tallest freestanding tower soars 1,815 feet (553 m) above Toronto, Canada. The CN Tower was designed to withstand 260-mph (418-kph) gusts.

Empire State Building
New York City

At 1,454 feet (443 m), the Empire State Building is the world's best-known skyscraper. For more than 40 years it was the tallest building in the world. Construction took only one year and 45 days.

Netherlands North Sea Protection Works
Netherlands

This is not just one structure but a complex system of dams, floodgates, storm surge barriers, and other engineered works that protect the country against destructive floods.

Golden Gate Bridge
San Francisco

Once the world's tallest suspension bridge, the Golden Gate Bridge hangs from two 746-foot (227-m) towers and is supported by enough cable to circle Earth three times.

Itaipu Dam
Brazil and Paraguay

Five miles (8 km) wide and as high as a 65-story building, the main dam is made of concrete while the flanking wings are made of earth and rock fill. The dam could power most of California.

Panama Canal
Panama

To build the Panama Canal, 42,000 workers dredged, blasted, and excavated from Colón to Balboa. They moved enough earth and rubble to bury the island of Manhattan to a depth of 12 feet (4 m)—or enough to open a 16-foot-(5-m) wide tunnel to Earth's center.

Top 10 Longest Suspension Bridges in North America

Name/Location	Completed	Length of main span
Verrazano-Narrows Lower New York Bay, NY	1964	4,260 ft. (1,298 m)
Golden Gate San Francisco Bay, CA	1937	4,200 ft. (1,280 m)
Mackinac Lakes Michigan and Huron, MI	1957	3,800 ft. (1,158 m)
George Washington Hudson River at New York City, NY	1931	3,500 ft. (1,067 m)
Tacoma Narrows II Puget Sound at Tacoma, WA	1950, 2007	2,800 ft. (853 m)
Carquinez (Alfred Zampa Memorial) Carquinez Strait, CA	2003	2,388 ft. (728 m)
San Francisco—Oakland Bay San Francisco Bay, CA	1936	2,310 ft. (704 m)
Bronx—Whitestone East River, New York City, NY	1939	2,300 ft. (701 m)
Pierre Laporte Saint Lawrence River at Quebec City, QC	1970	2,190 ft. (668 m)
Delaware Memorial (twin) Delaware River near Wilmington, DE	1951, 1968	2,150 ft. (655 m)

Longest Road Tunnels in the World

Name/Location	Completed	Tunnel length
Lærdal-Aurland Norway	2000	15.2 mi. (24.5 km)
Zhongnanshan China	2007	11.2 mi. (18.0 km)
St. Gotthard Switzerland	1980	10.5 mi. (16.9 km)
Arlberg Austria	1978	8.7 mi. (14.0 km)
Fréjus France/Italy	1980	8.0 mi. (12.9 km)
Hsuehshan Taiwan	2007	8.0 mi. (12.9 km)
Maijishan China	2009	7.6 mi. (12.3 km)
Mont Blanc France/Italy	1965	7.3 mi. (11.7 km)
Gudvanga Norway	1991	7.1 mi. (11.4 km)
Folgefonna Norway	2001	7.0 mi. (11.2 km)
Baojiashan China	2009	7.0 mi. (11.2 km)

World's 10 Tallest Dams

Name	Country	Height above lowest formation
*Rogun	Tajikistan	1,099 ft. (335 m)
*Bakhtiari	Iran	1,033 ft. (315 m)
Jinping I and Jinping II	China	1,001 ft. (305 m)
Nurek	Tajikistan	984 ft. (300 m)
Xiaowan	China	958 ft. (292 m)
Grande Dixence	Switzerland	935 ft. (285 m)
Xiluodu	China	912 ft. (278 m)
Inguri	Georgia	892 ft. (272 m)
Vajont	Italy	859 ft. (262 m)
Manuel M. Torres (also known as Chicoasén)	Mexico	856 ft. (261 m)

*Planned or under construction as of mid-2013

Top 10 Tallest Completed Buildings in the World

Name/Location	Height
Burj Khalifa — Dubai, United Arab Emirates	2,717 ft. (828 m)
Makkah Clock Royal Tower Hotel — Mecca, Saudi Arabia	1,971 ft. (601 m)
One World Trade Center — New York, New York, United States	1,776 ft. (541 m)
Taipei 101 — Taipei, Taiwan	1,667 ft. (508 m)
Shanghai World Financial Center — Shanghai, China	1,614 ft. (492 m)
International Commerce Centre — Hong Kong, China	1,585 ft. (483 m)
Petronas Tower 1 — Kuala Lumpur, Malaysia	1,483 ft. (452 m)
Petronas Tower 2 — Kuala Lumpur, Malaysia	1,483 ft. (452 m)
Zifeng Tower — Nanjing, China	1,476 ft. (450 m)
Willis (formerly Sears) Tower — Chicago, Illinois, United States	1,451 ft. (442 m)

Exploring Museums

Museums are buildings that preserve and display important pieces of history, culture, and human knowledge. They let us explore everything from Renaissance paintings to baseball cards, from mummies to lightning. Read about these famous museums and learn a little of what's inside each one. Visit them online if you can't get there in person!

British Museum

Location: London, England

What's Inside: This London landmark holds seven million objects representing civilizations and cultures from prehistory to modern times. World-famous exhibits include the Rosetta Stone, an ancient (196 BCE) Egyptian tablet that helped us understand Egyptian hieroglyphics.

Website: britishmuseum.org

The Exploratorium

Location: San Francisco, California, United States

What's Inside: "Don't touch" is definitely NOT the rule here. This hands-on museum has hundreds and hundreds of interactive exhibits to let visitors explore sound, light, motion, electricity, perception, the weather, and so much more up close.

Website: exploratorium.edu

Guggenheim Museum Bilbao

Location: Bilbao, Spain

What's Inside: This museum has an impressive collection of art from all over the world, mostly from the last half of the twentieth century. Equally impressive is the spectacular titanium-and-glass building itself, designed by world-famous architect Frank Gehry.

Website: guggenheim.org/bilbao

The Louvre

Location: Paris, France

What's Inside: The most-visited museum in the world, the Louvre is home to 35,000 art objects dating from ancient times to the 19th century. Visitors flock to Leonardo da Vinci's *Mona Lisa* and the famous sculptures *Winged Victory* and *Venus de Milo*.

Website: louvre.fr/en/

Metropolitan Museum of Art

Location: New York, New York, United States

What's Inside: The Met is so gigantic that its Egyptian art section contains an entire temple, which was shipped to America as a gift. The massive museum contains art from every period in history and every part of the world. In the Newbery Award—winning novel *From the Mixed-up Files of Mrs. Basil E. Frankweiler*, two kids hide out at the Met for days after running away from home.

Website: metmuseum.org

Museum of Modern Art

Location: New York, New York, United States

What's Inside: This New York City landmark holds one of the world's best collections of modern art, including Van Gogh's *The Starry Night*, Monet's *Water Lilies*, and Warhol's *Campbell's Soup Cans*.

Website: moma.org

National Baseball Hall of Fame and Museum

Location: Cooperstown, New York, United States

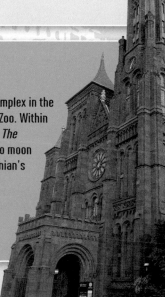

What's Inside: This popular upstate New York attraction is the center of the world of baseball, past and present. There are thousands of newspaper clippings, photos, and baseball cards plus special displays dedicated to Babe Ruth, Jackie Robinson, and women's baseball. Thirty glass-enclosed lockers, one for each Major League team, contain team jerseys and other items.

Website: baseballhall.org

Smithsonian Institution

Location: Washington, DC, United States

What's Inside: The Smithsonian is the largest museum complex in the world, composed of 19 different museums and the National Zoo. Within the complex you can check out Dorothy's red slippers from *The Wizard of Oz*, the lunar landing "dune buggy" from the Apollo moon missions, and millions of other items and displays. Smithsonian's newest museum, the National Museum of African American History and Culture (NMAAHC), is scheduled to open in late 2015. You can start exploring at nmaahc.si.edu right now.

Website: si.edu

Half the population of the world lives in just six countries: China, India, the United States, Indonesia, Brazil, and Pakistan. By the year 2050, Nigeria will join that group in the United States' place and another country will be out.

POPULATION

Nigeria has the largest population in Africa and the seventh largest in the world. And it's going to move up the ladder. According to Pew Research, by 2050 Nigeria will be the third most populous country, replacing the United States. It is projected to grow 176%, the most dramatic population growth for any country.

Here's something else that's dramatic: Nigeria is a land of young people. Half the population is under 20 years old. They're educated, eager for change, and ready to make a mark on their country and the world.

Nigeria has been called a "rising star," and one of its own rising stars is long jump champion Ese Brume. Ese won a gold medal in 2014 at the Commonwealth Games at age 19 and had previously won three national championships. Her longest jump on record is 22 feet (6.7 m), a distance equal to the height of some three-story buildings.

You might say Nigeria and Ese Brume are both running ahead. Keep an eye out for Ese at the Summer Olympics in Rio de Janeiro, Brazil, in August 2016. Read stats about Nigeria in Flags & Facts: Countries of the World on p. 301.

Population by Continent

Country	Population
Asia	4,388,026,000
Africa	1,177,263,000
Europe	744,623,000
North America	569,096,000
South America	413,535,000
Oceania*	37,575,000

*Includes Australia, New Zealand, Tasmania, Papua New Guinea, and thousands of other smaller islands

The continent of Antarctica is not listed above because it has no permanent population. Scientists, researchers, and tourists come and go.

5 Most Populous Countries

Country	Population
China	1,366,994,000
India	1,266,884,000
United States	323,849,000
Indonesia	258,316,000
Brazil	205,824,000

5 Least Populous Countries

Country	Population
Holy See (Vatican City)	842
Nauru	10,000
Tuvalu	11,000
Palau	21,000
Monaco	31,000

Country and continent populations based on US Census International Data Base 2016 projections.

5 Most Densely Populated Countries

Country	Persons per sq. mi. (persons per sq km)
Monaco	39,507.7 (15,254)
Singapore	20,988.7 (8,103.8)
Holy See (Vatican City)	4,956.3 (1,913.8)
Bahrain	4,478.3 (1,729.1)
Maldives	3,420.8 (1,320.8)

5 Most Sparsely Populated Countries

Country	Persons per sq. mi. (persons per sq km)
Mongolia	4.9 (1.9)
Namibia	6.9 (2.7)
Australia	7.6 (2.9)
Iceland	8.2 (3.2)
Mauritania	8.8 (3.4)

5 Largest World Urban Centers

City	Population (includes surrounding densely populated areas)
Tokyo, Japan	37,832,900
New Delhi, India	24,953,300
Shanghai, China	22,991,100
Mexico City, Mexico	20,843,500
São Paulo, Brazil	20,830,900

The world population is projected to be approximately 7.3 billion in 2016, more than double its number in 1956.

10 Most Populous States

State	Population
California	38,802,500
Texas	26,956,958
Florida	19,893,297
New York	19,746,227
Illinois	12,880,580
Pennsylvania	12,787,209
Ohio	11,594,163
Georgia	10,097,343
North Carolina	9,943,964
Michigan	9,909,877

10 Least Populous States

State	Population
Wyoming	584,153
Vermont	626,562
Alaska	736,732
North Dakota	739,482
South Dakota	853,175
Delaware	935,614
Montana	1,023,579
Rhode Island	1,055,173
New Hampshire	1,326,813
Maine	1,330,089

US Population Growth 1790–2016

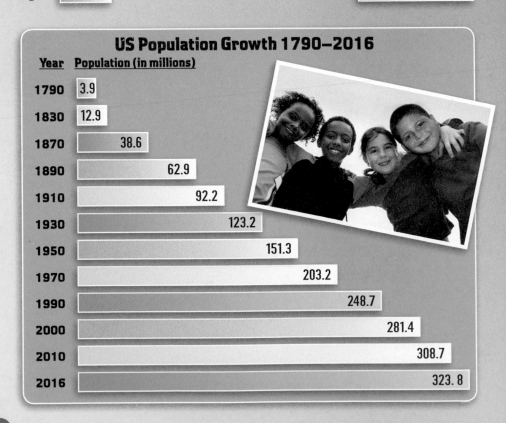

Year	Population (in millions)
1790	3.9
1830	12.9
1870	38.6
1890	62.9
1910	92.2
1930	123.2
1950	151.3
1970	203.2
1990	248.7
2000	281.4
2010	308.7
2016	323. 8

10 Most Populous US Cities

City	Population
New York, NY	8,405,837
Los Angeles, CA	3,884,307
Chicago, IL	2,718,782
Houston, TX	2,195,914
Philadelphia, PA	1,553,165
Phoenix, AZ	1,513,367
San Antonio, TX	1,409,019
San Diego, CA	1,355,896
Dallas, TX	1,257,676
San Jose, CA	998,537

10 Fastest-Growing US Cities

City	Projected percentage increase 2014–2015
Austin, TX	2.51
Ft. Worth, TX	2.10
Dallas, TX	2.04
Raleigh, NC	2.02
Charlotte, NC	1.98
San Antonio, TX	1.93
Houston, TX	1.74
Denver, CO	143
Seattle, WA	1.30
San Francisco, CA	0.95

When it comes to cutting-edge ideas, no group has the edge on DARPA (US Defense Advanced Research Projects Agency), the group that develops new technologies for the military. The Internet started under DARPA's direction, in the late 1960s. It was originally called ARPANET.

WildCat and **BigDog** are robots DARPA created with Boston Dynamics to help human soldiers on a variety of missions. These headless, four-legged 'bots can walk, run, and carry heavy loads over rough ground. BigDog is about the size of a small pony. It can carry up to 400 pounds (181 kg) of cargo and climb steep hills. WildCat can run at 16 mph (25 km/h)—faster than any human. Bad guys, better watch your backs!

MILITARY

Big Dog is a robot, but real canines have served their country heroically. In 2012, Congress called for the creation of a recognition system for military dogs. How would you design an award system for dogs? Take a look at the official list of medals and awards for human heroes on page 79 for ideas.

Best-Armed Nations

The world's strongest militaries are built with manpower, financial resources, training, and equipment.

Country	Active Troops	Defense Spending ($ in billions, rounded)	Tanks	Ships	Combat Aircraft
China	2,333,000	$112,173	6,840	139	1,385 +
United States	1,492,000	600,400	5,838	169	1,098
India	1,325,000	36,297	2,874 +	38	800
North Korea	1,190,000	Not available	3,500 +	75	489 +
Russia	845,000	68,163	2,550	96	923
South Korea	655,000	31,846	2,414	45	203
Pakistan	644,000	5,890	2,501 +	19	273
Iran	523,000	17,749	1,663 +	29	295 +
Turkey	511,000	10,742	2,504	33	352
Vietnam	482,000	3,800	1,270	4	97

Bring in the 'Bots

In today's military, high-tech devices help keep soldiers out of harm's way.

Explosive Ordnance Disposal (EOD) is a military unit that includes robots designed to handle chemical, biological, radiological, nuclear, and explosive threats.

Precision Urban Hopper is a GPS-guided robot that can hop more than 25 feet (7.6 m) in the air, allowing it to jump over fences and barricades. It's designed especially to be used in cities.

MQ-1 Predator is a plane that can be piloted remotely for surveillance and attack.

Branches of the US Military

Army
The oldest and largest branch of the United States military serves to defend and protect the nation at home and abroad. The most elite units, Army Rangers and Special Forces, train in advanced combat methods.

Navy
Members are especially skilled to handle any operations on and under the sea and in the air. Navy Divers and SEALs undergo specialized training for the most complex warfare operations.

Marines
The smallest branch of the nation's military is known for being the first on the ground in combat. Marines live by a strict code of honor, courage, and commitment.

Air Force
The technologically advanced members of the Air Force specialize in air and space operations to protect American interests.

Coast Guard
During peacetime, this branch protects national waterways, providing law enforcement, environmental cleanup, as well as search and rescue operations. During wartime, Coast Guard members serve with the Navy.

Beyond the Call of Duty

Military medals, or decorations, are awarded for bravery in and out of combat, loss of life or injury in combat, and other reasons. Most medals can be awarded to a member of any branch of the armed forces. The top 12 awards are listed in order, beginning with the highest.

Military Medals
1. Congressional Medal of Honor
2. Army Distinguished Service Cross, Navy Cross, Air Force Cross
3. Distinguished Service Medal
4. Silver Star
5. Defense Superior Service Medal
6. Legion of Merit
7. Distinguished Flying Cross
8. Soldier's Medal, Navy and Marine Corps Medal, Airman's Medal, Coast Guard Medal
9. Gold Lifesaving Medal
10. Bronze Star
11. Purple Heart
12. Defense Meritorious Service Medal

Liquid Body Armor is made of Kevlar soaked with shear thickening fluid (STF), silica particles mixed with polyethylene glycol. The material's liquid form makes it lightweight and flexible, but it hardens in milliseconds if struck by a bullet or shrapnel.

Hawaiians use hand movements in the hula and in the *shaka* sign, a greeting that means "hello," or "way to go." Deaf people in Hawaii have their own sign language. Learn about spoken languages in this chapter and about American Sign Language on page 59.

LANGUAGES

Like dinosaurs and dodo birds, languages can die out. Experts say 25 percent of world languages may soon be lost forever because too few people speak them regularly. One tribal language in the Himalayas has only eight speakers. When these people are gone, the language will disappear.

Hawaiian is the second official language in our 50th state, after English, but less than one percent of the population speaks it. Hawaii's ethnic diversity puts a number of other languages in the mix, including Japanese and Tagalog. To protect the Hawaiian language and identity, educators and community leaders started a language immersion program in the public schools. Students and teachers speak Hawaiian and read Hawaiian textbooks, although kids learn English beginning in grade 5. The program, called Ka Papahana Kaiapuni, goes all the way through high school.

Parents say kids come home and teach them Hawaiian. At performances like the one in the picture, they also keep Hawaiian culture alive.

Common Words and Phrases in Select Languages

MANDARIN CHINESE

Hello	Ni hao (nee how)
Good-bye	Zai jian (zay gee-en)
Yes	Shide (sure-due)
No	Bu shi (boo sure)
Please	Qing (ching)
Thank you	Xiexie (shieh-shieh)
You're welcome	Bukeqi (boo-keh-chee)
Excuse me	Duibuqi (doo-ee-boo-chee)

SPANISH

Hello	Hola (OH-lah)
Good-bye	Adiós (ah-dee-OHSS)
Good morning	Buenos días (BWAY-nohs DEE-ahs)
Good afternoon	Buenas tardes (BWAY-nahs TAHR-dehs)
Good evening	Buenas noches (BWAY-nahs NOH-chehs)
Yes	Sí (SEE)
No	No (NOH)
Please	Por favor (por fa-VOHR)
Thank you	Gracias (GRAH-see-ahs)
You're welcome	De nada (DE nada)
What's going on?	¿Qué pasa? (kay PAH-sah)
How are you?	¿Cómo está usted? (COH-mo es-TAH oo-STEHD)

GERMAN

Hello	Guten Tag (GOO-tin TAHK)
Good-bye	Auf Wiedersehen (ahf VEE-dehr-zeh-hehn)
Good morning	Guten Morgen (GOO-tin MOR-gun)
Yes	Ja (yah)
No	Nein (nine)
Please	Bitte (BIT-uh)
Thank you	Danke (DAHN-keh)
You're welcome	Bitte schön (BIT-uh shane)

Privet!

góðan dag

82

salut

ITALIAN

Hi, 'bye (informal)	Ciao (chow)
Good-bye	Arrivederci (ah-ree-vay-DEHR-chee)
Good morning, good afternoon, or a general hello	Buongiorno (bwohn JOOR-noh)
Yes	Si (SEE)
No	No (NOH)
Please	Per favore (purr fa-VO-ray)
Thank you	Grazie (GRAH-tsee-ay)
You're welcome	Prego (PRAY-go)
How are you?	Come sta? (KOH-may STAH)
Fine, very well	Molto bene (MOHL-toh BAY-nay)
Excuse me	Scusi (SKOO-zee)

EGYPTIAN ARABIC

Good morning	Sabah el khair (sa-BAH el KHAIR)
Good-bye	Ma'a salama (MA sa-LA-ma)
Yes	Aiwa (AYE-wa)
No	La (la)
Please	Min fadlak (min FAD-lak)
Thank you	Shukran (SHU-kran)
No problem	Ma fee mushkila (ma FEE mush-KI-la)
How are you?	Izzayak? (iz-ZAY-ak)
What is your name?	Ismak ay? (IS-mak AY)

JAPANESE

Hi	Konnichiwa (koh-nee-chee-wah)
Good-bye	Ja mata (jahh mah-tah)
Yes	Hai (hah-ee)
No	Iie (EE-eh)
Good morning	Ohayō gozaimasu (oh-hah-yohh goh-zah-ee-mahs)
Excuse me	Sumimasen (soo-mee-mah-sehn)
Pleased to meet you	Yoroshiku (yoh-roh-shee-koo)
One	Ichi (ee-chee)
Thank you	Dōmo arigatō (dohh-moh ah-ri-gah-toh)

hoi

FRENCH

Hello	Bonjour (bohn-ZHOOR)
Good-bye	Au revoir (oh reh-VWAH)
Yes	Oui (wee)
No	Non (no)
Excuse me	Pardonnez-moi (par-dough-nay MWAH)
Please	S'il vous plaît (see voo PLAY)
Thank you	Merci (mare-SEE)
How are you?	Comment allez-vous? (co-mahn-tah-lay VOO)

KOREAN

Hello	Anyŏng haseyo (ahn-n'yohng hah-say-yoh)
Good-bye	Anyŏng-hi kyeseyo (ahn-n'yohng-he kuh-say-yoh)
Please	Jwe-song-ha-ji-mahn (chey-song-hah-gee-mon)
Thank you	Kamsahamnida (kahm-sah-hahm-need-dah)
Excuse me	Miam hamnida (Me-ahn hahm-nee-dah)
One	Hana (hah-nah)
Ten	Yeol (yuhl)

xin chào

Hi

NIGERIAN
(four of the major Nigerian language groups)

English	Fulani	Hausa	Ibo	Yoruba
I'm fine	Jam tan (JAM-taan)	Kalau (KA-lay-U)	Adimnma (ah-DEE-mm-NMAA)	A dupe (ah-DEW-pay)
one	gogo (GO-quo)	daya (DA-ya)	otu (o-TOO)	eni (EE-nee)
two	didi (DEE-dee)	biyu (BEE-you)	abua (ah-BOO-ah)	eji (EE-gee)
three	tati (TA-tea)	uku (OO-coo)	ato (ah-TOE)	eta (EE-ta)
nine	jeenayi (gee-NA-yee)	tara (TAA-ra)	iteghete (IT-egg-HE-tee)	esan (EE-san)
ten	sappo (SAP-poe)	goma (GO-ma)	iri (EE-ree)	ewa (EE-wa)

Which Languages Are Spoken Most?

The following languages have the most speakers in the world. The languages combine individual varieties and dialects that may have different names. The numbers include only first-language (mother tongue) speakers.

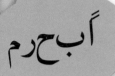

Language	Estimated Number of Speakers (in millions)
Chinese	1,197
Spanish	414
English	335
Hindi	260
Arabic	237
Portuguese	203
Russian	167
Japanese	122
Javanese	85
Lahnda	83
German (standard)	78
Korean	77
French	75
Telugu	74
Marathi	72
Turkish	71
Tamil	69
Vietnamese	68
Italian	64
Urdu	64

dzień dobry

talofa

hej

alô

Portugal isn't the only place where people speak Portuguese. About 150 million people speak it in Brazil, where it is the official language.

Every year, more than a million people visit the Anne Frank House in Amsterdam, the Netherlands. In a secret part of the house invisible from the street, eight Jewish people hid from Adolf Hitler's Nazis for two years before being discovered. One was a high-spirited teenager named Anne Frank. She died in a concentration camp in 1945, but the diary she left behind has become one of the world's most beloved books.

The Nazis persecuted Anne's family because of their religion. Sadly, religious intolerance and hatred go on today, some say in more than half the world's countries. As long as persecution continues against any religion, the basic freedom of everyone is threatened.

Anne's spirit and bravery in the face of unspeakable cruelty remain an inspiration. So does her message of hope: "In spite of everything, I still believe that people are really good at heart."

You can visit the Anne Frank House online at annefrank.org to see photographs and take a tour of the Franks' hiding place, the Secret Annex.

RELIGION

Crowds line up to visit the Anne Frank House in Amsterdam (right of the building with red shutters). The Franks lived in secret rooms on the two top floors.

Major Religions of the World

Buddhism

Buddhism began about 525 BCE, reportedly in India. This religion is based on the teachings of Gautama Siddhartha, the Buddha, who achieved enlightenment through intense meditation. The Buddha taught that though life is full of pain, you can break the cycle and achieve peace by being mindful, meditating, and doing good deeds. There are Buddhists all over the world, but mostly in Asia. The Buddha's teachings can be read in spiritual texts, or scriptures, called sutras.

Christianity

Christianity is the world's biggest religion, with over 2 billion worshippers. It is based on the teachings of Jesus Christ, who lived between 8 BCE and 29 CE. The Old and New Testaments of the Bible are the key scriptures. Christians believe that Jesus Christ is the son of God, who died on the cross to save humankind and later rose from the dead.

Hinduism

To Hindus, there is one overarching divine principle, with a variety of gods such as Vishnu, Shiva, and Shakti representing different parts of it. Hindus believe that by being mindful and doing good deeds you can break meaningless cycles and improve the purity of your actions, known as your karma. Hinduism was founded about 1500 BCE. The main scriptures are called Vedas.

Islam

Islam was founded in 610 CE by Muhammad. People who practice Islam are called Muslims. They believe in one God, Allah, who gave the spiritual writings of the Qur'an (also known as the Koran) to Muhammad so he could teach truth and justice to all people. There are two major Muslim groups, the Shiites and the Sunni.

Judaism

Judaism was founded about 2000 BCE. The prophet Abraham is recognized as the founder. Jews believe in one god. They believe God created the universe, and they believe in being faithful to God and in following God's laws as outlined in key scriptures such as the Torah and the Hebrew Bible. There are people practicing Judaism all over the world. Many of them are in Israel and the United States.

5 Largest World Religions

Religion	Members
Christianity	2,347,171,000
Islam	1,633,173,000
Hinduism	987,513,000
Buddhism	509,048,000
Chinese folk religions	436,179,000

The first Muslim settlers began arriving in America in the late nineteenth century. Many of these first immigrants bypassed big population centers and settled in the Midwest. The Mother Mosque in Cedar Rapids, Iowa, claims to be the first mosque in the United States. It was built in 1934.

Head injuries called concussions are increasing in kids playing soccer and lacrosse as well as football and ice hockey. Smart mouthguards could help. Read about all kinds of sports in this chapter.

SPORTS

Concussions are brain injuries caused by a hard hit on the head. They aren't usually fatal, but they can lead to permanent brain damage. Student athletes today are six times as likely to have a concussion as kids playing ten years ago. And it's not just football players who are at greater risk. Concussions are increasing in soccer and lacrosse, too.

New smart mouthguards could be a game-changer. They look like ordinary mouthguards, but they collect impact information from the head through the upper jaw and send it wirelessly to coaches' tablets or smartphones. The coaches can pull players out and get medical help quickly if the impact is high. They can also correct players who are using dangerous moves, such as tackling with the crown of their helmet.

PRO FOOTBALL

League Leaders 2014

Passing Yards
Drew Brees, New Orleans Saints	4,952
Ben Roethlisberger, Pittsburgh Steelers	4,952

Rushing Yards
DeMarco Murray, Dallas Cowboys	1,845

Receiving Yards
Antonio Brown, Pittsburgh Steelers	1,698

Touchdowns
Marshawn Lynch, Seattle Seahawks	17

Super Bowl XLIX

On February 1, 2015, the National Football League (NFL) staged its championship football game, Super Bowl XLIX, between the Seattle Seahawks, winners of the National Football Conference (NFC), and the New England Patriots, winners of the American Football Conference (AFC), at University of Phoenix Stadium in Glendale, AZ. The Patriots won 28—24. Quarterback Tom Brady was named MVP, the third time he has won that title. He completed 37 of 50 pass attempts for 328 yards and four touchdowns. New England intercepted Seattle's final pass attempt of the game at the 1-yard line to secure the victory.

New England Patriots (AFC) 28
Seattle Seahawks (NFC) 24

Manning's the Man

On December 22, 2013, Denver Broncos quarterback Peyton Manning threw four touchdown passes in a 37—13 win over the Houston Texans. The final touchdown pass of the game was a 25-yard strike to his tight end Julius Thomas, and it established a new record of 51 for touchdown passes thrown by a quarterback in the regular season. The previous record was 50, held by New England Patriots quarterback Tom Brady. By the end of the 2014 season, Manning had increased the record to 55. He also holds the NFL career record for touchdown passes, with 530.

COLLEGE FOOTBALL

Bowl Championship Series (BCS)

National Championship Game 2014
Ohio State 42, Oregon 20

Major Bowl Games 2014–2015

Game	Location	Teams/Score
Sugar Bowl	New Orleans, LA	Ohio State 42, Alabama 35
Rose Bowl	Pasadena, CA	Oregon 52, Florida State 20
Cotton Bowl	Arlington, TX	Michigan State 42, Baylor 41
Peach Bowl	Atlanta, GA	TCU 42, Ole Miss 3
Orange Bowl	Miami, FL	Georgia Tech 49, Mississippi State 34
Fiesta Bowl	Glendale, AZ	Boise State 38, Arizona 30
Alamo Bowl	San Antonio, TX	UCLA 40, Kansas State 35
Belk Bowl	Charlotte, NC	Georgia 37, Louisville 14
Sun Bowl	El Paso, TX	Arizona State 36, Duke 31
Citrus Bowl	Orlando, FL	Missouri 33, Minnesota 17

Heisman Trophy 2014

Marcus Mariota, University of Oregon, is the 80th Heisman trophy winner and the first ever from the University of Oregon. As a junior, he completed 304 of 445 pass attempts for 4,454 yards and 42 touchdowns, while throwing only 4 interceptions. He led Oregon to a playoff win against Florida State, a game played for the first time under college football's new playoff system, before falling short in the National Championship game to Ohio State.

BASEBALL

Top Players 2014

Rookies of the Year
American League	José Abreu, Chicago White Sox
National League	Jacob deGrom, New York Mets

Managers of the Year
American League	Buck Showalter, Baltimore Orioles
National League	Matt Williams, Washington Nationals

Most Valuable Player Awards
American League	Mike Trout, Los Angeles Angels
National League	Clayton Kershaw, Los Angeles Dodgers

Cy Young Awards
American League	Corey Kluber, Cleveland Indians
National League	Clayton Kershaw, Los Angeles Dodgers

Gold Glove Winners 2014
(selected by managers and players)

American League
Pitcher	Dallas Keutchel, Houston Astros
Catcher	Salvador Perez, Kansas City Royals
First Baseman	Eric Hosmer, Kansas City Royals
Second Baseman	Dustin Pedroia, Boston Red Sox
Third Baseman	Kyle Seager, Seattle Mariners
Shortstop	JJ Hardy, Baltimore Orioles
	Alex Gordon, Kansas City Royals
	Nick Markakis, Baltimore Orioles
Outfielders	Adam Jones, Baltimore Orioles

National League
Pitcher	Zack Greinke, Los Angeles Dodgers
Catcher	Yadier Molina, St. Louis Cardinals
First Baseman	Adrian Gonzalez, Los Angeles Dodgers
Second Baseman	DJ LeMahieu, Colorado Rockies
Third Baseman	Nolan Arenado, Colorado Rockies
Shortstop	Andrelton Simmons, Atlanta Braves
	Christian Yelich, Miami Marlins
	Juan Lagares, New York Mets
Outfielders	Jason Heyward, Atlanta Braves

League Leaders 2014

American League

Batting Average	Jose Altuve, Houston Astros	.341
Home Runs	Nelson Cruz, Baltimore Orioles	40
Runs Batted In	Mike Trout, Los Angeles Angels	111
	Corey Kluber, Cleveland Indians	18
	Max Scherzer, Detroit Tigers	18
Wins	Jered Weaver, Los Angeles Angels	18
Earned Run Average	Felix Hernandez, Seattle Mariners	2.14
Saves	Fernando Rodney, Seattle Mariners	48

National League

Batting Average	Justin Morneau, Colorado Rockies	.319
Home Runs	Giancarlo Stanton, Miami Marlins	37
Runs Batted In	Adrian Gonzalez, Los Angeles Dodgers	116
Wins	Clayton Kershaw, Los Angeles Dodgers	21
Earned Run Average	Clayton Kershaw, Los Angeles Dodgers	1.77
Saves	Craig Kimbrel, Atlanta Braves	47

World Series 2014

On October 29, 2014, the San Francisco Giants beat the Kansas City Royals in the World Series in the seventh and final game. It was the first time since 1979 that a team won a deciding game seven on the road, and it marked the Giants' third World Series championship in the last five years. Madison Bumgarner was the star of the game. He also won the Series MVP award, going 2-0 with one save, 31 strikeouts, and an amazing 0.25 ERA. He won games 1 and 5 as the starting pitcher, throwing a complete game shutout in the latter, before finishing off the series with 5 shutout innings in relief. He only allowed a total of one earned run in all three of his games.

Little League World Series 2014

The International champs from the Asia-Pacific Region defeated the United States champs from the Great Lakes Region 8-4 in the championship game of the Little League World Series played in Williamsport, PA on Sunday, August 24, 2014. Asia-Pacific took the lead in the first inning, and never trailed after that. Dong Wan Sin went 2-3 with a home run to lead the International team to victory.

PRO BASKETBALL

NBA Championship Finals 2014

On June 15, 2014, the San Antonio Spurs won the NBA Championship with a 104—87 victory over the Miami Heat at AT&T Center in San Antonio, TX. It was the second year in a row the same two teams met in the finals, the Spurs avenging their loss the previous year by taking the series in five games, 4—1. Kawhi Leonard was the MVP, scoring 22 points with 10 rebounds and two assists in the final game.

NBA Top Scorers 2014

NAME	TEAM	GAMES	AVG. POINTS
1. Kevin Durant	OKC	81	32.0
2. Carmelo Anthony	NYK	77	27.4
3. LeBron James	MIA	77	27.1
4. Kevin Love	MIN	77	26.1
5. James Harden	HOU	73	25.4

WNBA Championship Finals 2014

On Friday, Sept 12, 2014, the Phoenix Mercury played the Chicago Sky at the Allstate Arena in Rosemont, IL. The Mercury won 87—82 to sweep the series. Diana Taurasi was named the series MVP, scoring 24 points. She became only the third player to win the award more than once.

WNBA Top Scorers 2014

NAME	TEAM	GAMES	AVG. POINTS (per game)
1. Maya Moore	MIN	34	23.9
2. Skylar Diggins	TUL	34	20.1
3. Candace Parker	LA	30	19.4
4. Angel McCoughtry	ATL	31	18.5
5. Tina Charles	NY	34	17.4

COLLEGE BASKETBALL

NCAA Men's Division I Championship 2015

The Duke Blue Devils came from a half-time tie to beat the Wisconsin Badgers 68—63 in a thrilling National Collegiate Athletic Association (NCAA) championship on April 6, 2015, at Lucas Oil Stadium in Indianapolis, IN. It was Duke's fifth title under Coach Mike Krzyzewski, famously known as "Coach K."

Duke freshman point guard Tyus Jones scored 23 total points, 19 of them in the second half, and 7 out of 7 free throws. Jones was named Most Valuable Player in the Final Four. In his last college game, senior power forward Frank Kaminsky scored 21 points for Wisconsin.

NCAA Men's Championship Game Leaders

	DUKE		WISCONSIN	
Points	Tyus Jones	23	Frank Kaminsky	21
Rebounds	Bronson Koenig	12	Frank Kaminsky	12
Assists	Quinn Cook	2	Frank Kaminsky	2

NCAA Women's Division I Championship 2015

In the women's division of the NCAA, the University of Connecticut Huskies defeated the Notre Dame Fighting Irish 63—53 on April 7, 2015, at the Amalie Arena in Tampa, FL. Under Coach Geno Auriemma, it was the team's third championship in a row and tenth total, the most in college basketball history. The team has won every championship game they've played in.

UConn forward Breanna Stewart scored 8 points and 15 rebounds. She was named Most Outstanding Player of the Final Four for the third time, becoming the first female player to achieve that honor.

NCAA Women's Championship Game Leaders

	UCONN		NOTRE DAME	
Points	Kaleena Mosqueda-Lewis	15		
	Moriah Jefferson	15	Brianna Turner	14
Rebounds	Breanna Stewart	15	Taya Reimer	11
Assists	Lindsay Allen	7	Morgan Tuck	7

Locations of the Modern-Day Summer Olympics

Year	Location	Year	Location
1896	Athens, Greece	1936	Berlin, Germany
1900	Paris, France	1940	*canceled*
1904	St. Louis, Missouri, USA	1944	*canceled*
1906	Athens, Greece (unofficial)	1948	London, UK
1908	London, UK	1952	Helsinki, Finland
1912	Stockholm, Sweden	1956	Melbourne, Australia
		1960	Rome, Italy
		1964	Tokyo, Japan
		1968	Mexico City, Mexico
		1972	Munich, Germany
		1976	Montreal, Canada
		1980	Moscow, USSR
		1984	Los Angeles, California, USA
		1988	Seoul, South Korea
		1992	Barcelona, Spain
		1996	Atlanta, Georgia, USA
1916	*canceled*	2000	Sydney, Australia
1920	Antwerp, Belgium	2004	Athens, Greece
1924	Paris, France	2008	Beijing, China
1928	Amsterdam, Holland	2012	London, UK
1932	Los Angeles, California, USA	2016	Rio de Janeiro, Brazil

Olympics 84
USA
40c
Airmail

Locations of the Modern-Day Winter Olympics

Year	Location	Year	Location
1924	Chamonix, France	1984	Sarajevo, Yugoslavia
1928	St. Moritz, Switzerland	1988	Calgary, Alberta, Canada
1932	Lake Placid, New York, USA	1992	Albertville, France
1936	Garmisch-Partenkirchen, Germany	1994	Lillehammer, Norway
		1998	Nagano, Japan
1940	*canceled*	2002	Salt Lake City, Utah, USA
1944	*canceled*	2006	Turin, Italy
1948	St. Moritz, Switzerland	2010	Vancouver, Canada
1952	Oslo, Norway	2014	Sochi, Russian Federation
1956	Cortina d'Ampezzo, Italy	2018	Pyeong Chang, South Korea
1960	Squaw Valley, California, USA		
1964	Innsbruck, Austria		
1968	Grenoble, France		
1972	Sapporo, Japan		
1976	Innsbruck, Austria		
1980	Lake Placid, New York, USA		

- The five Olympic rings represent the five major regions of the world—Africa, the Americas, Asia, Europe, and Oceania.

- In 1916, 1940, and 1944, the Olympics were canceled because of World War I and World War II.

- In 1928, Australian rower Henry Pearce stopped in the middle of his race to let a duck family pass by the front of his boat. Even with the delay, Pearce went on to win the gold.

Log on to www.olympic.org for Olympics news, history, tips from the champions, and much more!

SCIENCE
& TECHNOLOGY

Dr. Murthy Gudipati, of NASA's Jet Propulsion Laboratory in Pasadena, CA, thinks of a comet as deep-fried ice cream. A hard outer crust covers a cold, dense interior. Organic dust coats the top like chocolate sprinkles.

Dr. Gudipati and other scientists think about comets a lot. They believe these ice-and-dust balls are the oldest bodies in the solar system, and that they supplied much of the water for today's oceans. They may have even brought molecules of the organic matter that led to life on Earth.

Now scientists have been able to see comets as never before. Since its historic landing on Comet 67P/Churyumov-Gerasimenko in late 2014, the spacecraft *Rosetta* has been following the comet through deep space. *Rosetta*'s cameras have captured and beamed back spectacular photos taken from only a few miles away. *Rosetta*'s mission will end December 2015, but a new stage of comet study is just beginning.

Read more about space starting on the next page. Learn about remarkable advances in other areas of science and technology in this section.

Space

Our Solar System
(with distances from the Sun*)

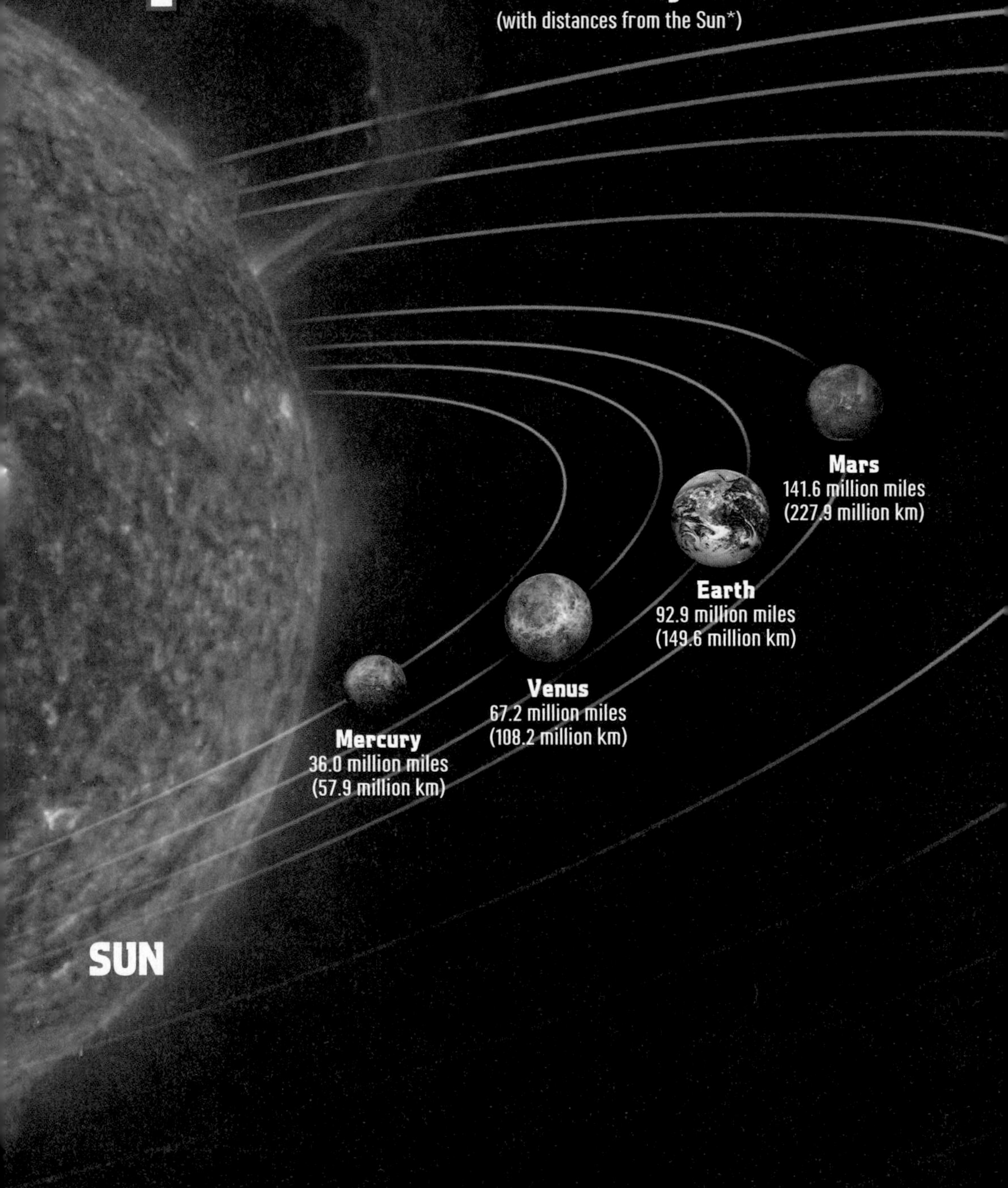

Mars
141.6 million miles
(227.9 million km)

Earth
92.9 million miles
(149.6 million km)

Venus
67.2 million miles
(108.2 million km)

Mercury
36.0 million miles
(57.9 million km)

SUN

*Distances rounded to nearest tenth

Neptune
2.8 billion miles
(4.5 billion km)

Uranus
1.8 billion miles
(2.9 billion km)

Saturn
885.9 million miles
(1. 4 billion km)

Jupiter
483.7 million miles
(778. 4 million km)

What's a Dwarf Planet?

A dwarf planet is usually smaller than a regular planet and lacks gravity powerful enough to "clear the neighborhood"— push space rocks away or pull them down to its surface. The first five recognized dwarf planets are Ceres, Pluto, Eris, Makemake, and Haumea. Scientists say there may be hundreds more.

Basic Facts about the Planets in Our Solar System

Planet	Average distance from Sun	Rotation period (hours)	Period of revolution (in Earth days)	Diameter relative to Earth	Average surface or effective temperature	Planetary satellites (moons)
Mercury	36.0 million miles (57.9 million km)	1,407.5 hours	88 days	38.2%	332°F (166°C)	0
Venus	67.2 million miles (108.2 million km)	5,832.4 hours*	224.7 days	94.9%	864°F (462°C)	0
Earth	92.9 million miles (149.6 million km)	23.9 hours	365.26 days	100%	59°F (15°C)	1
Mars	141.6 million miles (227.9 million km)	24.6 hours	687 days	53.2%	-80°F (-62°C)	2
Jupiter	483.7 million miles (778.4 million km)	9.9 hours	4,332.8 days	1,097%	-234°F (-148°C)	67
Saturn	885.9 million miles (1.4 billion km)	10.7 hours	10,755.7 days	914%	-288°F (-178°C)	at least 62
Uranus	1.8 billion miles (2.9 billion km)	17.2 hours*	30,687.2 days	398%	-357°F (-216°C)	at least 27
Neptune	2.8 billion miles (4.5 billion km)	16.1 hours	60,190 days	386%	-353°F (-214°C)	14

*Retrograde rotation: rotates backward, or in the opposite direction from most other planetary bodies.

Basic Facts about the Sun

Position in our solar system	center
Average distance from Earth	92,955,820 miles (149,597,891 km)
Distance from center of Milky Way galaxy	27,710 light-years
Rotation period	25.38 days
Equatorial diameter	864,400 miles (1,391,117 km)
Diameter relative to Earth	109 times larger
Temperature at core	27,000,000°F (15,000,000°C)
Temperature at surface	10,000°F (5,538°C)
Main components	hydrogen and helium
Expected life of hydrogen fuel supply	6.4 billion years

Top 10 Largest Bodies in the Solar System
Ranked by size of equatorial diameter

1. Sun
864,400 miles
(1,391,117 km)

2. Jupiter
88,846 miles
(142,984 km)

3. Saturn
74,898 miles
(120,536 km)

5. Neptune
30,776 miles
(49,528 km)

4. Uranus
31,764 miles
(51,118 km)

6. Earth
7,926 miles
(12,755 km)

7. Venus
7,521 miles
(12,104 km)

8. Mars
4,222 miles
(6,794 km)

9. Ganymede
(moon of Jupiter)
3,280 miles
(5,262 km)

10. Titan
(moon of Saturn)
3,200 miles
(5,149 km)

Astronomy Terms and Definitions

Light-year (distance traveled by light in one year)	5.880 trillion miles (9.462 trillion km)
Velocity of light (speed of light)	186,000 miles/second (299,338 km/s)
Mean distance, Earth to moon	238,855 miles (384,400 km)
Radius of Earth (distance from Earth's center to the equator)	3,963.19 miles (6,378 km)
Equatorial circumference of Earth (distance around the equator)	24,901 miles (40,075 km)
Polar circumference of Earth (distance around the poles)	24,860 miles (40,008 km)
Earth's mean velocity in orbit (how fast it travels)	18.5 miles/second (29.8 km/sec)

Fast Facts about Earth's Moon

Age	4.6 billion years
Diameter	2,160 miles (3,476 km)
Period of revolution	27 Earth days

Interesting features:
Earth's moon has no atmosphere or magnetic field.
Most rocks on the surface of Earth's moon seem to be
between 3 billion and 4.6 billion years old. Thus Earth's
moon provides evidence about the early history of our
solar system.

Top 10 Known Closest Comet Approaches to Earth prior to 2015

4. Halley
April 10, 1837
3,104,724.0 miles
(4,996,569 km)

5. Biela
December 9, 1805
3,402,182.5 miles
(5,475,282 km)

6. Comet of 1743
February 8, 1743
3,625,276.5 miles
(5,834,317 km)

7. Pons-Winnecke
June 26, 1927
3,662,458.7 miles
(5,894,156 km)

3. IRAS-Araki-Alcock
May 11, 1983
2,900,221.5 miles
(4,667,454 km)

8. Comet of 1014
February 24, 1014
3,783,301.1 miles
(6,080,633 km)

2. Tempel-Tuttle
October 26, 1366
2,128,687.8 miles
(3,425,791 km)

9. Comet of 1702
April 20, 1702
4,062,168.8 miles
(6,537,427 km)

1. Lexell
July 1, 1770
1,403,632.1 miles
(2,258,927 km)

10. Comet of 1132
October 7, 1132
4,155,124.7 miles
(6,687,025 km)

The Phases of the Moon

The moon's appearance from Earth changes as it moves in its orbit around Earth.

Waxing gibbous

First quarter

Waxing crescent

Full moon

New moon

Waning gibbous

Last quarter

Waning crescent

Major Constellations

Latin	English	Latin	English
Aries	Ram	Lynx	Lynx
Camelopardalis	Giraffe	Lyra	Harp
Cancer	Crab	Microscopium	Microscope
Canes Venatici	Hunting Dogs	Monoceros	Unicorn
Canis Major	Big Dog	Musca	Fly
Canis Minor	Little Dog	Orion	Orion
Capricornus	Goat	Pavo	Peacock
Cassiopeia	Queen	Pegasus	Pegasus
Centaurus	Centaur	Phoenix	Phoenix
Cetus	Whale	Pictor	Painter
Chamaeleon	Chameleon	Pisces	Fish
Circinus	Compass	Piscis Austrinus	Southern Fish
Columba	Dove	Sagitta	Arrow
Corona Australis	Southern Crown	Sagittarius	Archer
Corona Borealis	Northern Crown	Scorpius	Scorpion
Corvus	Crow	Sculptor	Sculptor
Crater	Cup	Scutum	Shield
Crux	Southern Cross	Serpens	Serpent
Cygnus	Swan	Sextans	Sextant
Delphinus	Dolphin	Taurus	Bull
Dorado	Goldfish	Telescopium	Telescope
Draco	Dragon	Triangulum	Triangle
Equuleus	Little Horse	Triangulum Australis	Southern Triangle
Gemini	Twins	Tucana	Toucan
Grus	Crane	Ursa Major	Big Bear
Hercules	Hercules	Ursa Minor	Little Bear
Horologium	Clock	Virgo	Virgin
Lacerta	Lizard	Volans	Flying Fish
Leo	Lion	Vulpecula	Little Fox
Leo Minor	Little Lion		

Galaxies Nearest to the Sun

1. Canis Major Dwarf Galaxy
25,000 light-years

2. Sagittarius Dwarf Elliptical Galaxy
70,000 light-years

3. Large Magellanic Cloud
179,000 light-years

4. Small Magellanic Cloud
210,000 light-years

It would take the spacecraft *Voyager* about 749,000,000 years to get to Canis Major Dwarf Galaxy, the closest galaxy to ours.

Stars Closest to Earth *

1. Proxima Centauri
4.22 light-years

2. Alpha Centauri A and B
4.35 light-years

3. Barnard's Star
5.9 light-years

4. Wolf 359
7.6 light-years

5. Lalande 21185
8.0 light-years

6. Sirius A and B
8.6 light-years

7. Luyten 726-8A and 726-8B
8.9 light-years

*besides the Sun

The smallest battery in the world is hundreds of times thinner than a hair on your head. The biggest battery can provide power to the whole city of Fairbanks, AK, population 12,000.

We use batteries to power smartphones, laptops, iPods, and even cars. Most electric cars are small and slow, designed more for pollution-free city driving than speed. However, engineers have developed a cool battery-powered race car that can go 155 miles per hour (250 kph) and accelerate from 0 to 62 miles per hour (100 kph) in three seconds. Drivers competed around the world throughout 2014 and 2015 in a new series called the Formula E Championship.

INVENTIONS

The first modern battery looked like a pile of coins. Who invented it, and what everyday electrical term comes from the inventor's name? Check out the time line on page 112 to find out!

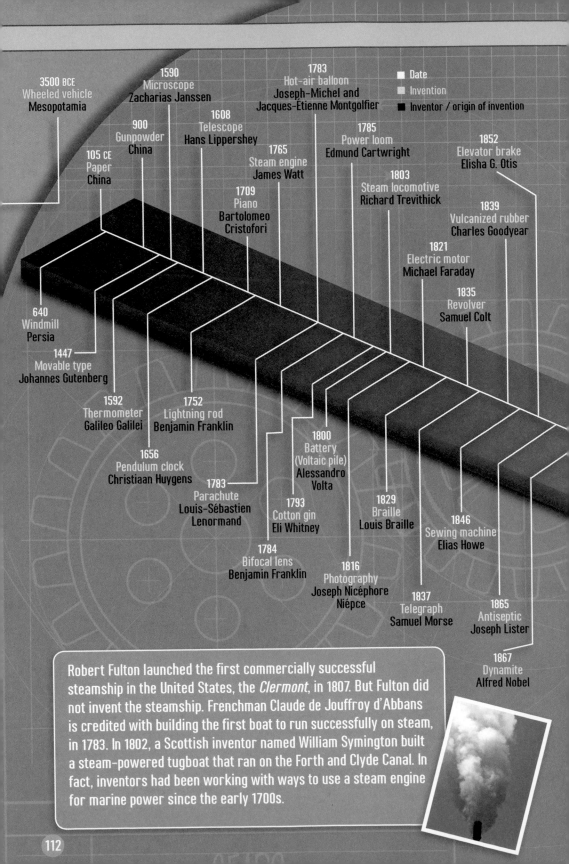

3500 BCE
Wheeled vehicle
Mesopotamia

1590
Microscope
Zacharias Janssen

1783
Hot-air balloon
Joseph-Michel and
Jacques-Étienne Montgolfier

■ Date
■ Invention
■ Inventor / origin of invention

900
Gunpowder
China

1608
Telescope
Hans Lippershey

1785
Power loom
Edmund Cartwright

1852
Elevator brake
Elisha G. Otis

105 CE
Paper
China

1765
Steam engine
James Watt

1803
Steam locomotive
Richard Trevithick

1839
Vulcanized rubber
Charles Goodyear

1709
Piano
Bartolomeo
Cristofori

1821
Electric motor
Michael Faraday

1835
Revolver
Samuel Colt

640
Windmill
Persia

1447
Movable type
Johannes Gutenberg

1592
Thermometer
Galileo Galilei

1752
Lightning rod
Benjamin Franklin

1800
Battery
(Voltaic pile)
Alessandro
Volta

1656
Pendulum clock
Christiaan Huygens

1783
Parachute
Louis-Sébastien
Lenormand

1793
Cotton gin
Eli Whitney

1829
Braille
Louis Braille

1846
Sewing machine
Elias Howe

1784
Bifocal lens
Benjamin Franklin

1816
Photography
Joseph Nicéphore
Niépce

1837
Telegraph
Samuel Morse

1865
Antiseptic
Joseph Lister

1867
Dynamite
Alfred Nobel

Robert Fulton launched the first commercially successful
steamship in the United States, the *Clermont*, in 1807. But Fulton did
not invent the steamship. Frenchman Claude de Jouffroy d'Abbans
is credited with building the first boat to run successfully on steam,
in 1783. In 1802, a Scottish inventor named William Symington built
a steam-powered tugboat that ran on the Forth and Clyde Canal. In
fact, inventors had been working with ways to use a steam engine
for marine power since the early 1700s.

Important Inventions and Their Inventors

These are just a few of the inventions that have shaped our world and changed our lives. The inventors listed are either those who received patents for the invention or the ones widely credited with introducing the version of the invention we use today. But in many cases, other inventors contributed to the invention by doing experiments or making earlier versions. Do some additional research for the whole story behind these inventions and others.

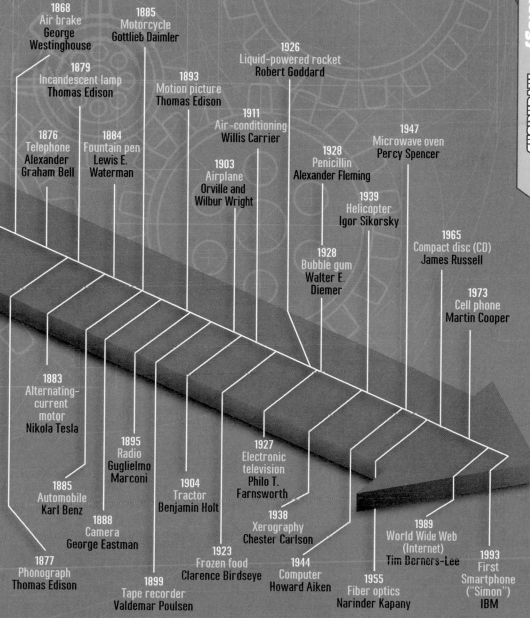

1868
Air brake
George
Westinghouse

1885
Motorcycle
Gottlieb Daimler

1926
Liquid-powered rocket
Robert Goddard

1879
Incandescent lamp
Thomas Edison

1893
Motion picture
Thomas Edison

1911
Air-conditioning
Willis Carrier

1947
Microwave oven
Percy Spencer

1876
Telephone
Alexander
Graham Bell

1884
Fountain pen
Lewis E.
Waterman

1928
Penicillin
Alexander Fleming

1903
Airplane
Orville and
Wilbur Wright

1939
Helicopter
Igor Sikorsky

1928
Bubble gum
Walter E.
Diemer

1965
Compact disc (CD)
James Russell

1973
Cell phone
Martin Cooper

1883
Alternating-
current
motor
Nikola Tesla

1895
Radio
Guglielmo
Marconi

1927
Electronic
television
Philo T.
Farnsworth

1885
Automobile
Karl Benz

1904
Tractor
Benjamin Holt

1938
Xerography
Chester Carlson

1888
Camera
George Eastman

1923
Frozen food
Clarence Birdseye

1989
World Wide Web
(Internet)
Tim Berners-Lee

1877
Phonograph
Thomas Edison

1944
Computer
Howard Aiken

1993
First
Smartphone
("Simon")
IBM

1899
Tape recorder
Valdemar Poulsen

1955
Fiber optics
Narinder Kapany

113

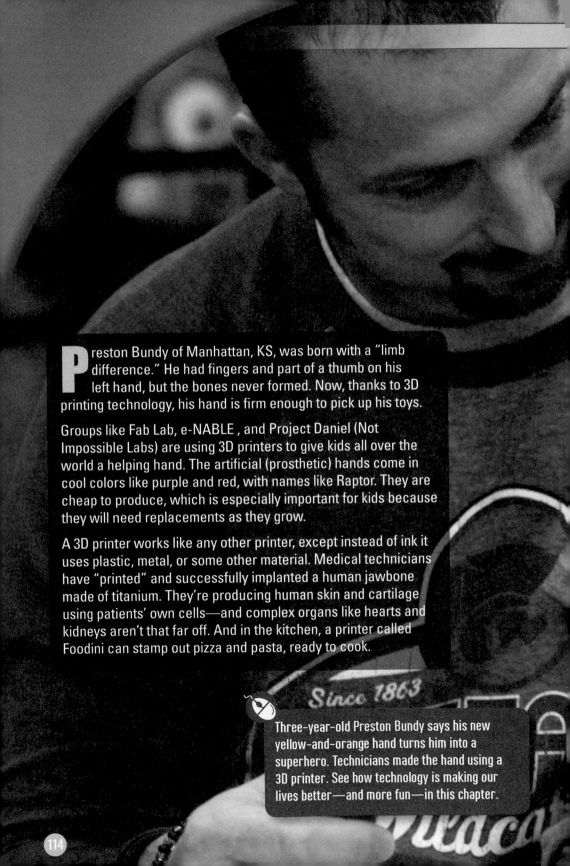

Preston Bundy of Manhattan, KS, was born with a "limb difference." He had fingers and part of a thumb on his left hand, but the bones never formed. Now, thanks to 3D printing technology, his hand is firm enough to pick up his toys.

Groups like Fab Lab, e-NABLE , and Project Daniel (Not Impossible Labs) are using 3D printers to give kids all over the world a helping hand. The artificial (prosthetic) hands come in cool colors like purple and red, with names like Raptor. They are cheap to produce, which is especially important for kids because they will need replacements as they grow.

A 3D printer works like any other printer, except instead of ink it uses plastic, metal, or some other material. Medical technicians have "printed" and successfully implanted a human jawbone made of titanium. They're producing human skin and cartilage using patients' own cells—and complex organs like hearts and kidneys aren't that far off. And in the kitchen, a printer called Foodini can stamp out pizza and pasta, ready to cook.

Three-year-old Preston Bundy says his new yellow-and-orange hand turns him into a superhero. Technicians made the hand using a 3D printer. See how technology is making our lives better—and more fun—in this chapter.

TECHNOLOGY

Top Ten World Internet Users

The Internet connects the farthest corners of the world. Here are the top ten Internet-using countries and how their usage grew between 2013 and 2014.

Rank	Country	Number of Internet Users	Percentage of Population with Internet	Year-over-Year Percentage Growth of Internet Users	Country's Share of World Internet Users
1	China	641,601,070	46.03%	4%	21.97%
2	United States	279,834,232	86.75%	7%	9.58%
3	India	243,198,922	19.19%	14%	8.33%
4	Japan	109,252,912	86.03%	8%	3.74%
5	Brazil	107,822,831	53.37%	7%	3.69%
6	Russia	84,437,793	59.27%	10%	2.89%
7	Germany	71,727,551	86.78%	2%	2.46%
8	Nigeria	67,101,452	37.59%	16%	2.30%
9	United Kingdom	57,075,826	89.90%	3%	1.95%
10	France	55,429,382	85.75%	3%	1.90%

Top 25 World Smartphone Users

The world connects online through laptops, tablets, and smartphones. Of course, we also talk and text on our phones . . . and listen to music, and monitor our heartbeats, and do a zillion other things. In 2016, there will be an estimated 2.15 billion smartphone users in the world. These 25 countries will lead in smartphone use.

Country	millions 2016	Country	millions 2016
China*	624.7	Italy	32.2
India	204.1	Philippines	29.7
USA**	198.5	Spain	26.9
Indonesia	69.4	Nigeria	26.8
Russia	65.1	Vietnam	24.6
Japan	61.2	Thailand	22.8
Brazil	58.5	Canada	21.7
Germany	50.8	Egypt	21.0
UK**	42.4	Colombia	18.2
Mexico	39.4	Poland	17.4
France	37.8	Australia	14.3
South Korea	34.5	Argentina	14.1
Turkey	32.4	Worldwide***	2155.0

Note: Individuals of any age who have at least one smartphone and use the smartphone(s) at least once per month
*excludes Hong Kong; ** forecast from August 2014; ***includes countries not listed.
Source: eMarketer, December 2014

Emoji means "picture" and "letter" in Japanese. You might use emojis in e-mails and texts to substitute for words or add punctuation and feeling. People like them so much there are emoji keyboards with no letters, only symbols.

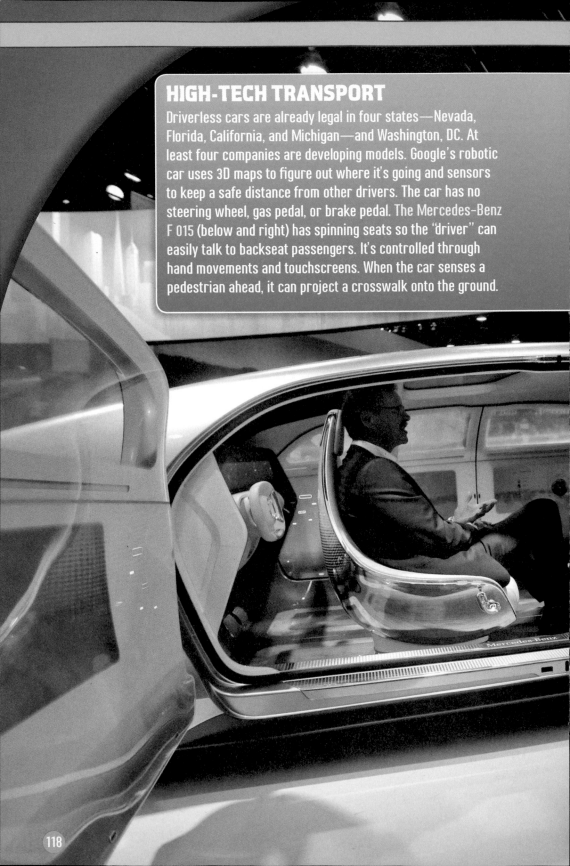

HIGH-TECH TRANSPORT

Driverless cars are already legal in four states—Nevada, Florida, California, and Michigan—and Washington, DC. At least four companies are developing models. Google's robotic car uses 3D maps to figure out where it's going and sensors to keep a safe distance from other drivers. The car has no steering wheel, gas pedal, or brake pedal. The Mercedes-Benz F 015 (below and right) has spinning seats so the "driver" can easily talk to backseat passengers. It's controlled through hand movements and touchscreens. When the car senses a pedestrian ahead, it can project a crosswalk onto the ground.

Tech Toys

SMART WHEELS

California-based IO Hawk's smart skateboard lets you step on and travel up to 6 mph (9.7 kph) for about 10—12 miles (16—19 km).

MAGIC MIRROR

Panasonic's Magic Mirror doesn't just show you what you look like. It tells you how you can look better, or at least different. It can analyze your skin and tell you to use more sunscreen and drink more water. It can show you how you look under outdoor and fluorescent light. It can even show you how you would look with a beard or mustache! In case you want to know.

THE LOGBAR RING

This wearable technology lets you control apps and devices by wagging your finger.

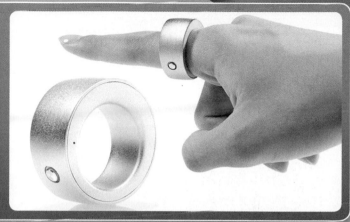

NIXIE

How to take a selfie from beyond your reach? Use a Nixie. It's a wristband with a flying camera built in. You launch it off your wrist. It takes a shot, and then it hovers until you catch it.

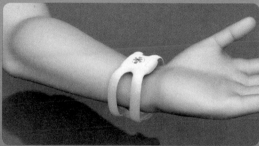

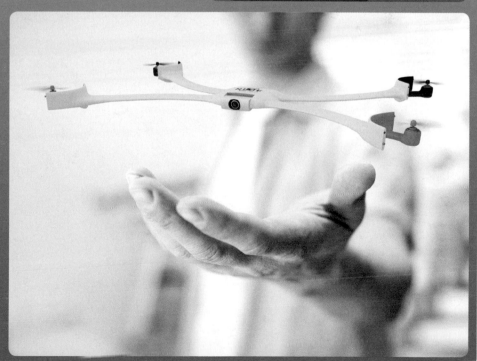

Tech Toys (continued)

UNPLUG YOUR HOUSE

Tesla, the electric car manufacturer, was scheduled to start production in 2015 of a battery big enough to run a whole house. The Toyota Mirai electric car runs on a battery that can be removed and used to power an average home for a week.

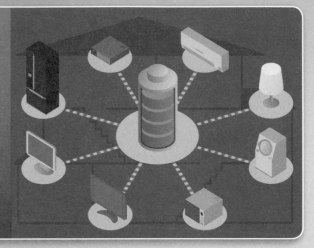

BAXTER

Healthcare workers treating dangerous contagious diseases wear protective equipment, but they could become infected if they make the slightest mistake taking it off. Baxter, a robot made especially for Ebola treatment, helps medical professionals take off their gear in a safe way. Workers can also remotely operate Baxter and other robots to monitor patients, move equipment, and dispose of contaminated material from a safe distance.

HEADSETS TAKE YOU THERE

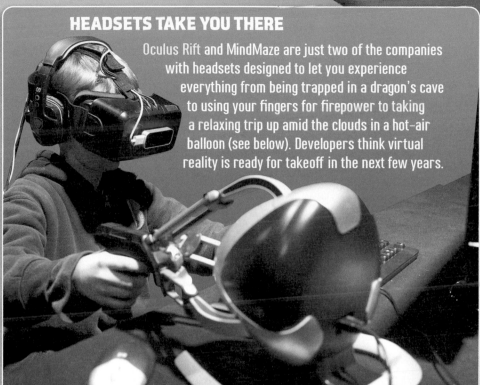

Oculus Rift and MindMaze are just two of the companies with headsets designed to let you experience everything from being trapped in a dragon's cave to using your fingers for firepower to taking a relaxing trip up amid the clouds in a hot-air balloon (see below). Developers think virtual reality is ready for takeoff in the next few years.

BIRD'S-EYE VIEW FROM YOUR CHAIR

Hot-air balloon rides are expensive and can be scary for those who are afraid of heights. A virtual ride lifts you into the clouds while you're firmly planted on the ground.

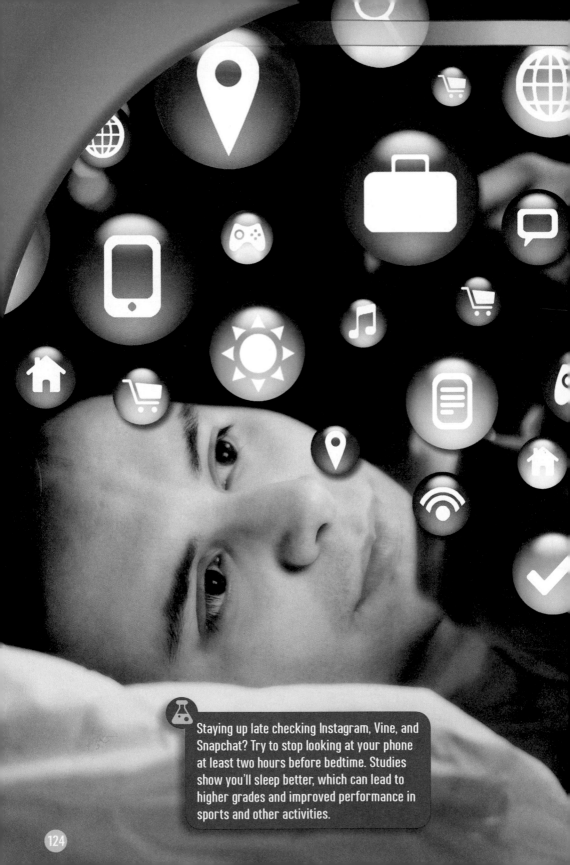

Staying up late checking Instagram, Vine, and Snapchat? Try to stop looking at your phone at least two hours before bedtime. Studies show you'll sleep better, which can lead to higher grades and improved performance in sports and other activities.

You snooze, you lose. Wrong. We all need our sleep. Getting plenty of sleep every night can improve memory, boost creativity, and help you step up your game on the field or court. Growing kids need their sleep even more than adults. However, a recent study of fourth- and seventh-graders in Massachusetts shows that many kids are losing sleep over their electronic gadgets. Kids in the study who said they slept near a smartphone, tablet, laptop, or TV got 18–21 minutes less sleep per night than kids without gadgets in their rooms.

If they were using their devices right before bedtime, their brains may have been too stimulated to settle down and sleep. Also, a glowing LED screen gives out blue light, a type of light whose wavelengths are similar to daylight. Our bodies think it's daytime and stop producing melatonin, the chemical that makes us sleepy.

Researchers advise powering down all electronics at least two hours before bedtime and leaving them in another room. On or off, never bring your phone into bed. A teenager in Texas stuck her phone under her pillow and woke up to find the phone melted and the bed on fire. (She was okay.) Give your phone some breathing space.

The 5 Kingdoms of Life

To understand living things, life scientists divide them into groups that share certain features. This process is called classification. A classification system created in 1735 by Carolus Linnaeus divides life-forms into five kingdoms: animals, plants, fungi, protista, and monera. Here are some (not all) of the types of life-forms within each kingdom.

ANIMAL KINGDOM	Vertebrates (such as mammals, birds, and reptiles), sponges, worms, insects and arthropods, crustaceans, and jellyfish
PLANT KINGDOM	Ferns, mosses, ginkgos, horsetails, conifers, flowering plants, liverworts, and bladderworts
FUNGI KINGDOM	Molds, mildews, blights, smuts, rusts, mushrooms, puffballs, stinkhorns, lichens, dung fungi, yeasts, morels, and truffles
PROTISTA KINGDOM	Yellow-green algae, golden algae, protozoa, green algae, brown algae, and red algae
MONERA KINGDOM	Bacteria and blue-green algae

The kingdoms are subdivided into smaller and more specific groups.

Most general → *Most specific*

Category	Example: Human Being
Kingdom	Animal
Phylum	Chordate
Subphylum	Vertebrate (animals with backbones)
Superclass	Vertebrate with jaws
Class	Mammal
Subclass	Advanced mammal
Infraclass	Placental mammal
Order	Primate
Family	Hominid
Genus	*Homo*
Species	*Homo sapiens*

The Domain System

In 1990, biologist Carl R. Woese and other scientists proposed a slightly different classification system. They suggested dividing living things into three domains, based on their cell structure. Domain Eukaryota includes multi-celled organisms: animals, plants, fungi, and protista. Domains Archaea and Bacteria are made up of microscopic one-celled organisms. The huge majority of all living things belong to these two domains. Scientists believe that Archaea are among the oldest forms of life on Earth.

Some Major Discoveries in Life Science

Year	Discovery
400 BCE	Aristotle classifies 500 species of animals into 8 classes.
1628 CE	William Harvey discovers how blood circulates in the human body.
1683	Anton van Leeuwenhoek observes bacteria.
1735	Carolus Linnaeus introduces the classification system.
1859	Charles Darwin publishes *On the Origin of Species*, which explains his theories of evolution.
1860	Gregor Mendel discovers the laws of heredity through experiments with peas and fruit flies.
1861	Louis Pasteur, the "father of bacteriology," comes up with a theory that certain diseases are caused by bacteria.
1953	James D. Watson and Francis H. Crick develop the double helix model of DNA, which explains how traits are inherited. Jonas Salk invents the polio vaccine.
1996	Dolly the sheep is cloned in Scotland.
2009	Doctors successfully treat blindness, brain disorders, and immune system deficiencies by inserting genes into patients' cells and tissues. However, the procedure remains controversial because of dangerous side effects.
2011	Early tests of a vaccine for malaria give scientists hope the disease can someday be wiped out. Malaria is carried by certain types of mosquitoes and is a leading cause of death for children in many countries.
2012	Scientists create artificial compounds called XNAs that can copy and store information and evolve, like DNA.
2013	Scientists recover the oldest human DNA ever found, from a 400,000-year-old thighbone.
2014–2015	An epidemic of the deadly virus Ebola breaks out in West Africa and claims more than 9,600 lives by early 2015. The majority of victims are in Guinea, Liberia, and Sierra Leone. In the race to find a cure for the disease, which kills about 60% of its victims, the first large-scale trials of two experimental vaccines begin in Liberia. Meanwhile, scientists are exploring the use of robots to help treat Ebola patients, to reduce risk to medical workers.

The Rock Cycle

Rocks don't grow like plants and animals, but they change from one form to another in a never-ending process called the **rock cycle**. Geologists, or scientists who study rocks, divide them into three groups.

Igneous

Igneous rock makes up about 95 percent of the upper part of Earth's crust. There are two kinds:

Granite

> **Intrusive** igneous rock forms when melted rock, or magma, cools beneath Earth's surface. Granite is a common type of intrusive igneous rock. Intrusive igneous rocks are constantly being pushed up to the surface by natural forces.

> **Extrusive** igneous rock forms when the melted rock erupts as lava and cools on Earth's surface. Basalt is a common type of extrusive igneous rock.

Basalt

Sedimentary

Igneous rocks on Earth's surface can be broken down into tiny pieces and moved around by wind, rain, and ocean waves. These little pieces, called sediments, pile up in water and are squeezed into layers with other sediments such as bits and pieces of plants or dead animals. Limestone is a common type of sedimentary rock.

Limestone

Metamorphic

Pressure and heat can flatten and fold igneous or sedimentary rock into a whole new shape, color, and mineral structure. Marble is a metamorphic rock that often comes from limestone.

Marble

Plymouth Rock in Plymouth, Massachusetts, is made of granite that scientists think was formed more than 600 million years ago. The famous landmark is much smaller today than it was in 1620, when the Pilgrims arrived from England. It has been worn down by erosion and chipped away by souvenir-hunting tourists.

What's the Difference Between Rocks and Minerals?

The difference is simple: Rocks are made of minerals, but minerals are not made of rocks. Minerals are chemical compounds found on, in, and below Earth's crust. There are about 4,000 known minerals on Earth.

Quartz is one of the most common minerals, making up about 12 percent of Earth's crust. Some quartz is so clear you can see straight through it. Other types are pink, green, yellow, or purple. The color varies depending on how the quartz was formed. But quartz does more than look pretty. Under certain conditions, quartz can generate electricity to power clocks, computers, TVs, heaters, and other devices.

A Scratch Test for Minerals

The Mohs scale, invented by German mineralogist Friedrich Mohs, ranks ten minerals on hardness based on their resistance to scratches. Minerals with higher numbers can scratch minerals with lower numbers.

Mineral	Rank
Talc	1
Gypsum	2
Calcite	3
Fluorite	4
Apatite	5
Orthoclase feldspar	6
Quartz	7
Topaz	8
Corundum	9
Diamond	10

Hard to Say

Here's how certain items would rank in hardness on the Mohs scale.

Fingernails	2.5
Gold, silver	2.5–3
Copper penny	3
Iron	4–5
Knife blade	5.5
Glass	6–7
Hardened steel file	7+

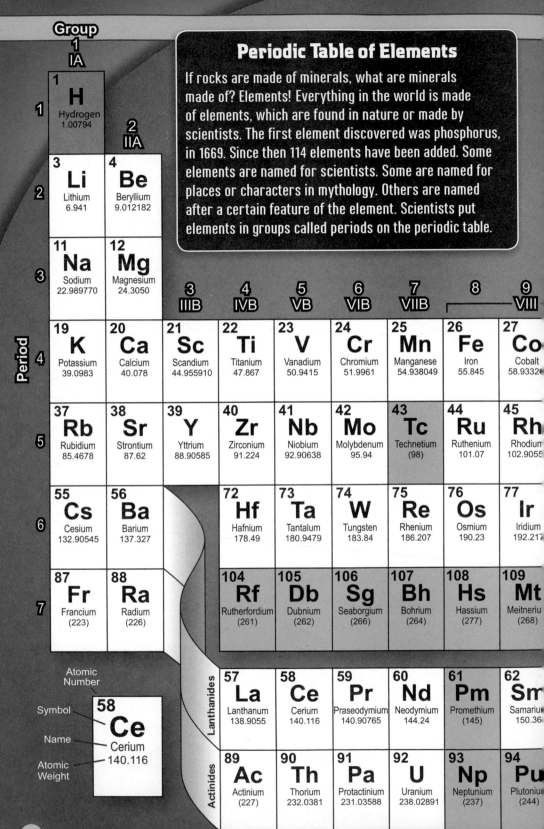

Periodic Table of Elements

If rocks are made of minerals, what are minerals made of? Elements! Everything in the world is made of elements, which are found in nature or made by scientists. The first element discovered was phosphorus, in 1669. Since then 114 elements have been added. Some elements are named for scientists. Some are named for places or characters in mythology. Others are named after a certain feature of the element. Scientists put elements in groups called periods on the periodic table.

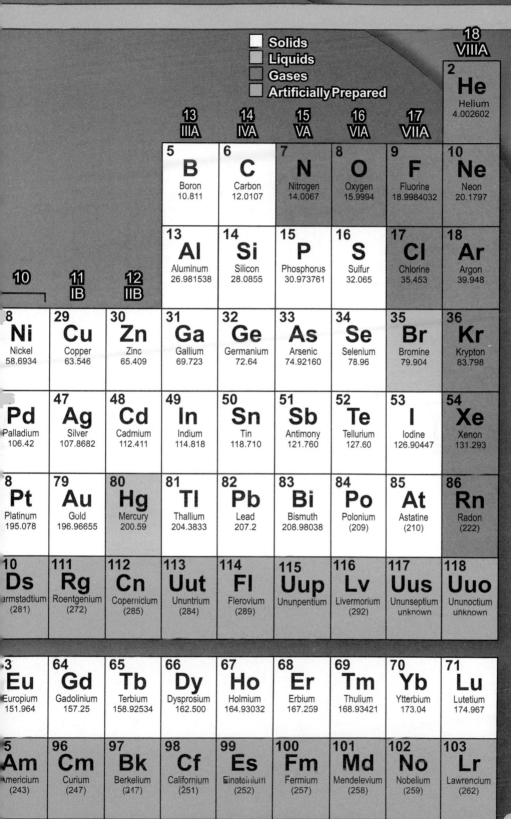

								18
								VIIIA
								2 **He** Helium 4.002602

Solids
Liquids
Gases
Artificially Prepared

13 IIIA	14 IVA	15 VA	16 VIA	17 VIIA	
5 **B** Boron 10.811	6 **C** Carbon 12.0107	7 **N** Nitrogen 14.0067	8 **O** Oxygen 15.9994	9 **F** Fluorine 18.9984032	10 **Ne** Neon 20.1797
13 **Al** Aluminum 26.981538	14 **Si** Silicon 28.0855	15 **P** Phosphorus 30.973761	16 **S** Sulfur 32.065	17 **Cl** Chlorine 35.453	18 **Ar** Argon 39.948

10	11 IB	12 IIB						
8 **Ni** Nickel 58.6934	29 **Cu** Copper 63.546	30 **Zn** Zinc 65.409	31 **Ga** Gallium 69.723	32 **Ge** Germanium 72.64	33 **As** Arsenic 74.92160	34 **Se** Selenium 78.96	35 **Br** Bromine 79.904	36 **Kr** Krypton 83.798
Pd Palladium 106.42	47 **Ag** Silver 107.8682	48 **Cd** Cadmium 112.411	49 **In** Indium 114.818	50 **Sn** Tin 118.710	51 **Sb** Antimony 121.760	52 **Te** Tellurium 127.60	53 **I** Iodine 126.90447	54 **Xe** Xenon 131.293
8 **Pt** Platinum 195.078	79 **Au** Gold 196.96655	80 **Hg** Mercury 200.59	81 **Tl** Thallium 204.3833	82 **Pb** Lead 207.2	83 **Bi** Bismuth 208.98038	84 **Po** Polonium (209)	85 **At** Astatine (210)	86 **Rn** Radon (222)
10 **Ds** Darmstadtium (281)	111 **Rg** Roentgenium (272)	112 **Cn** Coperniclum (285)	113 **Uut** Ununtrium (284)	114 **Fl** Flerovium (289)	115 **Uup** Ununpentium	116 **Lv** Livermorium (292)	117 **Uus** Ununseptium unknown	118 **Uuo** Ununoctium unknown

3 **Eu** Europium 151.964	64 **Gd** Gadolinium 157.25	65 **Tb** Terbium 158.92534	66 **Dy** Dysprosium 162.500	67 **Ho** Holmium 164.93032	68 **Er** Erbium 167.259	69 **Tm** Thulium 168.93421	70 **Yb** Ytterbium 173.04	71 **Lu** Lutetium 174.967
5 **Am** Americium (243)	96 **Cm** Curium (247)	97 **Bk** Berkelium (247)	98 **Cf** Californium (251)	99 **Es** Einsteinium (252)	100 **Fm** Fermium (257)	101 **Md** Mendelevium (258)	102 **No** Nobelium (259)	103 **Lr** Lawrencium (262)

 March 14, Pi Day, is also physicist Albert Einstein's birthday. Princeton University, where Einstein taught for many years, hosts an annual Einstein Birthday Party, with math puzzle contests, a parade, and plenty of Pizza Pi. For more about Pi Day, visit piday.org.

MATH

Every March 14, math becomes as easy as pi(e). It's Pi Day!

Pi is the ratio of a circle's circumference (the distance around the circle) to its diameter (the distance straight across its center). That ratio never changes. The distance around a circle is always a little over three times the distance straight across it.

Rounded to the nearest hundredth, pi equals 3.14 (see p. 138). So the perfect day to celebrate the unchanging dimensions of a circle is the 14th day of the third month of the year. And the perfect way to celebrate Pi Day is, of course, with pie! People enjoy small pies and large ones, apple pies and pizza pies, pies baked into numbers or the shape of the Greek letter pi (π). Sometimes people form a human pi, like the students in this picture.

MULTIPLICATION TABLE

	1	2	3	4	5	6	7	8	9	10	11	12
1	1	2	3	4	5	6	7	8	9	10	11	12
2	2	4	6	8	10	12	14	16	18	20	22	24
3	3	6	9	12	15	18	21	24	27	30	33	36
4	4	8	12	16	20	24	28	32	36	40	44	48
5	5	10	15	20	25	30	35	40	45	50	55	60
6	6	12	18	24	30	36	42	48	54	60	66	72
7	7	14	21	28	35	42	49	56	63	70	77	84
8	8	16	24	32	40	48	56	64	72	80	88	96
9	9	18	27	36	45	54	63	72	81	90	99	108
10	10	20	30	40	50	60	70	80	90	100	110	120
11	11	22	33	44	55	66	77	88	99	110	121	132
12	12	24	36	48	60	72	84	96	108	120	132	144

Squares and Square Roots

Multiplying a number by itself is also called squaring it (or raising it to its second power). For example, 3 squared (3^2) is 9. By the same token, the square root of 9 is 3. The symbol for square root is called a radical sign ($\sqrt{}$).

Examples of squaring
2 squared: $2^2 = 2 \times 2 = 4$
3 squared: $3^2 = 3 \times 3 = 9$
4 squared: $4^2 = 4 \times 4 = 16$

Examples of square Roots
Square root of 4: $\sqrt{4} = 2$
Square root of 9: $\sqrt{9} = 3$
Square root of 16: $\sqrt{16} = 4$

SQUARE ROOTS TO 40

$\sqrt{1}=1$	$\sqrt{36}=6$	$\sqrt{121}=11$	$\sqrt{256}=16$	$\sqrt{441}=21$	$\sqrt{676}=26$	$\sqrt{961}=31$	$\sqrt{1{,}296}=36$
$\sqrt{4}=2$	$\sqrt{49}=7$	$\sqrt{144}=12$	$\sqrt{289}=17$	$\sqrt{484}=22$	$\sqrt{729}=27$	$\sqrt{1{,}024}=32$	$\sqrt{1{,}369}=37$
$\sqrt{9}=3$	$\sqrt{64}=8$	$\sqrt{169}=13$	$\sqrt{324}=18$	$\sqrt{529}=23$	$\sqrt{784}=28$	$\sqrt{1{,}089}=33$	$\sqrt{1{,}444}=38$
$\sqrt{16}=4$	$\sqrt{81}=9$	$\sqrt{196}=14$	$\sqrt{361}=19$	$\sqrt{576}=24$	$\sqrt{841}=29$	$\sqrt{1{,}156}=34$	$\sqrt{1{,}521}=39$
$\sqrt{25}=5$	$\sqrt{100}=10$	$\sqrt{225}=15$	$\sqrt{400}=20$	$\sqrt{625}=25$	$\sqrt{900}=30$	$\sqrt{1{,}225}=35$	$\sqrt{1{,}600}=40$

Some Mathematical Formulas

To find the CIRCUMFERENCE of a:
- Circle—Multiply the diameter by π

To find the AREA of a:
- Circle—Multiply the square of the radius by π
- Rectangle—Multiply the base by the height
- Sphere (surface)—Multiply the square of the radius by π and multiply by 4
- Square—Square the length of one side
- Trapezoid—Add the two parallel sides, multiply by the height, and divide by 2
- Triangle—Multiply the base by the height and divide by 2

π (pi) = 3.1416
(See p. 138)

To find the VOLUME of a:
- Cone—Multiply the square of the radius of the base by π, multiply by the height, and divide by 3
- Cube—Cube (raise to the third power) the length of one edge
- Cylinder—Multiply the square of the radius of the base by π and multiply by the height
- Pyramid—Multiply the area of the base by the height and divide by 3
- Rectangular prism—Multiply the length by the width by the height
- Sphere—Multiply the cube of the radius by π, multiply by 4, and divide by 3

LARGE NUMBERS AND HOW MANY ZEROS THEY CONTAIN

Name	Zeros	Number	Name	Zeros	Number
million	6	1,000,000	sextillion	21	1,000,000,000,000,000,000,000
billion	9	1,000,000,000	septillion	24	1,000,000,000,000,000,000,000,000
trillion	12	1,000,000,000,000	octillion	27	1,000,000,000,000,000,000,000,000,000
quadrillion	15	1,000,000,000,000,000	nonillion	30	1,000,000,000,000,000,000,000,000,000,000
quintillion	18	1,000,000,000,000,000,000	decillion	33	1,000,000,000,000,000,000,000,000,000,000,000

NUMBERS GLOSSARY

COUNTING NUMBERS
Counting numbers, or natural numbers, begin with the number 1 and continue into infinity.

WHOLE NUMBERS
Whole numbers are the same as counting numbers except that the set of whole numbers begins with 0.

INTEGERS
Integers include 0, all counting numbers (called positive whole numbers), and all whole numbers less than 0 (called negative whole numbers).

RATIONAL NUMBERS
Rational numbers include any number that can be written in the form of a fraction (or a ratio), as long as the denominator (the bottom number of the fraction) is not equal to 0. All counting numbers and whole numbers are also rational numbers because all counting numbers and whole numbers can be written as fractions with a denominator equal to 1.

PRIME NUMBERS
Prime numbers are counting numbers that can be evenly divided by only two numbers: 1 and themselves.

Prime numbers between 1 and 1,000

2, 3, 5, 7, 11, 13, 17, 19, 23, 29, 31, 37, 41, 43, 47, 53, 59, 61, 67, 71, 73, 79, 83, 89, 97, 101, 103, 107, 109, 113, 127, 131, 137, 139, 149, 151, 157, 163, 167, 173, 179, 181, 191, 193, 197, 199, 211, 223, 227, 229, 233, 239, 241, 251, 257, 263, 269, 271, 277, 281, 283, 293, 307, 311, 313, 317, 331, 337, 347, 349, 353, 359, 367, 373, 379, 383, 389, 397, 401, 409, 419, 421, 431, 433, 439, 443, 449, 457, 461, 463, 467, 479, 487, 491, 499, 503, 509, 521, 523, 541, 547, 557, 563, 569, 571, 577, 587, 593, 599, 601, 607, 613, 617, 619, 631, 641, 643, 647, 653, 659, 661, 673, 677, 683, 691, 701, 709, 719, 727, 733, 739, 743, 751, 757, 761, 769, 773, 787, 797, 809, 811, 821, 823, 827, 829, 839, 853, 857, 859, 863, 877, 881, 883, 887, 907, 911, 919, 929, 937, 941, 947, 953, 967, 971, 977, 983, 991, 997

COMPOSITE NUMBERS
Composite numbers are all counting numbers that are not prime numbers. In other words, composite numbers are numbers that have more than two factors. (A factor is a number that divides another number evenly, with no remainder. The numbers 3 and 12 are factors of 12 because they can be divided evenly into 12. The other factors of 12 are 1, 2, 4, and 6.) The number 1, because it has only one factor (itself), is not a composite number.

Composite numbers between 1 and 100

4, 6, 8, 9, 10, 12, 14, 15, 16, 18, 20, 21, 22, 24, 25, 26, 27, 28, 30, 32, 33, 34, 35, 36, 38, 39, 40, 42, 44, 45, 46, 48, 49, 50, 51, 52, 54, 55, 56, 57, 58, 60, 62, 63, 64, 65, 66, 68, 69, 70, 72, 74, 75, 76, 77, 78, 80, 81, 82, 84, 85, 86, 87, 88, 90, 91, 92, 93, 94, 95, 96, 98, 99, 100

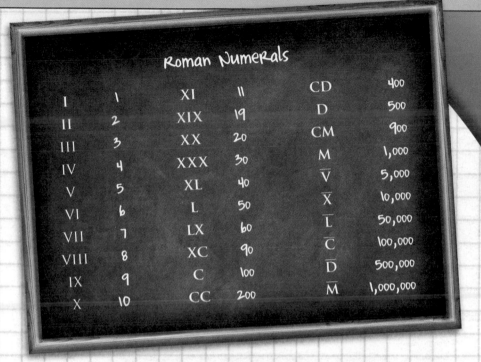

Roman Numerals

I	1	XI	11	CD	400
II	2	XIX	19	D	500
III	3	XX	20	CM	900
IV	4	XXX	30	M	1,000
V	5	XL	40	$\overline{V}$	5,000
VI	6	L	50	$\overline{X}$	10,000
VII	7	LX	60	$\overline{L}$	50,000
VIII	8	XC	90	$\overline{C}$	100,000
IX	9	C	100	$\overline{D}$	500,000
X	10	CC	200	$\overline{M}$	1,000,000

Fractions, Decimals, and Percents

To find the equivalent of a fraction in decimal form, divide the numerator (top number) by the denominator (bottom number). To change from a decimal to a percent, multiply by 100. To change from a percent to a decimal, divide by 100.

Fraction	Decimal	Percent
1/16 (= 2/32)	0.0625	6.25
1/8 (= 2/16)	0.125	12.5
3/16 (= 6/32)	0.1875	18.75
1/4 (= 2/8; = 4/16)	0.25	25.0
5/16 (= 10/32)	0.3125	31.25
1/3 (= 2/6; = 4/12)	0.333	33.3
3/8 (= 6/16)	0.375	37.5
7/16 (= 14/32)	0.4375	43.75
1/2 (= 2/4; = 4/8; = 8/16)	0.5	50.0
9/16 (= 18/32)	0.5625	56.25
5/8 (= 10/16)	0.625	62.5
2/3 (= 4/6; = 8/12)	0.666	66.6
11/16 (= 22/32)	0.6875	68.75
3/4 (= 6/8; = 12/16)	0.75	75.0
13/16 (= 26/32)	0.8125	81.25
7/8 (= 14/16)	0.875	87.5
15/16 (= 30/32)	0.9375	93.75
1 (= 2/2; = 4/4; = 8/8; = 16/16)	1.0	100.0

Geometry Glossary

Acute angle	Any angle that measures less than 90°	
Angle	Two rays that have the same endpoint form an angle	
Area	The amount of surface inside a closed figure	
Chord	A line segment whose endpoints are on a circle	
Circumference	The distance around a circle	
Congruent figures	Geometric figures that are the same size and shape	
Degree	A unit for measuring angles	
Diameter	A chord that passes through the center of a circle	
Endpoint	The end of a line segment	
Line of symmetry	A line that divides a figure into two identical parts if the figure is folded along the line	
Obtuse angle	Any angle that measures greater than 90°	
Perimeter	The distance around the outside of a plane figure	
Pi (π)	The ratio of the circumference of a circle to its diameter; when rounded to the nearest hundredth, pi equals 3.14	
Polygon	A simple closed figure whose sides are straight lines	
Protractor	An instrument used to measure angles	
Quadrilateral	A polygon with four sides	
Radius	A straight line that connects the center of a circle to any point on the circumference of the circle	
Ray	A straight line with one endpoint	
Rectangle	A four-sided figure with four right angles	
Right angle	An angle that measures 90°	
Square	A rectangle with congruent sides and 90° angles in all four corners	
Surface area	The total outside area of an object	
Symmetrical	Refers to a figure that, when folded along a line of symmetry, has two halves that superimpose exactly on each other	
Triangle	A three-sided figure	
Vertex	The common endpoint of two or more rays that form angles	
Vertices	The plural of vertex	

All About Polygons

Polygons are two-dimensional, or flat, shapes formed from three or more line segments.

Examples

Triangles

Triangles are polygons that have three sides and three vertices.

- **Right triangles** are formed when two of three line segments meet in a 90° angle. In a right triangle, the longest side has a special name: the hypotenuse.

- **Isosceles triangles** have two sides of equal length.

- **Scalene triangles** have no sides of equal length.

- **Equilateral triangles** have three sides of equal length.

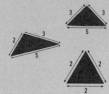

Quadrilaterals

Quadrilaterals are polygons that have four sides and four vertices.

- **Trapezoids** are quadrilaterals that have one pair of parallel sides.

- **Parallelograms** are quadrilaterals that have parallel line segments in both pairs of opposite sides.

- **Rectangles** are parallelograms formed by line segments that meet at right angles. A rectangle always has four right angles.

- **Squares** are rectangles that have sides of equal length and four right angles.

- **Rhombuses** are parallelograms that have sides of equal length but don't meet at right angles.

• • • • • • • • • Circles • • • • • • • • • • •

A circle is a set of points on a plane. Each point on the circle is at an equal distance from a common point inside the circle, called the center.

The distance from the center of the circle to any point on the circle is called the radius (r = radius).

A line segment drawn through the center of the circle to points on either side of the circle is called the diameter (d = diameter). The circle is bisected, or cut in two equal parts, along the diameter line. Diameter is equal to two times the radius (2r = diameter).

The distance around the circle is called the circumference (πd or π2r = circumference).

SIZE RELATIVE
TO THE EARTH

0.0   0.2   0.4   0.6

1.0   1.2

Scientists have now precisely measured
planets beyond our solar system. These
exoplanets include some "super-Earths"
with masses bigger than our planet's.
Read about how we measure things closer
to home in this chapter.

WEIGHTS & MEASURES

Using powerful space telescopes, NASA scientists have made the most precise measurements ever of a planet outside our solar system. The alien planet has a mass greater than Earth but less than Uranus or Neptune, which makes the planet a "super-Earth." There are many super-Earths in our galaxy, the Milky Way, but none in our solar system.

From this planet's density, scientists concluded that it is made of iron and rock, like Earth. However, this super-Earth is too hot to be habitable. From its closeness to its sun, scientists say its surface temperature must be about 1,400 degrees Fahrenheit (760 degrees Celsius).

Meanwhile, European astronomers have discovered 16 super-Earths, and one of these is the right distance from its sun to possibly support life. Researchers also think the biggest super-Earths might have oceans. Sooner or later, super-Earths may provide the answer to whether there is life elsewhere in space. Our ability to measure precisely objects hundreds of light-years away will be key in solving the mystery.

Simple Metric Conversion Table

To convert	To	Multiply by
centimeters	feet	0.0328
centimeters	inches	0.3937
cubic centimeters	cubic inches	0.0610
degrees	radians	0.0175
feet	centimeters	30.48
feet	meters	0.3048
gallons	liters	3.785
grams	ounces	0.0353
inches	centimeters	2.54
kilograms	pounds	2.205
kilometers	miles	0.6214
knots	miles/hour	1.151
liters	gallons	0.2642
liters	pints	2.113
meters	feet	3.281
miles	kilometers	1.609
ounces	grams	28.3495
pounds	kilograms	0.4536

Converting Household Measures

To convert	To	Multiply by
dozens	units	12
baker's dozens	units	13
teaspoons	milliliters	4.93
teaspoons	tablespoons	0.33
tablespoons	milliliters	14.79
tablespoons	teaspoons	3
cups	liters	0.24
cups	pints	0.50
cups	quarts	0.25
pints	cups	2
pints	liters	0.47
pints	quarts	0.50
quarts	cups	4
quarts	gallons	0.25
quarts	liters	0.95
quarts	pints	2
gallons	liters	3.79
gallons	quarts	4

Temperature Conversions

Fahrenheit	Celsius
475	246.1
450	232.2
425	218.3
400	204.4
375	190.6
350	176.7
325	162.8
300	148.9
275	135.0
250	121.1
225	107.2
212	100.0
110	43.3
105	40.6
100	37.8
95	35.0
90	32.2
85	29.4
80	26.7
75	23.9
70	21.1
65	18.3
60	15.6
55	12.8
50	10.0
45	7.2
40	4.4
35	1.7
32	0.0
30	−1.1
25	−3.9
20	−6.7
15	−9.4
10	−12.2
5	−15.0
0	−17.8
−5	−20.6
−10	−23.3
−15	−26.1
−20	−28.9
−25	−31.7
−30	−34.4
−35	−37.2
−40	−40.0
−45	−42.8

Fractions and Their Decimal Equivalents

1/2	0.5000	2/7	0.2857	5/9	0.5556
1/3	0.3333	2/9	0.2222	5/11	0.4545
1/4	0.2500	2/11	0.1818	5/12	0.4167
1/5	0.2000	3/4	0.7500	6/7	0.8571
1/6	0.1667	3/5	0.6000	6/11	0.5455
1/7	0.1429	3/7	0.4286	7/8	0.8750
1/8	0.1250	3/8	0.3750	7/9	0.7778
1/9	0.1111	3/10	0.3000	7/10	0.7000
1/10	0.1000	3/11	0.2727	7/11	0.6364
1/11	0.0909	4/5	0.8000	7/12	0.5833
1/12	0.0833	4/7	0.5714	8/9	0.8889
1/16	0.0625	4/9	0.4444	8/11	0.7273
1/32	0.0313	4/11	0.3636	9/10	0.9000
1/64	0.0156	5/6	0.8333	9/11	0.8182
2/3	0.6667	5/7	0.7143	10/11	0.9091
2/5	0.4000	5/8	0.6250	11/12	0.9167

Length or Distance
US Customary System

1 foot (ft.)	=	12 inches (in.)				
1 yard (yd.)	=	3 feet	=	36 inches		
1 rod (rd.)	=	5½ yards	=	16 ½ feet		
1 furlong (fur.)	=	40 rods	=	220 yards	=	660 feet
1 mile (mi.)	=	8 furlongs	=	1,760 yards	=	5,280 feet

An international nautical mile has been defined as 6,076.1155 feet.

Six Quick Ways to Measure If You Don't Have a Ruler

1. Most credit cards are 3⅜ inches by 2⅛ inches.
2. Standard business cards are 3½ inches long by 2 inches tall.
3. Floor tiles are usually manufactured in 12-inch squares.
4. US paper money is 6⅛ inches wide by 2⅝ inches tall.
5. The diameter of a quarter is approximately 1 inch, and the diameter of a penny is approximately ¾ of an inch.
6. A standard sheet of paper is 8½ inches wide by 11 inches long.

NATURE

The whale shark is the biggest fish in the world. A full-grown whale shark is as big as a bus and weighs more than an adult African elephant. It feeds by sucking tiny sea creatures into its wide-open mouth, filtering them through thousands of tiny teeth.

Luckily, this giant is gentle. In fact, whale sharks are so friendly that they let swimmers come close enough to hitch a ride. More and more tourists are visiting the Central American countries whose coastal waters are nesting grounds for whale sharks, hoping for a close-up look.

The increase in tourism has resulted in more tour boats and more possible boat-propeller injuries to the fish. During 3 months in 2014, tourist-boat operators in Panama hit whale sharks 27 times.

In July of that year, officials in eight countries passed new rules to protect whale sharks. These include guidelines for swimmers, such as staying at least six feet (1.8 m) away.

Large and small, living things need human attention. Read all about our amazing natural world in this section.

Animals

Show Some Spine

The simplest way to classify animals is to divide them into two groups: those with spinal columns, or backbones, and those without backbones. The bones in the spinal column are called vertebrae, so animals with backbones are called vertebrates. Vertebrates are far outnumbered by invertebrates, or animals without backbones. There are millions of species of invertebrates, compared with only 40,000 species of vertebrates.

All mammals, fish, birds, reptiles, and amphibians are vertebrates. Invertebrates include everything else: sponges, jellyfish, insects, spiders, clams, snails, worms, and many, many others.

Vertebrates
(Backbones)

Mammals

Fish

Reptiles

Amphibians

Birds

Invertebrates
(No Backbones)

Mollusks

Insects

Worms

Animals with the Most Known Species

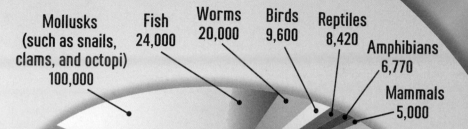

Mollusks (such as snails, clams, and octopi)
100,000

Fish 24,000

Worms 20,000

Birds 9,600

Reptiles 8,420

Amphibians 6,770

Mammals 5,000

Insects and Other Arthropods*
1,000,000+

*Animals with an exoskeleton, a segmented body, and jointed appendages

Longest Average Animal Life Spans

Animal	Maximum age (years)
Quahog (marine clam)	400
Giant tortoise	250
Sturgeon	150
Human	122
Orca	90
Blue whale	80
Elephant	75
Sea anemone	70
Golden eagle	60
Crocodile	60

Dinosaurs

For the better part of 200 million years, dinosaurs ruled the world. Yet until the 19th century, they didn't even have a name. In 1842, English scientist Sir Richard Owen concluded that recently discovered fossils of huge jaws and teeth must belong to reptiles unlike any living animals. He named them *Dinosauria* ("terrible lizards"). Some dinosaurs were enormous. *Supersaurus* could grow to a length of 130 feet (40 m)—as long as a 13-story building is tall—and weigh as much as 10 elephants. But other dinosaurs were the size of chickens. Most dinosaurs were herbivores, or plant eaters, and lived on land. They coexisted peacefully with mammals, most of which were small rodents.

How Big Were Dinosaurs?

Apatosaurus 75 ft. (23 m) long
Tyrannosaurus rex 40 ft. (12 m) long
Stegosaurus 30 ft. (9 m) long
Ankylosaurus 25 ft. (7.6 m) long
Triceratops 25 ft. (7.6 m) long

Which Dinosaurs Lived When?

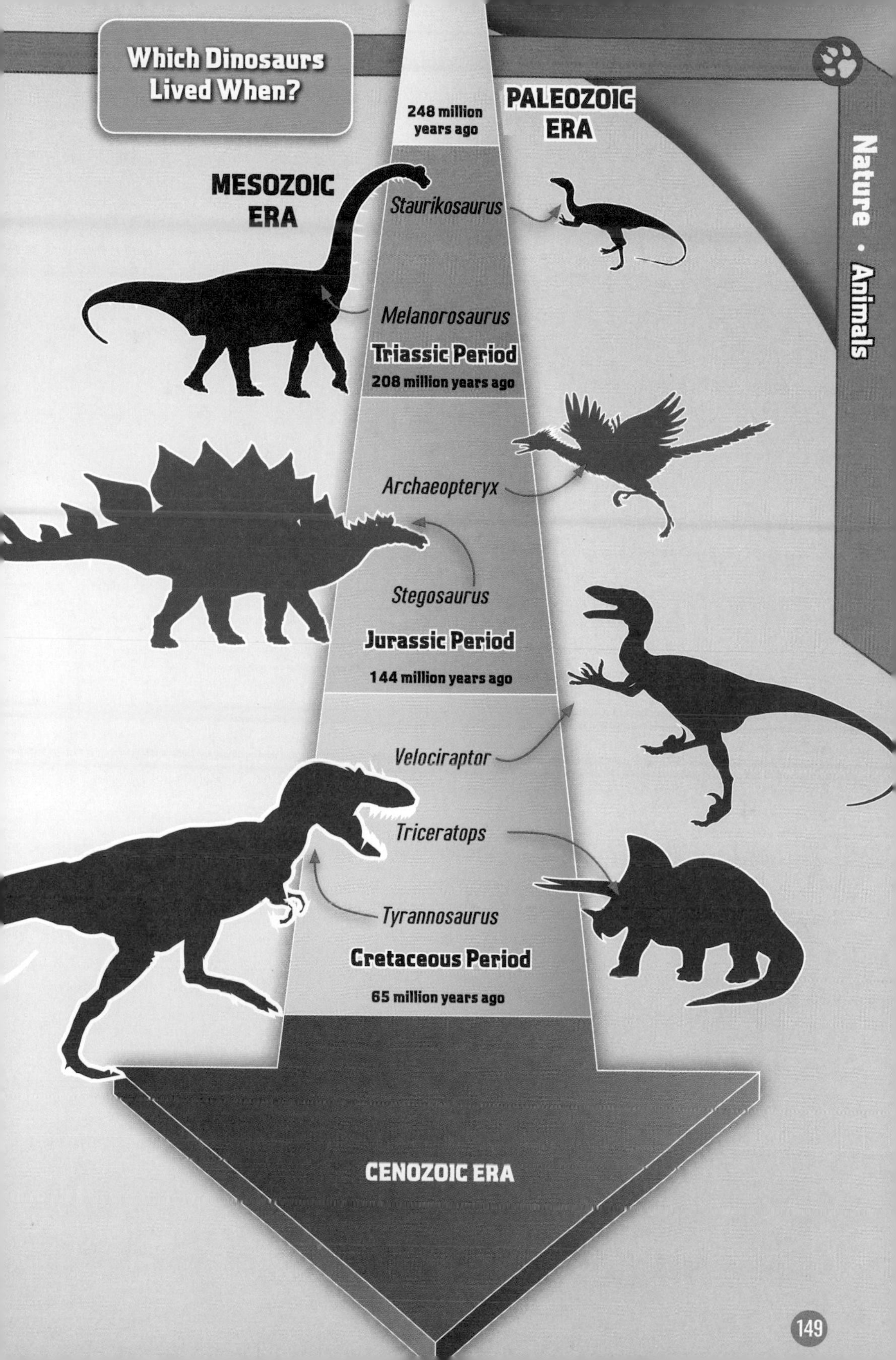

248 million years ago

PALEOZOIC ERA

MESOZOIC ERA

Staurikosaurus

Melanorosaurus

Triassic Period

208 million years ago

Archaeopteryx

Stegosaurus

Jurassic Period

144 million years ago

Velociraptor

Triceratops

Tyrannosaurus

Cretaceous Period

65 million years ago

CENOZOIC ERA

Gentle Giants and Menacing Meat-Eaters

Sauropods were the giants of the prehistoric world. The *antarctosaurus*, *diplodocus*, and *seismosaurus* were all sauropods. These dinosaurs had long necks, long tails, and huge stomachs and chests. Big as they were, the sauropods were peaceful plant-eaters.

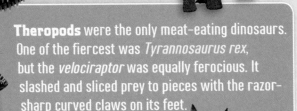

Theropods were the only meat-eating dinosaurs. One of the fiercest was *Tyrannosaurus rex*, but the *velociraptor* was equally ferocious. It slashed and sliced prey to pieces with the razor-sharp curved claws on its feet.

Stegosaurs' plates and spikes may have done more than keep away enemies. Scientists think blood flowing through the spikes could have been warmed or cooled by the air moving over the stegosaur's back, controlling body temperature.

Ankylosaurs were built for survival. Heavy, bony plates protected their bodies like armor on a tank. Some types had a mass of bone on their tails that they could use as a club.

Ceratopsians looked like rhinoceroses. Most had horns on their faces and a curved collar of bone around their neck. Horns over a *triceratops*'s eyes could reach 3 feet (90 cm) long.

What Killed the Dinosaurs?

Dinosaurs ruled for millions and millions of years. Then they were gone. What happened? One popular theory blamed the extinction on an enormous asteroid we now call Chicxulub, which crashed into Mexico's Yucatan Peninsula with the force of a billion atomic bombs about 65 million years ago. But now many scientists think half a million years before Chicxulub, volcanoes in western India caused climate changes, including cold periods, that made survival impossible for dinosaurs and most other species. The asteroid could have been the death blow to an animal kingdom that was already dying.

Mexico's Yucatan Peninsula

Studying the dinosaurs' extinction is important to understanding the impact of climate change and natural catastrophes on every living thing on Earth. Meanwhile, although dinosaurs may have died out, we see and hear their descendants every day: modern birds.

Spinosaurus Makes a Big Splash

Crocodile jaws full of cone-shaped teeth. Almost twice as long as a city bus. Heavier than two elephants. Bigger than *T. rex*, with a 7-foot (2m) sail on its back that made it look even more threatening. Meet *spinosaurus*, which may have been the largest predator that ever walked the earth—and possibly the only swimming dinosaur ever.

German scientist Ernst Stromer discovered the first *spinosaurus* fossils in Egypt about 100 years ago. They were kept in a museum in Munich, Germany, but destroyed when the building was bombed during World War II. More fossils were discovered in Morocco in 2008. These fossils showed adaptations to living in the water, such as big, flat feet that were perfect for paddling.

Insects

Insects come in an amazing number of shapes and colors, but all you have to do is count to three to tell them apart from other creatures. All insects have at least three pairs of legs and three body parts: the head, the thorax (midsection), and the abdomen. Scorpions, spiders, ticks, and mites look like insects, but they are arachnids.

There are about four times as many insects as every otherkind of animal combined. Why so many? Insects have adapted to survive.

They can live in the hottest, coldest, wettest, and driest places. Their small size lets them survive in tiny spaces with practically no food. Some insects can lay many thousands of eggs a day, so there are plenty of young to keep a species alive. Most have wings to fly away from danger.

Bugs may bug us, but only about 1 percent of insects are harmful. In fact many insects are more helpful then harmful. For example, bees, wasps, and butterflies help keep us supplied with fruits and vegetables and help keep our world beautiful by pollinating plants and flowers.

Top 10 Most Common Insects

Animal	Approximate number of known species
Beetles	350,000
Butterflies and moths	150,000
True flies	120,000
Ants, bees, and wasps	105,000
True bugs	40,000
Grasshoppers, crickets, and locusts	20,000
Caddis flies	7,000
Lacewings	4,000
Lice	2,900
Dragonflies	2,500

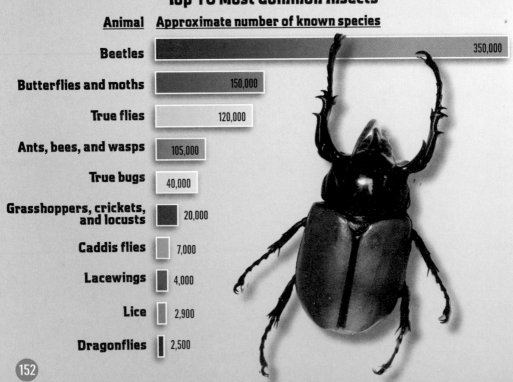

To hide from predators, walking sticks can blend into the twigs and branches on which they live. The largest kinds of walking sticks live in Asia and can grow to be more than 22 inches (56 cm) with their legs fully extended.

Dragonflies have up to 30,000 lenses in their eyes. Their amazing vision, expert flying skills, and fast speeds help them catch prey on the fly—with their feet.

Grasshoppers have about 900 muscles—over 200 more muscles than humans. Many insects can lift or pull objects 20 times their weight.

Fruit farmers love ladybugs because they eat aphids, tiny sap-eating insects that destroy crops. Predators hate their gross taste, which comes from a liquid produced from joints in their legs when threatened.

Mammals

There are about 5,000 kinds of mammals, including the species you see when you look in the mirror: human. Mammals are different from all other animals in two important ways:

• Babies feed on their mothers' milk.

• They have hair or fur.

Most mammals eat only plants, but big cats like the leopard and lion are exclusively meat-eaters. Humans and some other species are omnivores: they have flat teeth to grind plants, sharp teeth to pierce animal flesh, and the digestive systems to handle both kinds of food.

All mammals are warm-blooded. Their body temperature stays the same no matter how cold or warm their environment becomes. They also have large brains compared to their body size. Scientists say this lets certain mammals, like humans, chimps, and dolphins, learn more than other animals. In February 2010, a panel of scientists declared that dolphins are second only to humans in intelligence and are so bright they should be considered "nonhuman persons." In 2013, another study showed that dolphins can recognize the call of a departed tank mate for up to 20 years.

Fun Mammal Facts

Flying squirrels don't really fly. They stretch out a fold of skin between their forelimbs and hind limbs and glide from tree to tree.

Unlike kangaroos, koalas, and other marsupials, the short-tailed opossum does not have a pouch.

What do an armadillo's bony shell and a rhinoceros's thick hide have in common? They both protect against sharp-clawed predators.

The echidna and the platypus are the only mammals that don't give birth to live young. They're *monotremes* that lay eggs with leathery shells.

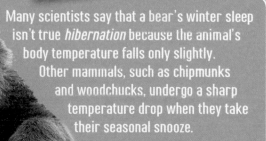

Many scientists say that a bear's winter sleep isn't true *hibernation* because the animal's body temperature falls only slightly. Other mammals, such as chipmunks and woodchucks, undergo a sharp temperature drop when they take their seasonal snooze.

Heaviest Land Mammals

Mammal	Weight
African elephant	15,000 lb. (6,804 kg)
Hippopotamus	9,920 lb. (4,500 kg)
White rhinoceros	7,920 lb. (3,600 kg)
Giraffe	3,000 lb. (1,361 kg)
Asian water buffalo	2,600 lb. (1,179 kg)
Arabian camel (dromedary)	1,520 lb. (689 kg)
Grizzly bear	1,500 lb. (680 kg)
Gorilla	500 lb. (227 kg)
Siberian tiger	500 lb. (227 kg)

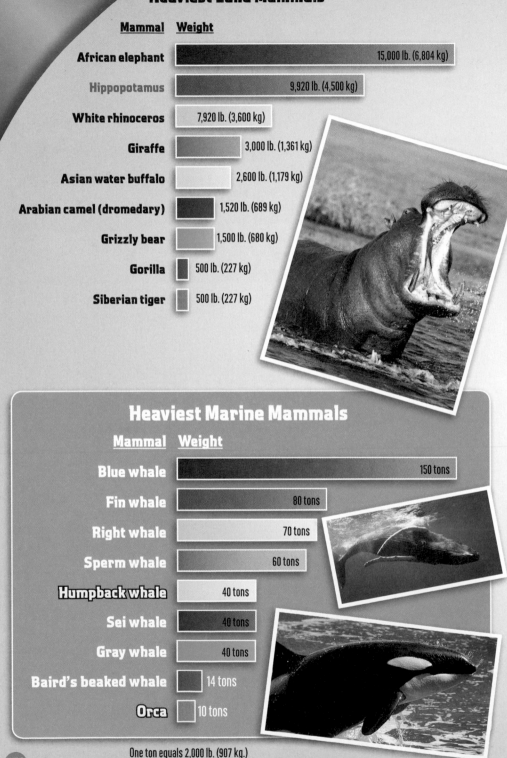

Heaviest Marine Mammals

Mammal	Weight
Blue whale	150 tons
Fin whale	80 tons
Right whale	70 tons
Sperm whale	60 tons
Humpback whale	40 tons
Sei whale	40 tons
Gray whale	40 tons
Baird's beaked whale	14 tons
Orca	10 tons

One ton equals 2,000 lb. (907 kg.)

Smallest Mammals

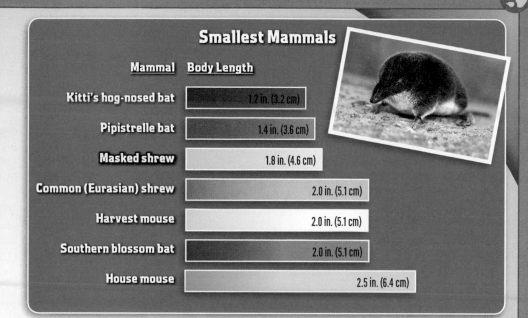

Mammal	Body Length
Kitti's hog-nosed bat	1.2 in. (3.2 cm)
Pipistrelle bat	1.4 in. (3.6 cm)
Masked shrew	1.8 in. (4.6 cm)
Common (Eurasian) shrew	2.0 in. (5.1 cm)
Harvest mouse	2.0 in. (5.1 cm)
Southern blossom bat	2.0 in. (5.1 cm)
House mouse	2.5 in. (6.4 cm)

Fastest Mammals

Mammal	Maximum speed
Cheetah	70 mph (113 kph)
Pronghorn antelope	61 mph (98 kph)
Springbok	55 mph (89 kph)
Blue wildebeest	50 mph (80 kph)
Lion	50 mph (80 kph)
Brown hare	48 mph (77 kph)
Red fox	30 mph (48 kph)

Birds

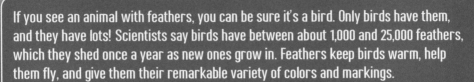

If you see an animal with feathers, you can be sure it's a bird. Only birds have them, and they have lots! Scientists say birds have between about 1,000 and 25,000 feathers, which they shed once a year as new ones grow in. Feathers keep birds warm, help them fly, and give them their remarkable variety of colors and markings.

Like mammals, birds are warm-blooded vertebrates. A bird's skeleton is strong because many of the bones are fused together. In humans and other animals, they're separate. At the same time, bird skeletons are lightweight because many of the bones are hollow.

Scientists believe that birds evolved from ancient reptiles—specifically, meat-eating dinosaurs such as *Tyrannosaurus rex* and the *velociraptor.* At one time these ferocious dinosaurs may have had feathers!

The feathers of this and of all birds are made of keratin, the same substance that covers a rhinoceros's bony horn and makes up human hair and nails.

Hummingbirds are the only birds that can fly backward. A hummingbird's heart beats 1,000 times a minute. In comparison, the range for a normal human is 60—100 beats a minute.

Parrots have a large *cerebrum*, the part of the brain that controls learning. Scientists say that may be why they can learn to talk.

Do you have eyes like a hawk? Not a chance! Hawks can see about eight times as well as humans.

Arctic terns migrate the farthest of any bird. Every year they travel about 22,000 miles (35,400 km) from the Arctic to their Antarctic winter home and back again.

All birds have wings, but not all birds can fly. Ostriches, the largest living birds, walk or run. Penguins swim, using their wings as flippers.

When a woodpecker digs for insects in the bark of a tree, it makes a loud hammering sound. It makes the same sound when trying to attract a mate or to claim territory from other birds. Some woodpeckers can make holes large enough to damage trees or even break them in half.

Fish and Other Marine Life

Not every animal that spends its life in the water is a fish—even if its name is *fish*! Jellyfish and starfish are not true fish. Clams, crabs, and scallops are called shellfish, but they're not really fish, either. Why not? None of these animals has a backbone. True fish are vertebrates. In fact, they were the first animals on Earth to have a backbone.

Fish are cold-blooded, which means their body temperature changes to match the temperature of their surroundings. Fish breathe through gills, which filter oxygen out of the water. Almost all fish have fins, which they use for swimming.

Most fish have skeletons made of bone, and most of these bony fish have an inflatable sac called a swim bladder below their backbone. The bladder gives them the buoyancy they need to stay afloat without moving. Sharks, rays, and some other fish have skeletons made of cartilage. These types of fish don't have a swim bladder. When they stop swimming, they sink. Sharks even have to keep swimming while they sleep!

There are more than 24,000 species of fish, with scientists discovering more all the time.

Most fish swim horizontally, but the sea horse swims vertically.

Hermit crabs constantly outgrow their shells and "borrow" new ones, usually abandoned snail shells.

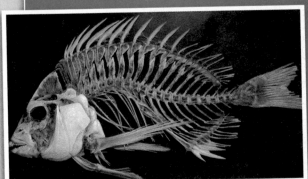

Barracudas and piranhas have razor-sharp teeth that can strip the flesh from a large mammal in minutes.

The *Paedocypris progenetica* is about the length of your fingernail. It's the smallest fish and one of the smallest vertebrates in the world. The tiny, transparent fish was found in a peat swamp in Indonesia.

Sharks have excellent eyesight, especially in the darkness. Bright colors such as yellow and orange seem to attract them. Based on documented attacks, the three most dangerous species of shark are the great white shark, the bull shark, and the tiger shark.

Clown fish stay safe from predators by hiding inside the poisonous stinging tentacles of certain sea anemones. Why aren't the clown fish stung? Scientists say they may be protected by a layer of slime on their skin.

Reptiles & Amphibians

Reptiles and amphibians have a lot in common. They're both vertebrates, they're both cold-blooded, and they've both been around for millions of years. However, there are important differences. Most amphibians hatch from eggs laid in water and then spend their adult lives on land. Reptiles are primarily land animals, although some, like sea turtles and sea snakes, spend their whole lives in the water.

Another difference is their skin. A reptile's skin is dry and scaly. Most amphibians have moist skin, which is often kept that way by a slimy coating of mucus.

Lizards and snakes are the most common reptiles, and there are thousands of different kinds of reptiles around the world. Alligators, crocodiles, and turtles are also reptiles. Frogs, toads, and salamanders are the most common amphibians.

Since about the 1980s, the population of some frog species has been declining. Scientists don't fully understand why. However, because frogs and all amphibians absorb gases and other chemicals directly through their skin, there is some worry that disappearing frogs could be an indication of serious environmental problems.

The Gila monster has a poisonous bite, but most other reptiles are harmless to humans.

To survive frigid winters, the gray tree frog can freeze solid without harming itself. A substance in its blood works like antifreeze to protect its organs and tissues.

One way to tell a frog from a toad is to look at its skin. A frog's skin is smooth and moist. A toad's is bumpy and dry.

For many years, scientists thought a chameleon changed colors to blend into its surroundings for protection from predators. Now some scientists think that chameleons change colors to stand out to other chameleons. Brighter colors are used to show dominance and attract mates, while dull colors signal surrender.

Tigers Take a Small Leap Forward

About a hundred years ago there were 100,000 wild tigers living in 23 countries. Now there are only about 3,000 tigers living in 11 countries, their numbers slashed by habitat loss and poachers.

But now in India, where 70 percent of the world's tigers live, officials say the wild tiger population has risen from 1,411 in 2008, to 2,226 in 2015. India's government says increased enforcement against poachers and better security for protected tiger parks are key reasons for the success.

Officials use camera traps to observe and count the tigers. They identify the animals by the patterns of their stripes, which are as unique as fingerprints. Although officials are excited by the increase, they warn that it's too soon to celebrate. The number is still very small.

Hope for Mountain Gorillas?

Most mountain gorillas live in the mountains or high forests of central Africa, where for many years they have been threatened by dangerous loss of habitat, hunting, disease, and war. Not long ago scientists feared the species would soon be extinct. However, because of wildlife management and conservation efforts, the mountain gorilla population has grown from 620 animals in 1989 to around 880 today.

Trying to Save Lolita

In 2005, a special group of Southern Resident orcas were included on the Endangered Species List—all but one. Lolita, who has lived and performed at the Miami Seaquarium since 1970, didn't qualify for the list because she was in captivity. Reports say she was taken from her pod in Penn Cove, WA, as a calf.

Supporters finally got her on the list in 2015. Now they want her returned to her native waters of Puget Sound. But her owners are afraid she may not survive in the wild and want to keep her where she is. Keiko, another whale released from captivity, did not survive reentry. There isn't always a clear solution as to how best to save endangered species.

Animal Multiples

ants: colony

bears: sleuth, sloth

bees: grist, hive, swarm

birds: flight, volery

cats: clowder, clutter

chicks: brood, clutch

clams: bed

cows: drove

cranes: sedge, seige

crows: murder

doves: dule

ducks: brace, team

elephants: herd

elks: gang

finches: charm

fish: drought, school, shoal

foxes: leash, skulk

geese: flock, gaggle, skein

gnats: cloud, horde

goats: trip

gorillas: band

hares: down, husk

hawks: cast

hens: brood

hogs: drift

horses: pair, team

hounds: cry, mute, pack

kangaroos: troop

kittens: kindle, litter

larks: exaltation

lions: pride

locusts: plague

magpies: tiding

mules: span

nightingales: watch

oxen: yoke

oysters: bed

parrots: company

partridges: covey

peacocks: muster, ostentation

pheasants: bouquet, nest

pigs: litter

ponies: string

quail: bevy, covey

rabbits: nest

seals: pod

sheep: drove, flock

sparrows: host

storks: mustering

swans: bevy, wedge

swine: sounder

toads: knot

turkeys: rafter

turtles: bale

vipers: nest

whales: gam, pod

wolves: pack, route

woodcocks: fall

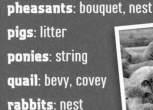

Names of Male, Female, and Young Animals

Animal	Male	Female	Young
Bear	Boar	Sow	Cub
Cat	Tom	Queen	Kitten
Chicken	Rooster	Hen	Chick
Cow	Bull	Cow	Calf
Deer	Buck	Doe	Fawn
Dog	Dog	Bitch	Pup
Donkey	Jack	Jenny	Foal
Duck	Drake	Duck	Duckling
Elephant	Bull	Cow	Calf
Fox	Dog	Vixen	Kit
Goose	Gander	Goose	Gosling
Horse	Stallion	Mare	Foal
Lion	Lion	Lioness	Cub
Rabbit	Buck	Doe	Bunny
Sheep	Ram	Ewe	Lamb
Swan	Cob	Pen	Cygnet
Swine	Boar	Sow	Piglet
Tiger	Tiger	Tigress	Cub
Whale	Bull	Cow	Calf
Wolf	Dog	Bitch	Pup

Popular Pets in the United States

The American Pet Products Association (APPA) reported in its 2015—2016 survey that 79.7 million (65%) American households own a pet.

Animal	Millions of households owning
Any pet	79.7
Dog	54.4
Cat	42.9
Freshwater fish	12.3
Bird	6.1
Small animal	5.4
Reptile	4.9
Horse	2.5
Saltwater fish	1.3

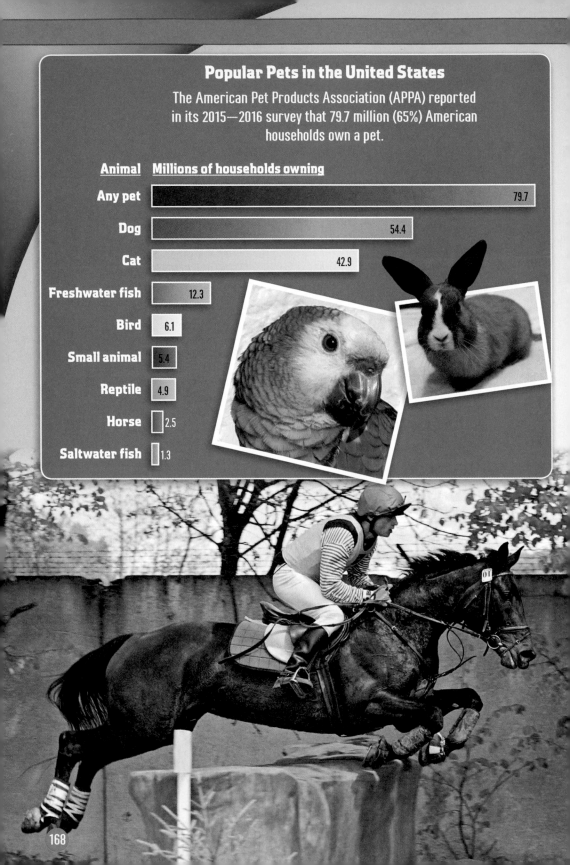

Top 10 Registered US Dog Breeds

Labrador retriever

German shepherd

Golden retriever

Bulldog

Beagle

Yorkshire terrier

Poodle

Boxer

French bulldog

Rottweiler

Top 10 Registered US Cat Breeds

Exotic

Persian

Maine coon

Ragdoll

British shorthair

American shorthair

Abyssinian

Sphynx

Siamese

Scottish fold

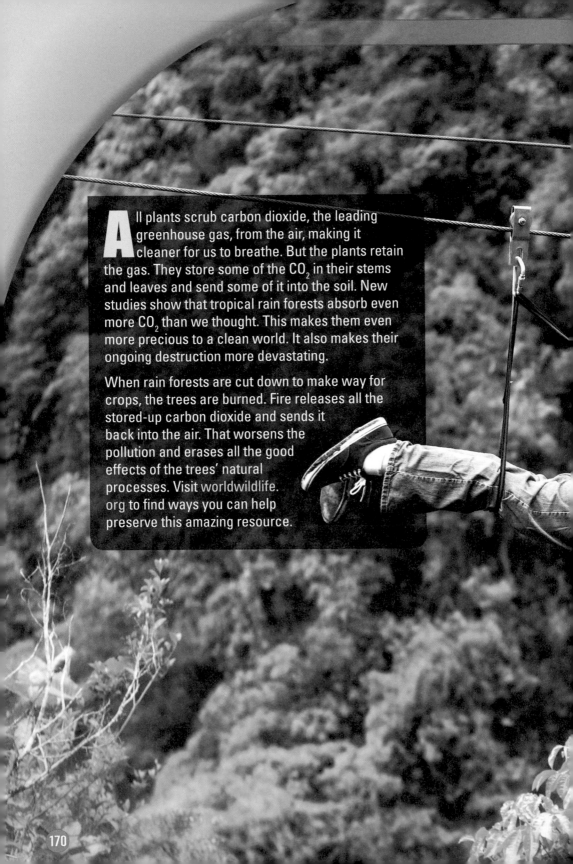

All plants scrub carbon dioxide, the leading greenhouse gas, from the air, making it cleaner for us to breathe. But the plants retain the gas. They store some of the CO_2 in their stems and leaves and send some of it into the soil. New studies show that tropical rain forests absorb even more CO_2 than we thought. This makes them even more precious to a clean world. It also makes their ongoing destruction more devastating.

When rain forests are cut down to make way for crops, the trees are burned. Fire releases all the stored-up carbon dioxide and sends it back into the air. That worsens the pollution and erases all the good effects of the trees' natural processes. Visit worldwildlife. org to find ways you can help preserve this amazing resource.

PLANTS

Forests provide food and fuel for millions of people and habitat for about 80 percent of the world's biodiversity. Plus, they're slowing climate change. Treasure those trees! Where are the biggest forests in the world? See page 173.

Biological Classification of Plants

PLANT KINGDOM

Filicinophyta
FERNS

Lycopodophyta
CLUB MOSSES

Ginkgophyta
GINKGO

Gnetophyta
WELWITSCHIA,
EPHEDRA, GNETUM

Psilophyta
WHISKFERNS

Cycadophyta
CYCADS

Bryophyta
BRYOPHYTES

Sphenophyta
HORSETAILS

Coniferophyta
CONIFERS

Angiospermophyta
FLOWERING PLANTS

KEY
These colors show the classification groupings in the chart.

- **PHYLUM or DIVISION**
- **CLASS**
- **ORDER**

Hepaticae
LIVERWORTS

Monocotyledoneae
MONOCOTYLEDONS

Musci
MOSSES

Dicotyledoneae
DICOTYLEDONS

Anthocerotae
HORNWORTS

Liliaceae	LILY, TULIP
Orchidaceae	ORCHIDS
Poaceae	WHEAT, BAMBOO
Iridaceae	IRIS, GLADIOLUS
Arecaceae	COCONUT PALM, DATE PALM
Bromeliaceae	BROMELIAD, PINEAPPLE
Cyperaceae	SEDGES
Juncaceae	RUSHES
Musaceae	BANANA
Amaryllidaceae	DAFFODIL, AMARYLLIS
Ranunculaceae	BUTTERCUP, DELPHINIUM

Brassicaceae	CABBAGE, TURNIP
Rosaceae	APPLE, ROSE
Fabaceae	BEAN, PEANUT
Magnoliaceae	MAGNOLIA, TULIP TREE
Apiaceae	CARROT, PARSLEY
Solonaceae	POTATO, TOMATO
Lamiaceae	MINT, LAVENDER
Asteraceae	SUNFLOWER, DANDELION
Salicaceae	WILLOW, POPLAR
Cucurbitaceae	MELON, CUCUMBER
Malvaceae	HIBISCUS, HOLLYHOCK
Cactaceae	CACTUS

Where Do Plants Grow?

Plants grow everywhere in the world, except where there is permanent ice. However, different types of plants grow best in different regions. A region's plant life depends on the climate, the amount of water and sun, the type of soil, and other features. For instance, plants in the tundra grow close to the ground, away from the region's icy winds. Desert plants have thick skins to hold in every drop of water. This map shows five major regions where certain kinds of plants grow best, and the areas where the climate is too harsh for any plant life at all.

Region	Types of Plants
Aquatic	Cattails, seaweed
Grassland	Short and tall grasses
Forest	Trees, shrubs, ferns, wildflowers
Tundra	Small shrubs, mosses
Desert	Many kinds of cacti
Permanent ice	No plant life

173

The United Nations says there are about 1,900 kinds of edible insects in the world. Two billion people eat them every day, and now the UN wants more of us to put the bite on bugs. Insects are a cheap, plentiful source of nutrition, which is especially important for poorer nations with growing populations. Raising insects also requires much less land and energy than raising livestock.

According to a cookbook called *Creepy Crawly Cuisine*, some of the most commonly eaten insects include beetles, butterflies and moths, bees and wasps, ants, grasshoppers, crickets and locusts, and stinkbugs. Beetles have the most protein. Stinkbugs taste like apples (if you can get past the smell).

Crickets, which have as much calcium as milk, are hopping to the top of the list of bugs most likely to be eaten in the United States. Hopper Bars, made with ground crickets, are sold at Whole Foods. Cricket chips, made of ground crickets mixed with beans and rice, came out in late 2014. They're called "Chirps".

If insect legs and antennae turn you off, try foods made with insects ground into flour or meal instead. Cricket meal has 70 grams of protein per serving.

HUMAN BODY

Systems of the Human Body

Skeletal System

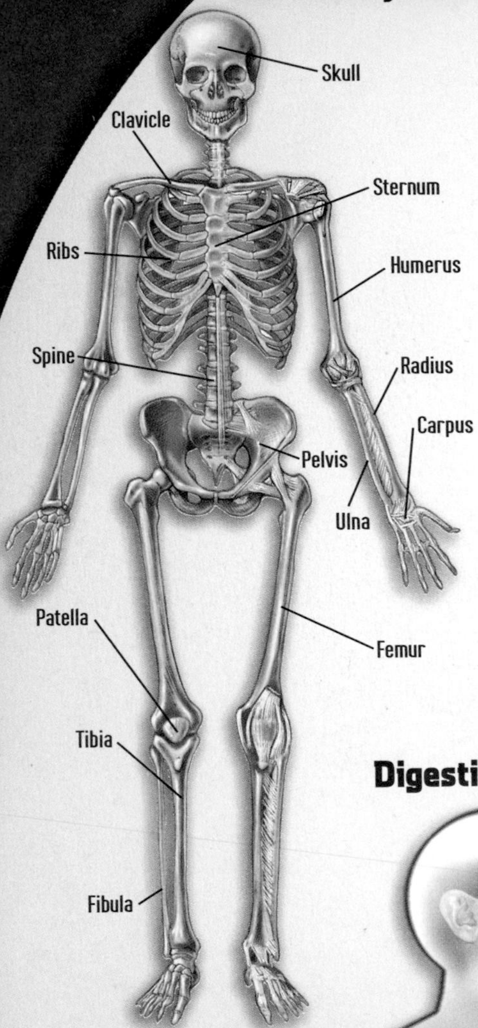

- Skull
- Clavicle
- Sternum
- Ribs
- Humerus
- Spine
- Radius
- Carpus
- Pelvis
- Ulna
- Patella
- Femur
- Tibia
- Fibula

Muscular System

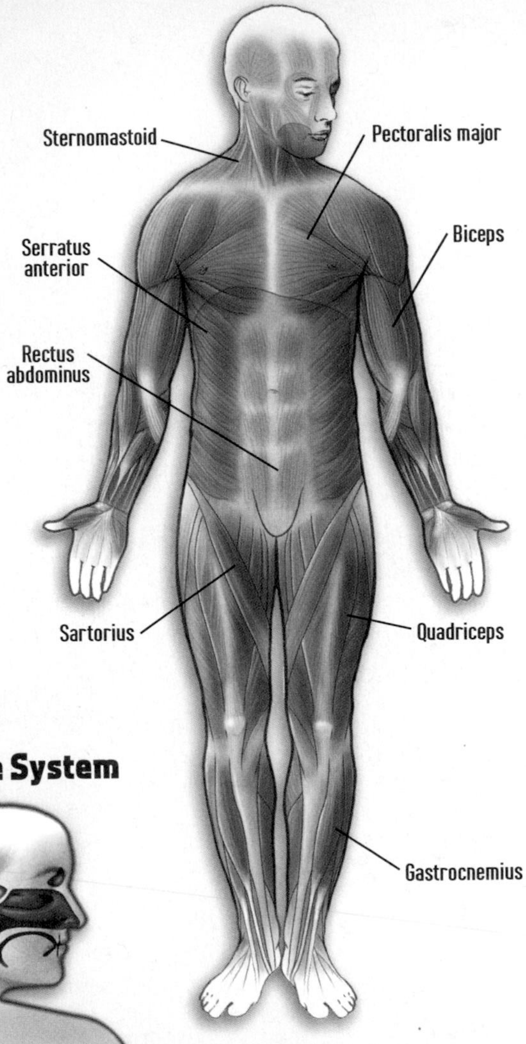

- Sternomastoid
- Pectoralis major
- Serratus anterior
- Biceps
- Rectus abdominus
- Sartorius
- Quadriceps
- Gastrocnemius

Digestive System

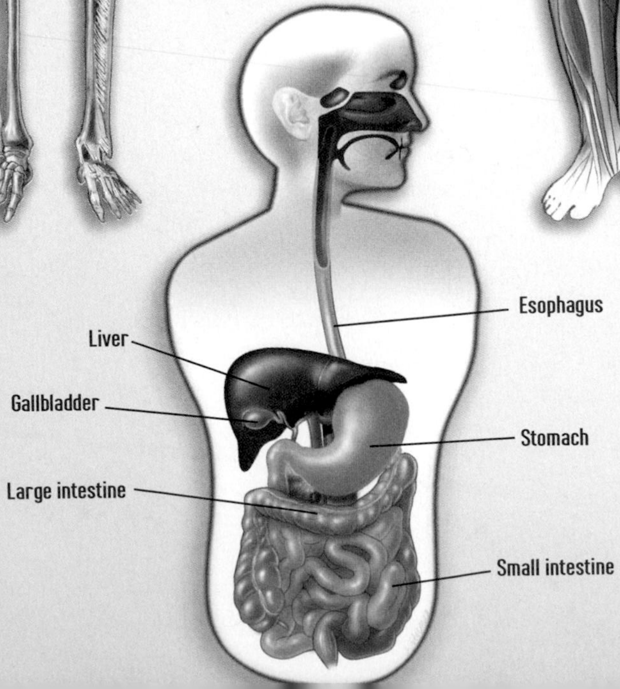

- Esophagus
- Liver
- Gallbladder
- Stomach
- Large intestine
- Small intestine

Nervous System

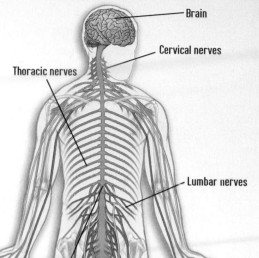

Brain

Cervical nerves

Thoracic nerves

Lumbar nerves

Spinal cord

Circulatory System

- Veins carry blood to the heart

- Arteries carry blood away from the heart

Heart

Respiratory System

Nasal cavity

Windpipe (trachea)

Oral cavity

Voice box (larynx)

Lungs

What kinds of foods should you eat every day to stay healthy, and how much of each kind do you need? MyPlate, the US government's official food graphic, tells you at a glance what should be on your plate. The graphic was created to help everyone remember to choose fruits, grains, vegetables, protein, and dairy as they plan their daily meals. Get tips, recipes, and calculate your personal calorie needs at ChooseMyPlate.gov.

The most popular fruit in the world is one you may think is a vegetable—the tomato. Scientifically speaking, a tomato is considered a fruit because it comes from a flowering plant that contains seeds. Sixty million tons of tomatoes are produced every year.

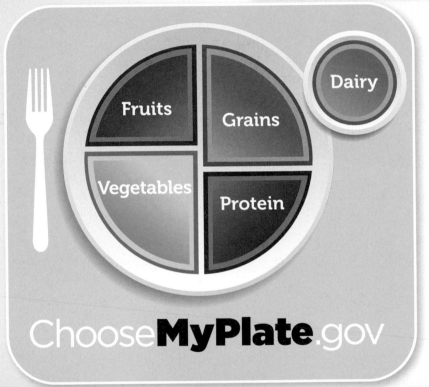

ChooseMyPlate.gov

Grains	Vegetables	Fruits	Dairy	Protein
At least half of the bread, cereal, and pasta you eat should be whole grain.	Fresh or frozen, dark green, orange, light green, yellow—mix it up! Limit the starchy kind, like potatoes.	Enjoy a couple of pieces of fruit a day, but go easy on the fruit juice. It's loaded with sugar.	Choose nonfat or lowfat milk, cheese, and yogurt.	Choose meat, fish, or poultry, but make sure your protein is lean. Nuts, seeds, and beans are also good protein sources.

Oils Oils aren't a food group, but you need some for good health. Nuts and fish are good sources. Be sure to limit sugars and solid fats, such as butter. Read the labels—you might be surprised!

Kids' Top Five Favorite Outdoor Activities

According to a 2014 study by the Outdoor Foundation, these are the favorite activities of kids between the ages of 6 and 17:

1. Running   2. Biking   3. Fishing   4. Hiking   5. Skateboarding

The study shows that kids 6–12 as a group and girls in particular are becoming more active in outdoor activities. That's good news! Experts say the best way to keep your body healthy and fit, as well as limit risk of certain diseases, is to exercise at least an hour a day. Find an activity you love and have fun moving in a healthy direction.

Your Amazing Body, by the Numbers

Your heart pumps blood along 60,000 miles (97,000 km) of veins and arteries. It beats 100,000 times a day—that's 36 million times a year and more than 3 billion times in an average lifetime.

Your brain weighs only about 3 pounds (1.4 kg), but it has about 100 billion nerve cells. Nerves help you think, move, dream, feel happy or sad, and regulate unconscious activities, such as digesting food and breathing.

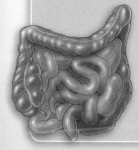

Your digestive system consists of about 30 feet (9 m) of tubes that carry food along a journey from top to bottom, squeezing out nutrients to keep you healthy and processing waste materials.

Your skin is your body's largest organ, weighing about 8 pounds (3.6 kg) and measuring about 22 square feet (2 sq m). Be good to your skin by keeping it clean and well protected from the sun.

Every year, tons and tons of plastic litter wash into the oceans through rivers and streams. Massive amounts collect in the gyres, huge revolving water systems in the five major oceans.

The most famous one is the North Pacific Gyre, where halfway between California and Hawaii the plastic extends over an area twice the size of Texas. The site is nicknamed the Great Pacific Garbage Patch.

Dutch teenager Boyan Slat, shocked by the floating plastic he saw while diving in Greece, decided to invent a process to clean up the Garbage Patch. His idea was to build floating barriers anchored deep down in the sea bed. The barriers, combined with the ocean's movement, would guide the debris toward a platform, where it could be removed.

China   Russia
Japan   Canada
US
Great Pacific Garbage Patch
Pacific Ocean
Hawaii

Boyan started a foundation called The Ocean Cleanup, raising money to fund the project and attracting scientists to join him. Boyan hopes to have the first platform working by 2020. Follow his progress on theoceancleanup.com.

Plastic bottles make up about half of the plastic litter that washes out to sea. Even tiny pieces of plastic act like sponges to soak up harmful chemicals in the water. When birds and fish eat the pieces, they're eating chemicals, too. San Francisco, CA, has become the first US city to ban plastic grocery bags.

ENVIRONMENT

Rising Carbon Dioxide Levels

The amount of the main greenhouse gas in the atmosphere, carbon dioxide (CO_2), has been steadily rising for more than a century. Experts say the increase comes mostly from the burning of fossil fuels for energy.

Carbon Dioxide in the Atmosphere, 1903–2014

Year	CO_2 (parts per million)
1903	295
1915	301
1927	306
1943	308
1960	317
1970	326
1980	339
1990	354
2000	367
2005	377
2006	379
2007	381
2008	383
2009	385
2013	396
2014	399

10 Worst Carbon Dioxide-Producing Countries

Country	Millions of Metric Tons Produced Annually
China	8,715.3
United States	5,490.6
Russia	1,788.1
India	1,725.8
Japan	1,180.6
Germany	748.5
Iran	624.9
South Korea	611.0
Canada	552.6
Saudi Arabia	513.5

Something's in the Air

There are six common air pollutants: ground level ozone, carbon monoxide, sulfur and nitrogen oxides, lead, and particulate matter, such as soot and smoke. The charts on this page show the urban areas with the lowest and highest year-round levels of particle pollution. Find out more at lung.org.

Most Polluted US Cities/Urban Areas
(by year-round particle pollution)

Rank	City
1	Fresno-Madera, CA
2	Visalia-Porterville-Hanford, CA
3	Los Angeles-Long Beach, CA*
3	Bakersfield, CA*
4	Modesto-Merced, CA
6	Pittsburgh-New Castle-Weirton, PA-OH-WV
7	El Centro, CA
8	Phoenix-Mesa-Scottsdale, AZ**
8	St. Louis-St. Charles-Farmington, MO-IL**
8	El Paso-Las Cruces, TX-NM**

*Tie   **Three-way tie

Cleanest US Cities/Urban Areas
(by year-round particle pollution)

Rank	City
1	Prescott, AZ
2	Cheyenne, WY*
2	Farmington, NM*
4	Casper, WY
5	St. George, UT
6	Flagstaff, AZ
7	Redding-Red Bluff, CA
8	Duluth, MN-WI
9	Kahului-Wailuku-Lahaina, HI
10	Rapid City-Spearfish, SD

*Tie

RECYCLE

Around We Go

In the United States, we recycle about 34 percent of our municipal solid waste (MSW). More than 30 percent of the raw material used in glass production comes from recycled glass. That's good news, but we can do better. Even recycling a tiny amount makes a huge difference:

- Recycling one glass bottle saves enough energy to light a 100-watt lightbulb for four hours.

- If every American household recycled the Sunday newspaper, more than half a million trees would be saved—every week!

- Recycling one aluminum can saves enough energy to run a TV for three hours.

- Manufacturing one ton of recycled paper takes about 60 percent of the energy to make a ton of paper from raw pulp.

- In 2010, Americans recycled about 53 billion aluminum cans. That's more than 100,000 every minute. If they were lined up end to end on the ground, the cans could circle the earth 169 times.

Always Recycle These Items

Acid batteries	Electronic equipment	Newspaper	Steel cans
Aluminum cans	Glass (particularly bottles and jars)	Oil	Tires
Appliances		Paint	Wood
Building materials	Lead	Paper	Writing/copy paper
Cardboard	Magazines	Plastic bags	Yard waste
Chemicals	Metal	Plastic bottles	

Some of these items have special rules for handling or disposal. Look online for your local recycling office. Check out the Environmental Protection Agency (EPA) website at epa.gov for a state-by-state list of locations and other helpful information.

Plastic foam does not break down like other materials. It can stay in the environment for 500 years. That's why New York City; Portland, OR; and Seattle, WA, have officially banned plastic foam containers and packing peanuts. More than 70 cities in California have restrictions on foam containers. New York planned to start using compostable plates in school cafeterias instead of plastic foam trays starting May 1, 2015.

Bike It or Hike It!

Every time you travel, you have choices about how you impact the environment. When you go, go green!

Take the bus. A bus carrying 40 passengers takes one-sixth the energy of one car carrying each passenger, while replacing six city blocks' worth of cars.

Skateboard, walk, or ride your bike whenever safety and weather permit. These are the greenest ways to travel, and they're great for your health.

Suggest that the adults in your family drive less or carpool. Driving 25 fewer miles (40 km) every week can eliminate 1,500 pounds (680 kg) of carbon dioxide from the air. Riding with two or more people two days a week can eliminate 1,590 pounds (721 kg) from the air.

Shrink Your Carbon Footprint

The Environmental Protection Agency (EPA) is calling on kids to help reduce climate change and its effects on people and the environment. Visit epa.gov/climateforaction to check out your carbon footprint and learn what other "steps" you can take.

Scientists have declared 2014 the hottest year on record. Although parts of the United States were cooler than usual, the average global temperature was the highest since 1880, when scientists started keeping track.

Levels of carbon dioxide, the main greenhouse gas, have been rising at the same time. Most scientists now agree that there is a direct link between pollution caused by human activities and global warming, and the effects are getting worse fast. Nine of the ten warmest years on record have happened since 2000.

If it's hot on land, scientists say they are "stunned" at how fast the ocean is warming. Warm water expands, increasing coastal flood danger. As carbon dioxide dissolves, it releases acid, threatening marine life. Scientists have committed to research projects around the globe in 2015 to try to find badly needed solutions fast.

WEATHER

2000

2014

The graph shows how temperatures have been rising, hitting their peak in 2014. A chart on page 181 shows that carbon dioxide levels have been rising to match. Scientists say pollution caused by humans is influencing global warming at an alarming rate.

The numbers below are based on 30-year averages of temperature, wind, snowfall, rainfall, and humidity at weather stations in the 48 continental states (not Alaska and Hawaii).

5 Driest Places

Location	Annual Precipitation
Yuma, AZ	3.01 in. (7.65 cm)
Las Vegas, NV	4.49 in. (11.40 cm)
Bishop, CA	5.02 in. (12.75 cm)
Bakersfield, CA	6.49 in. (16.48 cm)
Alamosa, CO	7.25 in. (18.41 cm)

5 Wettest Places

Location	Annual Precipitation
Mount Washington, NH	101.91 in. (258.85 cm)
Quillayute, WA	101.72 in. (258.37 cm)
Astoria, OR	67.13 in. (170.51 cm)
Mobile, AL	66.29 in. (168.38 cm)
Pensacola, FL	64.28 in. (163.27 cm)

5 Coldest Places

Location	Average Temperature
Mount Washington, NH	27.2°F (-2.66°C)
International Falls, MN	37.4°F (3.00°C)
Marquette, MI	38.7°F (3.72°C)
Duluth, MN	39.1°F (3.94°C)
Caribou, ME	39.2°F (4.00°C)

5 Hottest Places

Location	Average Temperature
Key West, FL	78.1°F (25.61°C)
Miami, FL	76.7°F (24.83°C)
Yuma, AZ	75.3°F (24.05°C)
West Palm Beach, FL	75.3°F (24.05°C)
Fort Wayne, FL	74.9°F (23.83°C)

What is a Front?

The line where cold and warm air masses collide is called a front. A cold front occurs when cold air pushes warm air out of its way. Cold fronts can bring stormy and even severe weather. A warm front occurs when warm air pushes away cold air, and it can bring gray, drizzly weather. (On a weather map, a cold front is indicated by a blue line with triangles below. Warm fronts are shown as red lines with half-circles above.)

Worldwide Weather Extremes

Highest Recorded Temperatures by Continent

Temperature	Continent	Location	Date
131°F (55°C)	Africa	Kebili, Tunisia	July 7, 1931
134°F (56.7°C)	North America	Death Valley, California, United States	July 10, 1913
129.2°F (54°C)	Asia	Tirat Tsvi, Israel	June 21, 1942
123°F (50.5°C)	Australia	Oodnadatta, South Australia	January 2, 1960
120°F (48.9°C)	South America	Rivadavia, Argentina	December 11, 1905
118.4°F (48°C)	Europe	Athens, Greece (and Elefsina, Greece)	July 10, 1977
59°F (15°C)	Antarctica	Vanda Station	May 1, 1974

Lowest Recorded Temperatures by Continent

Temperature	Continent	Location	Date
-129°F (-89.4°C)	Antarctica	Vostok Station	July 21, 1983
-90°F (-67.8°C)	Asia	Oimekon, Russia	February 6, 1933
-90°F (-67.8°C)	Asia	Verkhoyansk, Russia	February 5 and 7, 1892
-81.4°F (-63°C)	North America	Snag, Yukon Territory, Canada	February 3, 1947
-72.6°F (-58.1°C)	Europe	Ust-Shchugor, Russia	December 31, 1978
-27°F (-32.8°C)	South America	Sarmiento, Argentina	June 1, 1907
-11°F (-23.9°C)	Africa	Ifrane, Morocco	February 11, 1935
-9.4°F (-23.0°C)	Australia	Charlotte Pass, New South Wales	June 29, 1994

Highest Average Annual Precipitation by Continent

Amount	Continent	Location
467.4 in. (1,187.2 cm)	Asia	Mawsynram, India
405.0 in. (1,028.7 cm)	Africa	Debundscha, Cameroon
354.0 in. (899.2 cm)	South America	Quibdo, Colombia
316.3 in. (803.4 cm)	Australia	Bellenden Ker, Queensland, Australia
276.0 in. (700.0 cm)	North America	Henderson Lake, BC, Canada
183.0 in. (464.8 cm)	Europe	Crkvica, Bosnia, and Herzegovina

Lowest Average Annual Precipitation by Continent

Amount	Continent	Location
0.03 in. (0.08 cm)	South America	Arica, Chile
0.08 in. (0.20 cm)	Antarctica	Amundsen-Scott South Pole Station
0.10 in. (0.25 cm)	Africa	Wadi Halfa, Sudan
1.20 in (3.05 cm	North America	Bataques, Mexico
1.80 in. (4.57 cm)	Asia	Aden, Yemen
4.05 in. (10.28 cm)	Australia	Mulka (Troudaninna), South Australia
6.40 in. (16.26 cm)	Europe	Astrakhan, Russia

The *Titanic* was the biggest, fanciest ocean liner in the world. It was called "unsinkable," but of course that wasn't true. The ship sank in the North Atlantic on April 15, 1912, after an iceberg punched a hole in its hull. More than 1,500 people died, mostly because the 20 lifeboats it carried were not adequate for all the passengers and crew.

One thing is sure: *Titanic II* will have enough lifeboats. It will also have air-conditioning. Australian billionaire Clive Palmer is building a cruise ship that will look exactly like the original, inside and out, but will offer a few modern comforts. Palmer hopes to launch in 2016.

Meanwhile, scientists say the rusted wreck of the *Titanic* will disappear in the next 15–20 years, destroyed by rust-eating bacteria. There's no chance it will be raised before then, but you can visit onlinetitanicmuseum.com to dive deep into the ship's history.

DISASTERS

Historians say the *Titanic* disaster could have been avoided entirely if the officer on duty had taken quicker action. He waited half a minute to change course after being warned that an iceberg was in the ship's path. Read about other disasters caused by human error and natural events in this chapter.

What Makes an Earthquake?

At certain places, there are breaks in the rocks that make up Earth's surface. These places are called faults. An earthquake is a shock wave that occurs when the tectonic plates beneath a fault rub or crash together. The US Geological Survey estimates that there are several million earthquakes a year. Most are too small to be detected.

Deadliest Earthquakes

Date	Place	Number of Deaths
Jan. 24, 1556	Shaanxi, China	830,000
May 20, 526 CE	Antioch, Syria	250,000
July 28, 1976	Tangshan, China	242,769
Aug. 9, 1138	Aleppo, Syria	230,000
Dec. 26, 2004	near Sumatra, Indonesia	227,898
Jan. 12, 2010	near Port-au-Prince, Haiti	220,000
Dec. 22, 856 CE	Damghan, Iran	200,000
Dec. 16, 1920	Gansu, China	200,000
March 23, 893 CE	Ardabil, Iran	150,000

Hero Dogs

The California-based Search Dog Foundation (SDF) trains dogs to help humans after disasters. SDF has sent dogs to more than 80 emergencies and disasters, including Hurricane Katrina, the 2010 Haiti earthquake, and the Japan earthquake and tsunami of 2011. In Haiti, canine search teams helped bring 12 people to safety. SDF recruits dogs from shelters and rescue groups, looking for young dogs with drive, energy, and focus. The dogs are mostly Labrador retrievers, golden retrievers, border collies, and mixes. In 2014, SDF had plans in place for the first national search and rescue dog training center in the United States. Visit searchdogfoundation.org to learn more.

What Makes a Volcano?

A volcano is an opening in Earth's surface that allows hot melted rock, called magma, to escape from below the surface. Scientists say there are about 550 historically active volcanoes.

Gently curved shield volcanoes build up over thousands of years. Mauna Loa is a shield volcano on the island of Hawaii. It rises about 56,000 feet (17 km) above the ocean floor.

Some of the most famous volcanoes in the world are stratovolcanoes, including Mt. Vesuvius, Krakatau, and Mt. Mayon, the most active volcano in the Philippines.

10 Deadliest Volcanic Eruptions

Date	Volcano	Number of Deaths
April 10–12, 1815	Mt. Tambora, Indonesia	92,000
Aug. 26–28, 1883	Krakatau, Indonesia	36,000
May 8, 1902	Mt. Pelee, Martinique	28,000
Nov. 13, 1985	Nevado del Ruiz, Colombia	23,000
Aug. 24, 79 CE	Mt. Vesuvius, Italy	16,000
May 21, 1792	Mt. Unzen, Japan	14,500
1586 (month and day unknown)	Kelut, Indonesia	10,000
June 8, 1783	Laki, Iceland	9,350
May 19, 1919	Mt. Kelut, Indonesia	5,000
Dec. 15, 1631	Mt. Vesuvius, Italy	4,000

What Makes a Tsunami?

A tsunami is a wave that is often caused by an underwater earthquake. The wave travels across the ocean at speeds up to 600 miles per hour (970 kph), then crashes on shore with devastating power. On March 11, 2011, an underwater earthquake triggered a massive tsunami, which led to a nuclear power plant meltdown in Japan. Over 15,000 people were killed, mostly from the tsunami.

Wild Windstorms

Hurricanes

Hurricanes are huge storms with winds over 74 mph (119 kph) blowing around a center, or eye. Most hurricanes form over the mild waters of the southern Atlantic Ocean, the Caribbean Sea, or the Gulf of Mexico. Equally powerful storms that form over the western Pacific Ocean are called typhoons. If they form over the Indian Ocean, they're called cyclones.

Hurricane Katrina, which hit the Gulf Coast in 2005, was the costliest natural disaster in US history and the third-deadliest hurricane, causing $125 billion in damages and 1,836 deaths.

Tornadoes

Tornadoes are powerful storms with funnels of furious wind spinning from 40 mph (64 kph) to more than 300 mph (482.8 kph). The funnels touch down and rip paths of destruction on land. About 1,500 tornadoes hit the United States every year.

A group of tornadoes is called an outbreak. On April 3, 1974, a group of 148 tornadoes swept through 13 states and parts of Canada in the 1974 Super Outbreak. The storm's path on the ground covered almost 2,500 miles (4,023 km).

Major US Natural Disasters

Earthquake
When: April 18, 1906
Where: San Francisco, California
An earthquake accompanied by a fire destroyed more than 4 square miles (10 sq km) and left at least 3,000 dead or missing.

Hurricane
When: August 27–September 15, 1900
Where: Galveston, Texas
More than 6,000 died from the devastating combination of high winds and tidal waves.

Tornado
When: March 18, 1925
Where: Missouri, Illinois, and Indiana
Called the Great Tri-State Tornado, this twister caused 747 deaths and ripped along a path of 219 miles (352 km) after touching down near Ellington, Missouri.

Blizzard
When: March 11–14, 1888
Where: East Coast
Four hundred people died, and 40–50 inches (101.6–127 cm) of snow fell in the Blizzard of '88. Damage was estimated at $20 million.

Major US Disasters Caused by Humans

Aircraft
When: September 11, 2001
Where: New York, New York; Arlington, Virginia; Shanksville, Pennsylvania
Hijacked planes crashed into the World Trade Center, the Pentagon, and a field in Pennsylvania, causing nearly 3,000 deaths.

Fire
When: March 25, 1911
Where: New York, New York
The Triangle Shirtwaist Factory caught fire, trapping workers inside and causing 146 deaths.

Passenger Train
When: July 9, 1918
Where: Nashville, Tennessee
An inbound and an outbound train collided in a crash that witnesses heard miles away and took more than 100 lives. The crash was caused by errors and misunderstandings by both train crews.

Environmental
When: April 20, 2010
Where: Gulf of Mexico, 42 miles off the Louisiana coast
The Deepwater Horizon oil rig exploded, killing 11 workers and letting loose an underwater gush of about 4.9 million barrels of oil over 86 days. The spill was called the worst environmental disaster in US history. However, after a massive offshore and onshore cleanup effort, by 2011 Gulf fish, shrimp, and oysters were deemed safe to eat and most Gulf beaches were open.

HISTORY

The United Nations turns 70 on October 24, 2015, but the party got started early. Artists rocked the famous building in New York City on June 6, 2014, with so much excitement and energy that top UN officials jumped up onstage to jam with them.

Performers played Caribbean, African, and Bengali music blended with rock and hip-hop. One of the stars was Emmanuel Jal, a former child soldier in the Sudan who is now a professional musician and activist for kids. But the artists did much more than entertain. They urged everyone to use their own voices for a better future through MyWorld, the UN's global survey. The survey asked participants to choose their six top hopes for the world, such as clean water, enough food, and education for all people. The results will help influence world leaders as they make important decisions after 2015.

You can read the results at MyWorld.com through the end of December 2015. You can meet the people and learn about the events that changed history in this section. And you can sing out for positive change any way you can, anytime.

World History

Ancient History Highlights

Date	Event
4.5 billion BCE	Planet Earth forms.
3 billion BCE	First signs of life (bacteria and green algae) appear in oceans.
3.2 million BCE	*Australopithecus afarensis* roams Earth (remains, nicknamed Lucy, found in Ethiopia in 1974).
1.8 million BCE	*Homo erectus* ("upright man"). Brain size twice that of *australopithecine* species.
100,000 BCE	First modern *Homo sapiens* live in east Africa.
4500–3000 BCE	Sumerians in Tigris and Euphrates valleys develop city-state civilization. First phonetic writing.
3000–2000 BCE	Pharaonic rule begins in Egypt with King Menes. Great Sphinx of Giza constructed. Earliest Egyptian mummies created.
2000–1500 BCE	Israelites enslaved in Egypt.
1500–1000 BCE	Ikhnaton develops monotheistic religion in Egypt (circa 1375 BCE). His successor, Tutankhamun, returns to earlier gods. Moses leads Israelites out of Egypt into Canaan. Ten Commandments. End of Greek civilization in Mycenae with invasion of Dorians.
800–700 BCE	First recorded Olympic Games (776 BCE). Legendary founding of Rome by Romulus (753 BCE).
700–600 BCE	Founding of Byzantium by Greeks (circa 660 BCE). Building of Acropolis in Athens by Solon, Greek lawmaker (630–560 BCE).
600–500 BCE	Confucius (551–479 BCE) develops philosophy of Confucianism in China. Siddhartha Gautama or Buddha (563–483 BCE) founds Buddhism in India.
300–241 BCE	First Punic War (264–241 BCE). Rome defeats Carthaginians and begins domination of Mediterranean. Invention of Mayan calendar in Yucatán (more exact than older calendars). First Roman gladiatorial games (264 BCE). Archimedes, Greek mathematician (287–212 BCE).
250–201 BCE	Construction of the Great Wall of China begins.
149–146 BCE	Third Punic War. Rome destroys Carthage.
100–4 BCE	Julius Caesar (100–44 BCE) invades Britain and conquers Gaul (France). Spartacus leads slave revolt against Rome (73 BCE). Birth of Jesus (variously given 7 BCE to 4 BCE).

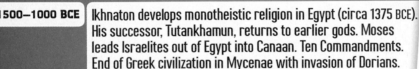

People of Ancient History

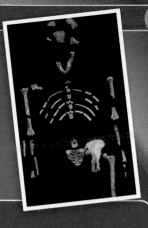

Lucy

In 1974, in Hadar, Ethiopia, scientists discovered a nearly complete skeleton of an *Australopithecus afarensis*, or early human being, which they named Lucy. The skeleton provided scientists with critical insight into the history of humans.

Tutankhamun

Tutankhamun, or King Tut, was one of the most famous *pharaohs*, or rulers, of ancient Egypt. He began ruling at age 10 and died at 19. There are no written records about his life. Until recently, most of the information known came from what Howard Carter discovered in King Tut's tomb in 1922. In 2010, results of a two-year study including DNA tests and CT scans of King Tut's mummy revealed the probable cause of his death as a leg injury complicated by bone disease and malaria.

Confucius

Confucius was a thinker and educator in ancient China. His beliefs and teachings about the way a person should live and treat others greatly influenced the Chinese culture and inspired the Ru school of Chinese thought. Later, his beliefs spread to other parts of the world, and his type of belief system came to be known as Confucianism.

Buddha

Siddhartha Gautama was born the son of a wealthy ruler in what is modern-day Nepal. One day, he was confronted with the suffering of people outside his kingdom, and he left his life of privilege. Siddhartha searched for enlightenment through meditation and eventually found his own path of balance in the world. He earned the title Buddha, or "Enlightened One," and spent the rest of his life helping others to reach enlightenment.

Julius Caesar

As a great politician, military leader, and dictator, Julius Caesar expanded the Roman Empire. He led Rome in conquering Gaul (France), ended the civil war, and instituted many social reforms. His rule ended with his assassination by many of his fellow statesmen on March 15, the Ides of March.

199

World History Highlights: 1—1499 CE

Date	Event
1—49 CE	Crucifixion of Jesus Christ (probably 30 CE).
312—337	Under Constantine the Great, eastern and western Roman empires reunite and new capital, Constantinople, is established.
350—399	Huns invade Europe (circa 360).
622—637	Muhammad flees from Mecca to Medina. Muslim empire grows (634). Arabs conquer Jerusalem (637).
c. 900	Vikings discover Greenland.
c. 1000	Viking raider Leif Ericson discovers North America, calls it Vinland. Chinese invent gunpowder.
1211—1227	Genghis Khan invades China, Persia, and Russia.
1215	King John of England forced by barons to sign Magna Carta, limiting royal power.
1231—1252	Inquisition begins as Pope Gregory IX creates special court to locate and punish heretics. Torture used (1252).
1251	Kublai Khan comes to prominence in China.
1271—1295	Marco Polo of Venice travels to China.
c. 1325	Renaissance begins in Italy.
1337—1453	English and French fight for control of France in Hundred Years' War.
1347—1351	About 25 million Europeans die from "Black Death" (bubonic plague).
1368	Ming dynasty begins in China.
1429	Joan of Arc leads French against English.
1452	Leonardo da Vinci, painter of *Mona Lisa* and other masterpieces, born near Florence, Italy.
1492—1498	Columbus discovers Caribbean Islands and Americas, returns to Spain (1493). Second voyage to Dominica, Jamaica, Puerto Rico (1493—1496). Third voyage to Orinoco (1498).
1497	Vasco da Gama sails around Africa and discovers sea route to India (1498). John Cabot, employed by England, explores Canadian coast.

Constantine

Known as Constantine the Great, he served as the emperor of Rome from 312 to 337. He created a "new" Rome by bringing religious tolerance to the empire and laying a foundation for Western culture. He moved the center of the empire from Rome to the Greek colony of Byzantium, which he renamed Constantinople.

Muhammad

As a prophet from Mecca, Muhammad worked to restore the faith of Abraham. He spread the religion of Islam and the belief in one true God, Allah. His teachings were recorded in the Koran. As his teachings spread, many aristocrats in Mecca began to oppose him. Muhammad fled to Medina, an event that marks the beginning of the Muslim calendar. In 629, he won over his opposition in Mecca. By the time he died in 632, most of the Arabian Peninsula followed his political and religious ideas.

Genghis Khan

Born around 1162 in Mongolia, Genghis Khan was a warrior and ruler who united the tribes of Mongolia and founded the Mongol Empire. He spent his life establishing and increasing his empire by conquering China, Russia, and parts of Persia.

Joan of Arc

At the age of thirteen, Joan of Arc heard the voices of saints telling her to help the French king defeat the English. She presented herself to the king and led the French army to victory at Orléans, forcing the English out of the region. She was later captured by the English, accused of heresy, and burned at the stake. Joan of Arc was hailed as a hero in France for her bravery and made a saint.

Leonardo da Vinci

Italian-born Leonardo da Vinci was one of the most farsighted, multitalented, and relentless thinkers of the time. He was a great artist, inventor, engineer, mathematician, architect, scientist, and musician whose works and insights influenced generations.

World History Highlights: 1500–1899

Date	Event
1509	Henry VIII becomes king of England.
1513	Juan Ponce de León explores Florida and Yucatán Peninsula for Spain.
1517	Martin Luther pins his 95 theses on door of Wittenberg Castle Church in Wittenberg, Germany, starting Protestant Reformation.
1520	Ferdinand Magellan discovers Strait of Magellan and Tierra del Fuego for Spain.
1547	Ivan IV, known as Ivan the Terrible, crowned czar of Russia.
1558	Elizabeth I, Henry VIII's daughter, becomes queen of England.
1585–1587	Sir Walter Raleigh's men reach Roanoke Island, Virginia.
1588	Spanish Armada attempts to invade England and is defeated.
1609	Henry Hudson explores Hudson River and Hudson Bay for England.
1632	Italian astronomer Galileo Galilei is first person to view space through a telescope and confirms belief that Earth revolves around Sun.
1687	Sir Isaac Newton publishes his theories on gravity and his laws of motion.
1721	Peter I, known as Peter the Great, crowned czar of Russia.
1756	Seven Years' War breaks out, involving most European countries.
1778	James Cook sails to Hawaii.
1789	Parisians storm Bastille prison, starting French Revolution.
1804	Scottish explorer John Ross begins expedition to find Northwest Passage in Arctic.
1821	Mexico gains its independence from Spain.
1845	Irish potato crops are ruined by blight, or fungus, creating famine that causes millions to starve to death or emigrate to America.
1859	Charles Darwin publishes On the Origin of Species.
1898	Spanish-American War begins.

Ferdinand Magellan

As a Portuguese explorer, Magellan sailed under both the Portuguese and Spanish flags. To find a route to India by sailing west, he sailed around South America to the Pacific Ocean, discovering the Strait of Magellan along the way. Although he was killed in the Philippines and did not complete the journey, his ships made it back to Spain and were the first to circumnavigate the globe.

Elizabeth I

Queen Elizabeth I ruled England, leading her country through war with wisdom and courage. She was a beloved queen who brought prosperity and a rebirth of learning to England, making the country a major European power. For this reason, the era in which she ruled became known as the Elizabethan Age.

Galileo

Galileo Galilei was a great Italian thinker whose contributions in philosophy, astronomy, and mathematics shaped the way we view the world. He helped develop the scientific method and establish the mathematical laws of falling motion. He advanced the development of the telescope to the point where he could use it to view objects in space and prove that Earth revolved around the Sun. His findings and beliefs were radical at the time and led to his excommunication from the Catholic Church.

Sir Isaac Newton

The contributions of this English physicist and mathematician laid the foundation of many modern sciences. Newton's discovery of white light and its composition of colors paved the way for studies in modern optics. His laws of motion gave a basis to modern physics and his law of universal gravity created a framework for classic mechanics.

Peter the Great

Crowned czar of Russia at the age of ten, Peter ruled jointly with his half brother until his brother's death. As sole ruler, Peter expanded the Russian empire to reclaim access to the Baltic Sea and establish trade with Europe. He reorganized government, founding the city of St. Petersburg as the new capital of Russia and creating the Russian army and navy.

World History Highlights: 1900–1999

Date	Event
1905	Albert Einstein formulates his theory of relativity.
1911	Marie Curie wins Nobel Prize for chemistry.
1914	Archduke Franz Ferdinand, heir to Austrian-Hungarian throne, assassinated in Sarajevo, setting off events that lead to World War I.
1918	Massive worldwide flu epidemic kills more than 20 million people.
1919	Treaty of Versailles signed, ending World War I.
1927	American Charles Lindbergh is first to fly solo across Atlantic Ocean.
1939	Germany invades Poland, sparking World War II. Britain and France declare war on Germany. United States remains neutral.
1941	Japan attacks United States by bombing American ships at Pearl Harbor, Hawaii. United States declares war on Japan and enters World War II.
1945	Germany surrenders. United States drops atomic bombs on two Japanese cities, Hiroshima and Nagasaki. World War II ends. United Nations, international peacekeeping organization, formed.
1948	Israel proclaims its independence. Gandhi, nonviolent leader of Indian Nationalist movement against British rule, assassinated.
1950	North Korea invades South Korea, starting Korean War.
1964	United States begins sending troops to Vietnam to assist South Vietnam during Vietnamese civil war.
1973	Paris Peace Accords signed, ending Vietnam War.
1989	Chinese army shoots and kills protestors in China's Tiananmen Square. Berlin Wall, separating East and West Germany, torn down.
1991	President Frederik Willem de Klerk negotiates to end apartheid in South Africa. Union of Soviet Socialist Republics (USSR) dissolved into independent states.
1994	Nelson Mandela elected president of South Africa in first free elections.
1997	Mother Teresa, champion of poor in Calcutta, India, dies.

Albert Einstein

Called the greatest scientist of the 20th century, physicist Albert Einstein developed revolutionary theories about how the world works, especially the connection between matter and energy. Einstein's knowledge was applied to the development of the atomic bomb, which he said saddened him. Today calling somebody an "Einstein" means that he or she is a genius. However, young Albert Einstein didn't get good grades in every subject. His problems mastering French caused him to fail a college entrance examination.

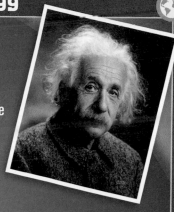

Marie Curie

Polish-French chemist Marie Curie is best known for discovering the radioactive element radium, for which she won a Nobel Prize. She also discovered an element called polonium, named for her birthplace, Poland. Although radium is used to treat and diagnose diseases, repeated or excessive exposure can cause serious illness and even death. After years of working with radium, Marie Curie died in 1934 from radiation poisoning.

Mohandas Gandhi

To the people of India, Mohandas Gandhi was the Mahatma, or Great Soul. Gandhi believed in tolerance for all religious beliefs. He led peaceful protests to bring about social change and freedom from British rule. India was granted freedom in 1947, but fighting between Hindus and Muslims continued. Gandhi spoke out against the fighting, angering many and resulting in his assassination. In America, Dr. Martin Luther King Jr. modeled his nonviolent strategy of fighting racism on Gandhi's methods.

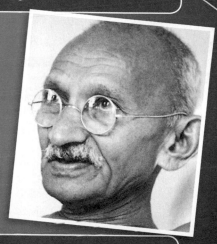

MADRE TERESA

ITALIA 900

M. TEMO

Mother Teresa

Born Agnes Gonxha Bojaxhiu, Mother Teresa was a Roman Catholic nun who became known as the "Saint of the Gutters" for her work with poor people. She founded a religious order in India to provide food, schools, health care, and shelters for the poor, sick, and dying. Mother Teresa received numerous awards for her work, including the Nobel Peace Prize. In 2003, Pope John Paul II approved the first step toward declaring Mother Teresa a saint in the Roman Catholic Church.

World History Highlights: 2000–Present

Date	Event
2001	Hijackers deliberately cause four passenger planes to crash in the United States, resulting in 2,977 deaths (September 11). The Taliban government in Afghanistan collapses after bombing campaign by US forces and ground war by Northern Alliance.
2002	East Timor formally declares its independence from Indonesia and becomes a separate state.
2003	British and US forces launch war against Iraq (March 19), claiming dictator Saddam Hussein has weapons of mass destruction.
2004	A powerful earthquake off the coast of Indonesia results in a devastating tsunami in the Indian Ocean. About 225,000 people are killed.
2005	Angela Merkel is elected chancellor of Germany, the first woman to win the office. Ellen Johnson-Sirleaf is elected president of Liberia, becoming the first female head of state in Africa.
2006	Iraqi dictator Saddam Hussein is captured and later tried and executed for crimes against humanity. Montenegro declares itself an independent state from Serbia.
2008	Aging leader Fidel Castro steps down as president of Cuba. Kosovo declares independence from Serbia.
2009	Swine flu (the H1N1 virus) breaks out in Mexico.
2010	A massive earthquake strikes Haiti, destroying large areas of capital, Port-au-Prince, killing about 220,000 people and leaving 1 million homeless (January 12). Protests in Tunisia, Egypt, and Libya lead to the removal or death of longtime dictators.
2011	US forces in Pakistan kill Osama bin-Laden, Al-Qaeda leader and mastermind of the September 11, 2001, attacks. South Sudan declares its independence from Sudan and becomes the 54th nation in Africa.
2012	North Korea launches a rocket into Earth's orbit, heightening fears of that nation's nuclear capabilities. Human rights activist Aung San Suu Kyi is released from years of house arrest in Burma (Myanmar) and wins election to parliament.

Date	Event
2013	Argentine cardinal Jorge Mario Bergoglio is elected the 266th leader of the Catholic Church, taking the title Pope Francis.
2014	After more than 50 years, United States opens up relations with Cuba. Pakistani activist Malala Yousafzai wins the Nobel Peace Prize for her outspoken efforts in support of girls' education. The Centers for Disease Control officially announces an outbreak of the Ebola virus in Guinea (March 25). Germany wins the World Cup in Brazil.
2015	Islamic extremists attack editorial staff at a newspaper office in Paris because of cartoons of the Prophet Muhammad published by the paper. Altogether, 12 people are killed in the attack and the following chase.

Two Lives on the Line for Human Rights

Malala Yousafzai was just 11 the first time she spoke out for girls' rights to an education in Pakistan. Her view angered the Taliban, the radical group that controlled her region at the time, who outlawed education for girls. Four years later, a Taliban gunman shot Malala in the head on the school bus. She recovered after surgery in Great Britain and went on to become world famous for her outspoken support of the right of young people everywhere to an education. In 2012, Pakistan passed its first Right to Education bill. In 2014, Malala became the youngest person to win the Nobel Peace Prize.

Aung San Suu Kyi fought the brutal military rule in her native Burma (Myanmar) by forming a group called the National League for Democracy (NLD). The NLD wanted to bring about democratic change through peaceful protests, but the government arrested Suu Kyi and some of her followers. They kept her under house arrest—a prisoner in her own home—for most of 15 years. She became a symbol of peaceful protest around the world, and policies in Burma finally began to ease. In 2012, Suu Kyi was released and won a seat in parliament under the NLD party, which was now recognized. She also traveled to Oslo, Sweden, to accept the Nobel Peace Prize she had been awarded in 1991 but had not been free to claim.

The base of the Iwo Jima Memorial in Arlington, VA, contains the locations and dates of every major Marine Corps battle since the corps was founded in 1775. The memorial is one of only eight public places where the American flag is authorized by the president to fly 24/7.

REA·1950·   REVOLU   798–1801×TRIPOLI·1801–

UNCOMMON VALOR WAS A COMMON VIRTUE

US HISTORY

The United States Marine Corps Memorial, or the Iwo Jima Memorial, celebrates a crucial American victory near the end of World War II. The bronze statue was modeled on "Raising the Flag at Iwo Jima," a photograph taken by combat photographer Joe Rosenthal. It has become one of the most famous and frequently reproduced pictures in the world.

The six servicemen in the picture planted the flag on the highest point of the tiny island on February 23, 1945. The sight of the flag inspired troops fighting on the slopes below and watching from American ships offshore. In the ferocious battle that continued for more than a month, three of the men pictured died.

The Iwo Jima Memorial honors all the Marines who have lost their lives serving the United States. The year 2015 marks the 70th anniversary of the Battle of Iwo Jima, the end of World War II, and the beginning of strong friendships among former enemies.

WAR OF 1812 1815 × FLORIDA INDIAN WARS 1835-1842 ×

DECLARATION OF INDEPENDENCE

(Phrases in red are key ideas.)

IN CONGRESS, JULY 4, 1776

THE UNANIMOUS DECLARATION OF THE THIRTEEN UNITED STATES OF AMERICA

When in the Course of human events, it becomes necessary for one people to dissolve the political bands which have connected them with another, and to assume among the powers of the earth, the separate and equal station to which the Laws of Nature and of Nature's God entitle them, a decent respect to the opinions of mankind requires that they should declare the causes which impel them to the separation.

We hold these truths to be self-evident, that all men are created equal, that they are endowed by their Creator with certain unalienable Rights, that among these are Life, Liberty and the pursuit of Happiness. —That to secure these rights, Governments are instituted among Men, deriving their just powers from the consent of the governed, —That whenever any Form of Government becomes destructive of these ends, it is the Right of the People to alter or to abolish it, and to institute new Government, laying its foundation on such principles and organizing its powers in such form, as to them shall seem most likely to effect their Safety and Happiness. Prudence, indeed, will dictate that Governments long established should not be changed for light and transient causes; and accordingly all experience hath shewn, that mankind are more disposed to suffer, while evils are sufferable, than to right themselves by abolishing the forms to which they are accustomed. But when a long train of abuses and usurpations, pursuing invariably the same Object evinces a design to reduce them under absolute Despotism, it is their right, it is their duty, to throw off such Government, and to provide new Guards for their future security. —Such has been the patient sufferance of these Colonies; and such is now the necessity which constrains them to alter their former Systems of Government. The history of the present King of Great Britain is a history of repeated injuries and usurpations, all having in direct object the establishment of an absolute Tyranny over these States. To prove this, let Facts be submitted to a candid world.

He has refused his Assent to Laws, the most wholesome and necessary for the public good.

He has forbidden his Governors to pass Laws of immediate and pressing importance, unless suspended in their operation till his Assent should be obtained; and when so suspended, he has utterly neglected to attend to them.

He has refused to pass other Laws for the accommodation of large districts of people, unless those people would relinquish the right of Representation in the Legislature, a right inestimable to them and formidable to tyrants only.

He has called together legislative bodies at places unusual, uncomfortable, and distant from the depository of their public Records, for the sole purpose of fatiguing them into compliance with his measures.

He has dissolved Representative Houses repeatedly, for opposing with manly firmness his invasions on the rights of the people.

He has refused for a long time, after such dissolutions, to cause others to be elected; whereby the Legislative powers, incapable of Annihilation, have returned to the People at large for their exercise; the State remaining in the mean time exposed to all the dangers of invasion from without, and convulsions within.

He has endeavoured to prevent the population of these States; for that purpose obstructing the Laws for Naturalization of Foreigners; refusing to pass others to encourage their migrations hither, and raising the conditions of new Appropriations of Lands.

He has obstructed the Administration of Justice, by refusing his Assent to Laws for establishing Judiciary powers.

He has made Judges dependent on his Will alone, for the tenure of their offices, and the amount and payment of their salaries.

He has erected a multitude of New Offices, and sent hither swarms of Officers to harrass our people, and eat out their substance.

He has kept among us, in times of peace, Standing Armies without the Consent of our legislatures.

He has affected to render the Military independent of and superior to the Civil power.
He has combined with others to subject us to a jurisdiction foreign to our constitution, and unacknowledged by our laws; giving his Assent to their Acts of pretended Legislation:

For Quartering large bodies of armed troops among us:

For protecting them, by a mock Trial, from punishment for any Murders which they should commit on the Inhabitants of these States:

For cutting off our Trade with all parts of the world:

For imposing Taxes on us without our Consent:

For depriving us in many cases, of the benefits of Trial by Jury:

For transporting us beyond Seas to be tried for pretended offences:

For abolishing the free System of English Laws in a neighbouring Province, establishing therein an Arbitrary government, and enlarging its Boundaries so as to render it at once an example and fit instrument for introducing the same absolute rule into these Colonies:

For taking away our Charters, abolishing our most valuable Laws, and altering fundamentally the Forms of our Governments:

For suspending our own Legislatures, and declaring themselves invested with power to legislate for us in all cases whatsoever.

He has abdicated Government here, by declaring us out of his Protection and waging War against us.

He has plundered our seas, ravaged our Coasts, burnt our towns, and destroyed the lives of our people.

He is at this time transporting large Armies of foreign Mercenaries to compleat the works of death, desolation and tyranny, already begun with circumstances of Cruelty & perfidy scarcely paralleled in the most barbarous ages, and totally unworthy the Head of a civilized nation.

He has constrained our fellow Citizens taken Captive on the high Seas to bear Arms against their Country, to become the executioners of their friends and Brethren, or to fall themselves by their Hands.

He has excited domestic insurrections amongst us, and has endeavoured to bring on the inhabitants of our frontiers, the merciless Indian Savages, whose known rule of warfare, is an undistinguished destruction of all ages, sexes and conditions.

In every stage of these Oppressions We have Petitioned for Redress in the most humble terms: Our repeated Petitions have been answered only by repeated injury. A Prince whose character is thus marked by every act which may define a Tyrant, is unfit to be the ruler of a free people.

Nor have We been wanting in attentions to our Brittish brethren. We have warned them from time to time of attempts by their legislature to extend an unwarrantable jurisdiction over us. We have reminded them of the circumstances of our emigration and settlement here. We have appealed to their native justice and magnanimity, and we have conjured them by the ties of our common kindred to disavow these usurpations, which, would inevitably interrupt our connections and correspondence. They too have been deaf to the voice of justice and of consanguinity. We must, therefore, acquiesce in the necessity, which denounces our Separation, and hold them, as we hold the rest of mankind, Enemies in War, in Peace Friends.

We, therefore, the Representatives of the united States of America, in General Congress, Assembled, appealing to the Supreme Judge of the world for the rectitude of our intentions, do, in the Name, and by Authority of the good People of these Colonies, solemnly publish and declare, That these United Colonies are, and of Right ought to be Free and Independent States; that they are Absolved from all Allegiance to the British Crown, and that all political connection between them and the State of Great Britain, is and ought to be totally dissolved; and that as Free and Independent States, they have full Power to levy War, conclude Peace, contract Alliances, establish Commerce, and to do all other Acts and Things which Independent States may of right do. And for the support of this Declaration, with a firm reliance on the protection of divine Providence, we mutually pledge to each other our Lives, our Fortunes and our sacred Honor.

THE BILL OF RIGHTS
(Phrases in red are key ideas.)

THE FIRST 10 AMENDMENTS TO THE CONSTITUTION
(The first 10 amendments, known collectively as the Bill of Rights, were adopted in 1791.)

AMENDMENT I
Congress shall make no law respecting an establishment of religion, or prohibiting the free exercise thereof; or abridging the freedom of speech, or of the press; or the right of the people peaceably to assemble, and to petition the Government for a redress of grievances.

AMENDMENT II
A well regulated Militia, being necessary to the security of a free State, the right of the people to keep and bear Arms, shall not be infringed.

AMENDMENT III
No Soldier shall, in time of peace be quartered in any house, without the consent of the Owner, nor in time of war, but in a manner to be prescribed by law.

AMENDMENT IV
The right of the people to be secure in their persons, houses, papers, and effects, against unreasonable searches and seizures, shall not be violated, and no Warrants shall issue, but upon probable cause, supported by Oath or affirmation, and particularly describing the place to be searched, and the persons or things to be seized.

AMENDMENT V
No person shall be held to answer for a capital, or otherwise infamous crime, unless on a presentment or indictment of a Grand Jury, except in cases arising in the land or naval forces, or in the Militia, when in actual service in time of War or public danger; nor shall any person be subject for the same offence to be twice put in jeopardy of life or limb; nor shall be compelled in any criminal case to be a witness against himself, nor be deprived of life, liberty, or property, without due process of law; nor shall private property be taken for public use, without just compensation.

AMENDMENT VI
In all criminal prosecutions, the accused shall enjoy the right to a speedy and public trial, by an impartial jury of the State and district wherein the crime shall have been committed, which district shall have been previously ascertained by law, and to be informed of the nature and cause of the accusation; to be confronted with the witnesses against him; to have compulsory process for obtaining witnesses in his favor, and to have the Assistance of Counsel for his defence.

AMENDMENT VII
In Suits at common law, where the value in controversy shall exceed twenty dollars, the right of trial by jury shall be preserved, and no fact tried by jury, shall be otherwise re-examined in any Court of the United States, than according to the rules of the common law.

AMENDMENT VIII
Excessive bail shall not be required, nor excessive fines imposed, nor cruel and unusual punishments inflicted.

AMENDMENT IX
The enumeration in the Constitution, of certain rights, shall not be construed to deny or disparage others retained by the people.

AMENDMENT X
The powers not delegated to the United States by the Constitution, nor prohibited by it to the States, are reserved to the States respectively, or to the people.

Some Important Supreme Court Decisions

Marbury v. Madison (1803)
The Court struck down a law "repugnant to the Constitution" for the first time and set the precedent for judicial review of acts of Congress.

Dred Scott v. Sanford (1857)
Dred Scott, a Missouri slave, sued for his liberty after his owner took him into free territory. The Court ruled that Congress could not bar slavery in the territories. This decision sharpened sectional conflict about slavery.

Plessy v. Ferguson (1896)
This case was about the practice of segregating railroad cars in Louisiana. The Court ruled that as long as equal accommodations were provided, segregation was not discrimination and did not deprive black Americans of equal protection under the Fourteenth Amendment. This decision was overturned by *Brown v. Board of Education* (1954).

Brown v. Board of Education (1954)
Chief Justice Earl Warren led the Court to decide unanimously that segregated schools violated the equal protection clause of the Fourteenth Amendment. Efforts to desegregate Southern schools after the Brown decision met with massive resistance for many years.

Miranda v. Arizona (1966)
The Court ruled that Ernesto Miranda's confession to certain crimes was not admissible as evidence because he had been denied his right to silence and to legal counsel. Now police must advise suspects of their "Miranda rights" when they're taken into custody.

Roe v. Wade (1973)
In a controversial decision, the Court held that state laws restricting abortion were an unconstitutional invasion of a woman's right to privacy.

Chief Justices of the US Supreme Court

Chief Justice	Tenure	Appointed by
John Jay	1789–1795	George Washington
John Rutledge	1795	George Washington
Oliver Ellsworth	1796–1800	George Washington
John Marshall	1801–1835	John Adams
Roger B. Taney	1836–1864	Andrew Jackson
Salmon P. Chase	1864–1873	Abraham Lincoln
Morrison R. Waite	1874–1888	Ulysses S. Grant
Melville W. Fuller	1888–1910	Grover Cleveland
Edward D. White	1910–1921	William H. Taft
William H. Taft	1921–1930	Warren G. Harding
Charles E. Hughes	1930–1941	Herbert Hoover
Harlan F. Stone	1941–1946	Franklin D. Roosevelt
Fred M. Vinson	1946–1953	Harry S Truman
Earl Warren	1953–1969	Dwight D. Eisenhower
Warren E. Burger	1969–1986	Richard M. Nixon
William H. Rehnquist	1986–2005	Ronald Reagan
John G. Roberts Jr.	2005–	George W. Bush

c. 1000	Viking explorer Leif Ericson explores North American coast and founds temporary colony called Vinland.
1492	On first voyage to America, Christopher Columbus lands at San Salvador Island in Bahamas.

1513	Juan Ponce de León discovers Florida. Vasco Nuñez de Balboa crosses Panama and sights Pacific Ocean.
1520	Ferdinand Magellan, whose ships were first to circumnavigate world, discovers South American straits, later named after him.
1521	Hernán Cortéz captures Mexico City and conquers Aztec Empire.
1534–1539	Jacques Cartier of France explores coast of Newfoundland and Gulf of St. Lawrence. Hernando de Soto conquers Florida and begins three-year trek across Southeast.
1540	Francisco Vásquez de Coronado explores Southwest, discovering Grand Canyon and introducing horses to North America.

1541	Hernando de Soto discovers Mississippi River.

1572	Sir Francis Drake of England makes first voyage to Americas, landing in Panama.
1585	Sir Walter Raleigh establishes England's first American colony at Roanoke.
1603	Samuel de Champlain of France explores St. Lawrence River, later founds Québec.
1607	First permanent English settlement in America established at Jamestown, Virginia. Capt. John Smith imprisoned by Native Americans and saved by Pocahontas, daughter of Chief Powhatan.
1609	Henry Hudson sets out in search of Northwest Passage. Samuel de Champlain sails into Great Lakes.
1620	Pilgrims and others board *Mayflower* and travel to Plymouth, Massachusetts. They draw up Mayflower Compact.
1626	Dutch colony of New Amsterdam founded on Manhattan Island, bought from Native Americans for about $24.
1675	Thousands die in King Philip's War between New Englanders and five Native American tribes.
1692	Witchcraft hysteria breaks out in Salem, Massachusetts, leading to 20 executions.

1754	French and Indian War begins.
1763	Treaty of Paris ends French and Indian War.
1765	Parliament passes Stamp Act (tax on newspapers, legal documents, etc.) and Quartering Act (requiring housing of British soldiers in colonists' homes).
1770	Five Americans, including Crispus Attucks, perish in Boston Massacre (March 5).
1773	British Parliament passes Tea Act, leading to Boston Tea Party (Dec. 16).
1775	American Revolution begins with battles of Lexington and Concord (April 19). Second Continental Congress appoints George Washington as commander of Continental Army.
1776	Second Continental Congress approves Declaration of Independence (July 4).
1777	Congress adopts Stars and Stripes flag and endorses Articles of Confederation. Washington's army spends winter at Valley Forge, Pennsylvania.
1783	Treaty of Paris signed, officially ending American Revolution (Sept. 3).
1787	Constitution accepted by delegates to Constitutional Convention in Philadelphia (Sept. 17).
1803	Louisiana Purchase from France doubles size of United States.

1804	Lewis and Clark expedition sets out from St. Louis, Missouri. New Jersey begins gradual emancipation of slaves. Alexander Hamilton killed in duel with Aaron Burr.
1812	War of 1812 with Britain begins by close vote in Congress.
1815	War of 1812 ends.
1825	Erie Canal opens.

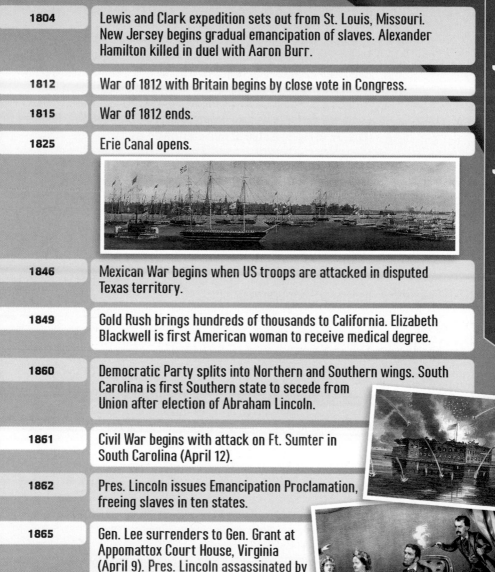

1846	Mexican War begins when US troops are attacked in disputed Texas territory.
1849	Gold Rush brings hundreds of thousands to California. Elizabeth Blackwell is first American woman to receive medical degree.
1860	Democratic Party splits into Northern and Southern wings. South Carolina is first Southern state to secede from Union after election of Abraham Lincoln.
1861	Civil War begins with attack on Ft. Sumter in South Carolina (April 12).
1862	Pres. Lincoln issues Emancipation Proclamation, freeing slaves in ten states.
1865	Gen. Lee surrenders to Gen. Grant at Appomattox Court House, Virginia (April 9). Pres. Lincoln assassinated by John Wilkes Booth in Washington, DC.
1870	Fifteenth Amendment, guaranteeing right to vote for all male US citizens, is ratified (Feb. 3).
1898	After mysterious explosion of battleship *Maine* in Havana harbor (Feb. 15), Spanish–American War breaks out (April 25).

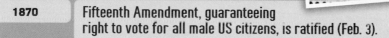

US History Highlights: 1900–1999

1903	Orville and Wilbur Wright conduct first powered flight near Kitty Hawk, NC (Dec. 17).
1909	Expedition team led by Robert E. Peary and Matthew Henson plants American flag at North Pole (April 6). W. E. B. DuBois founds National Association for the Advancement of Colored People (NAACP).
1917	Congress declares war on Germany (April 6) and Austria-Hungary (Dec. 7), bringing United States into World War I.
1918	Armistice Day ends World War I (Nov. 11).
1920	Nineteenth Amendment establishes women's right to vote (Aug. 26).
1927	Charles Lindbergh completes nonstop solo flight from New York to Paris (May 20–21).
1929	Stock market crash on "Black Tuesday" ushers in Great Depression (Oct. 29).
1932	Amelia Earhart is first woman to fly solo across Atlantic.
1941	Japanese planes attack Pearl Harbor, Hawaii, killing 2,400 US servicemen and civilians (Dec. 7). United States declares war on Japan (Dec. 8). Germany and Italy declare war on United States (Dec. 11). United States declares war on Germany and Italy (Dec. 11).
1945	Germany surrenders, ending war in Europe (May 7). Atomic bombs dropped on Hiroshima (Aug. 6) and Nagasaki (Aug. 9); Japan surrenders, ending World War II (Aug. 14).
1950	North Korea invades South Korea, beginning Korean War (June 25).
1954	Supreme Court orders school desegregation in *Brown v. Board of Education* decision (May 17).
1958	In response to Soviet launch of *Sputnik*, United States launches *Explorer I*, first American satellite.
1962	Lt. Col. John H. Glenn Jr. is first American to orbit Earth.

1963	Dr. Martin Luther King Jr. delivers his "I Have a Dream" speech in Washington, DC (Aug. 28). Pres. Kennedy assassinated in Dallas, Texas (Nov. 22).
1965	Black nationalist Malcolm X assassinated in New York City (Feb. 21). Pres. Johnson orders US Marines into South Vietnam (March 8).
1968	Dr. Martin Luther King Jr. is assassinated by James Earl Ray in Memphis, Tennessee (April 4). After winning California presidential primary, Sen. Robert F. Kennedy of New York is assassinated by Sirhan Sirhan in Los Angeles, California (June 5).
1969	Neil Armstrong and Edwin "Buzz" Aldrin of *Apollo 11* are first men to walk on Moon (July 20).
1972	Congress debates Equal Rights Amendment.
1974	Pres. Nixon resigns, elevating Vice Pres. Ford to presidency (Aug. 9).
1981	*Columbia* completes first successful space shuttle mission (April 12–14). Sandra Day O'Connor becomes first female Justice of Supreme Court.
1983	Sally Ride, aboard space shuttle *Challenger*, is first American female astronaut.
1986	Space shuttle *Challenger* explodes in midair over Florida on its tenth mission.
1991	US sends aircraft, warships, and 400,000 troops to Persian Gulf to drive Iraq's armed forces from Kuwait in Operation Desert Storm (Jan. 17). Ground war begins six weeks later and lasts only 100 hours (Feb. 24–28).
1993	Congress passes the North America Free Trade Agreement (NAFTA), removing trade barriers between Canada, the United States, and Mexico.
1996	President Bill Clinton wins reelection.
1998	Clinton is impeached for obstruction of justice by the House of Representatives. The charge stems from his relationship with a White House intern, Monica Lewinsky. He is acquitted by the US Senate in 1999 and serves out his second term.

US History Highlights: 2000-Present

2000 George W. Bush is elected president in an extremely close contest against Democratic nominee Al Gore (November).

2001 On Sept. 11, hijackers overtake four US planes, crashing two of them into World Trade Center in New York City. Another plane crashes into the Pentagon in Washington, DC. The fourth plane crash-lands in a Pennsylvania field after passengers storm the cockpit. In all, 2,977 lives are lost.

2003 The space shuttle *Columbia*, returning from a routine mission to the International Space Station, explodes as it reenters the earth's atmosphere (February 1). All 7 astronauts aboard are killed.

2004 George Bush is reelected president in a close race against Democratic nominee Sen. John Kerry.

2005 Hurricane Katrina strikes the Gulf Coast and devastates the city of New Orleans (August). The rainfall and storm surge overwhelm the city's levee system, and more than 80 percent of the city is flooded.

2008 A financial crisis brought on by banks making high-risk loans strikes markets in the United States. Congress passes bills to bail out the largest banks.

2009 Sen. Barack Obama, first African American presidential candidate to win the nomination of his party, is inaugurated as president (January 20).

Sonia Sotomayor is confirmed by the US Senate to the Supreme Court (August). She is the first Hispanic and third woman to serve as a Supreme Court justice.

2010 President Obama signs the Affordable Care Act into law, extending health insurance coverage to millions of uninsured Americans.

The Deepwater Horizon oil rig, operating off the Gulf Coast, explodes (April 20), killing 11 workers. The resulting spill is the worst in US history, with 3.19 million barrels of oil leaking into the Gulf.

2011	The last US troops leave Iraq (December). The economy's recovery from the financial crisis of 2008 proceeds slowly, with unemployment still over 8 percent. In response, the Occupy Wall Street protest movement spreads to 100 US cities and around the world.

2012	Mass shootings in Colorado, Wisconsin, and Connecticut prompt debate about gun control. A major storm system, averaging 900 miles in diameter, develops in the Caribbean (October) and strikes the East Coast. Property damage is estimated between $30 and $50 billion and "Superstorm Sandy" is blamed for 110 deaths.

2013	Barack Obama is inaugurated for a second term as president. Bombs at the Boston Marathon (April 15) kill 3 people and injure 260. One suspect is killed and another is taken into custody.

2014	The worst mudslide in the nation's history kills 43 people in Oso, Washington (March). The University of Connecticut men's and women's basketball teams both win the NCAA (April). It is the second time UConn has won both competitions in the same year. A police officer shoots and kills unarmed black teenager Michael Brown in Ferguson, Missouri (August). Violent protests follow the grand jury's decision not to charge the officer. President Barack Obama signs an executive order to prevent the deportation of five million illegal immigrants (November). People in New York City protest the decision not to charge police in the death of Eric Garner, an unarmed black man killed when he resisted arrest (December).

2015	The trial of surviving Boston Marathon bomber Dzhokhar Tsarnaev begins (January). A federal judge in Texas rules that President Obama's executive action on immigration imposes heavy burdens on the states (February).

Visit recipechallenge.epicurious.com for information on how to enter the next Healthy Lunchtime Challenge.

US GOVERNMENT

How do you score an invitation to dinner at the White House? It helps to be a king or queen of a foreign country, or a US senator or Supreme Court justice. Or you can get on the guest list starting in your own kitchen, like the kids in this picture. They were winners in the second annual Healthy Lunchtime Challenge, sponsored by Michelle Obama's Let's Move! program. Kids ages 8–12 from all 50 states, three territories, and the District of Columbia won a trip to our nation's capital, with their healthy, tasty, affordable recipes. The Kids' State Dinner was the highlight, where prize-winning recipes were on the menu.

Like official state dinners, this meal was about sharing important ideas as well as food. A speech by Mrs. Obama about helping others inspired winner **Braeden Mannering** to cook up something new. He launched Brae's Brown Bags (3B), a service through which he distributes lunch bags packed with snacks and bottled water to people in need. So far he's distributed more than 2,500 bags.

The Branches of Government

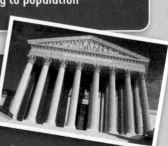

Executive

The President

- Head of state
- Shapes and conducts foreign policy and acts as chief diplomat
- Chief administrator of federal government
- Commander in chief of armed forces
- Has authority to pass or veto congressional bills, plans, and programs
- Appoints and removes nonelected officials
- Leader of his or her political party

Legislative

The Congress:
The Senate
The House of Representatives

- Chief lawmaking body
- Conducts investigations into matters of national importance
- Has power to impeach or remove any civil officer from office, including the president
- Can amend Constitution
- The Senate is made up of 100 senators—2 from each state
- The House of Representatives is made up of 435 congressional representatives, apportioned to each state according to population

Judicial

The Supreme Court

- Upholds the intentions of the Constitution
- Enforces commands of executive and legislative branches
- Interprets the laws of our nation
- Can declare laws unconstitutional

Highest Federal Salaries

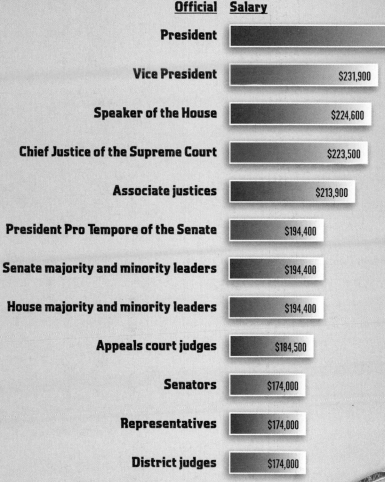

Official	Salary
President	$400,000
Vice President	$231,900
Speaker of the House	$224,600
Chief Justice of the Supreme Court	$223,500
Associate justices	$213,900
President Pro Tempore of the Senate	$194,400
Senate majority and minority leaders	$194,400
House majority and minority leaders	$194,400
Appeals court judges	$184,500
Senators	$174,000
Representatives	$174,000
District judges	$174,000

For most of the years between 1789 and 1855, members of Congress received no yearly salary at all. Instead they were paid $6.00 to $8.00 a day when Congress was in session. Benjamin Franklin proposed that elected government officials not be paid anything for their service, but his proposal didn't win much support.

How a Bill Introduced in the House of Representatives Becomes a Law

How a Bill Originates

The executive branch inspires much legislation. The president usually outlines broad objectives in the yearly State of the Union address.

Members of the president's staff may draft bills and ask congresspersons who are friendly to the legislation to introduce them.

Other bills originate independently of the administration, perhaps to fulfill a campaign pledge made by a congressperson.

How a Bill Is Introduced

Each bill must be introduced by a member of the House. The Speaker then assigns the bill to the appropriate committee. Committees are panels of members assigned to focus on a particular area, such as the military or education.

The committee conducts hearings during which members of the administration and others may testify for or against the bill.

If the committee votes to proceed, the bill goes to the Rules Committee, which decides whether to place it before the House.

The House Votes

A bill submitted to the House is voted on, with or without a debate. If a majority approves it, the bill is sent to the Senate.

Senate Procedure

The Senate assigns a bill to a Senate committee, which holds hearings and then approves, rejects, rewrites, or shelves the bill.

If the committee votes to proceed, the bill is submitted to the Senate for a vote, which may be taken with or without a debate.

Results

If the Senate does not change the House version of the bill and a majority approves it, the bill goes to the president for signing.

If the bill the Senate approves differs from the House version, the bill is sent to a House-Senate conference for a compromise solution.

If the conference produces a compromise bill and it is approved by both the House and Senate, the bill goes to the president for signing.

When a Bill Becomes Law

The bill becomes law if the president signs it. If the president vetoes the bill, two-thirds of both the House and Senate must approve it again before it can become law. If the bill comes to the president soon before Congress adjourns, the president may not do anything at all. If the bill is not signed before Congress adjourns, the bill dies. This is called the president's "pocket veto."

(A similar procedure is followed for bills introduced in the Senate.)

US Supreme Court

State Courts

Federal Courts

State Supreme Court

US Court of Appeals

State Court of Appeals

US District Court

State General Trial Court
(Jury Court)

Municipal Court
(misdemeanors and
minor civil cases)

**District or Justice
of the Peace Court**

The Sequence of Presidential Succession

If the president dies, resigns, is removed from office, or can't carry out his or her duties, the vice president assumes the president's duties. If the vice president dies or becomes unable to serve, who is next in line? The order of presidential replacements is below.

1. Vice President
2. Speaker of the House
3. President Pro Tempore of the Senate
4. Secretary of State
5. Secretary of the Treasury
6. Secretary of Defense
7. Attorney General
8. Secretary of the Interior
9. Secretary of Agriculture
10. Secretary of Commerce
11. Secretary of Labor
12. Secretary of Health and Human Services
13. Secretary of Housing and Urban Development
14. Secretary of Transportation
15. Secretary of Energy
16. Secretary of Education
17. Secretary of Veterans Affairs
18. Secretary of Homeland Security

Voting

Basic Laws and Requirements

- You must be 18 years of age or older before an election in order to vote in it.
- You must be an American citizen to vote.
- You must register before voting.
- You must show proof of residence in order to register.

How to Register

- Registering often only requires filling out a simple form.
- It does not cost anything to register.
- You need not be a member of any political party to register.
- To find out where to register, you can call your town hall or city board of elections.
- You can find out more about voting and registering at:

eac.gov

Voter Turnout:
Selected Presidential Elections 1960–2012

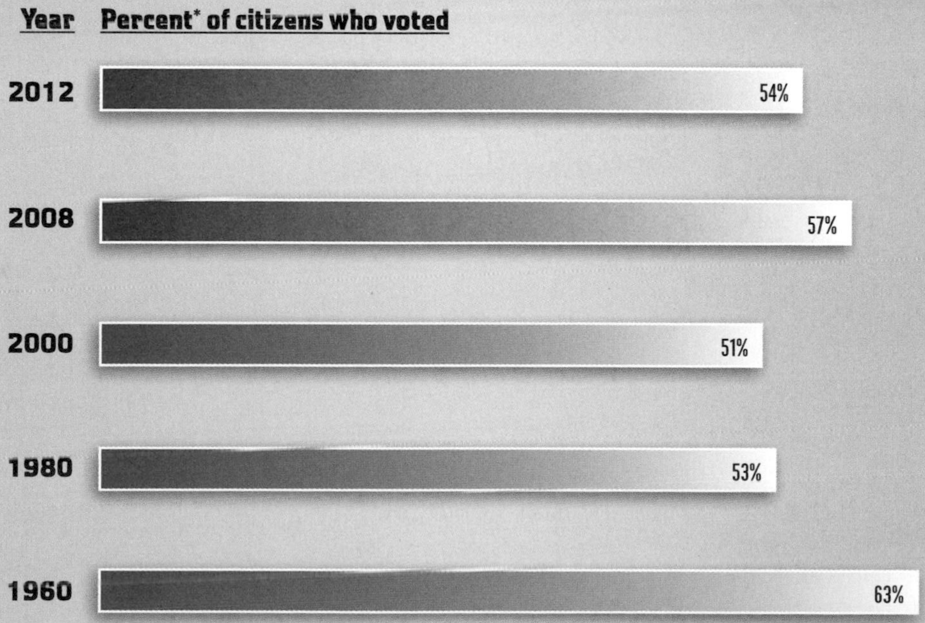

Year	Percent* of citizens who voted
2012	54%
2008	57%
2000	51%
1980	53%
1960	63%

* Rounded

The Electoral College

Although people turn out on Election Day and cast their votes for president, the president and vice president are only indirectly elected by the American people. In fact, the president and vice president are the only elected federal officials not chosen by direct vote of the people. These two officials are elected by the Electoral College, which was created by the framers of the Constitution.

Here is a basic summary of how the Electoral College works:
- There are 538 electoral votes.
- The votes are divided among the 50 states and the District of Columbia. The number of votes that each state has is equal to the number of senators and representatives for that state. (For example, California has 53 representatives and 2 senators; it has a total of 55 electoral votes.)
- During an election, the candidate who wins the majority of popular votes in a given state wins all the electoral votes from that state, except in Maine and Nebraska.
- A presidential candidate needs 270 electoral votes to win.

It is possible for a presidential candidate who has not won the most popular votes to win an election. This can happen if a candidate wins the popular vote in large states (ones with lots of electoral votes) by only a slim margin and loses the popular votes in smaller states by a wide margin. This has happened only four times: 1824, 1876, 1888, and 2000.

Electoral Votes for President

	= Republican
	= Democrat

US Presidents with the Most Electoral Votes

President		Year	Number of electoral votes	
Ronald Reagan		1984		525
Franklin D. Roosevelt		1936		523
Richard Nixon		1972		520
Ronald Reagan		1980		489
Lyndon B. Johnson		1964		486
Franklin D. Roosevelt		1932		472
Dwight D. Eisenhower		1956		457
Franklin D. Roosevelt		1940		449
Herbert Hoover		1928		444
Dwight D. Eisenhower		1952		442

In 2012, 18-year-old Chris Tumbeiro was named as one of California's 55 electors in that year's presidential election. He was the first high school student in US history to become a member of the Electoral College.

Who Is on Our Paper Money?

$1
George Washington

$2
Thomas Jefferson

$5
Abraham Lincoln

$10
Alexander Hamilton

$20
Andrew Jackson

$50
Ulysses S. Grant

$100
Benjamin Franklin

$500*
William McKinley

$1,000*
Grover Cleveland

$5,000*
James Madison

$10,000*
Salmon P. Chase

$100,000*
Woodrow Wilson

*Bills above $100 are no longer made.

Who Is on Our Coins?

Penny:
Abraham
Lincoln

Dime:
Franklin D.
Roosevelt

Half-dollar:
John F. Kennedy

Dollar:
Sacagawea

Nickel:
Thomas Jefferson

Quarter:
George Washington

Dollar:
Susan B. Anthony

1. George Washington
Born: Feb. 22, 1732, Westmoreland County, Virginia
Died: Dec. 14, 1799, Mount Vernon, Virginia
Term of office: April 30, 1789—March 3, 1797
Age at inauguration: 57
Party: Federalist
Vice President: John Adams
First Lady: Martha Dandridge Custis Washington

2. John Adams
Born: Oct. 30, 1735, Braintree (now Quincy), Massachusetts
Died: July 4, 1826, Braintree, Massachusetts
Term of office: March 4, 1797—March 3, 1801
Age at inauguration: 61
Party: Federalist
Vice President: Thomas Jefferson
First Lady: Abigail Smith Adams

3. Thomas Jefferson
Born: April 13, 1743, Shadwell, Virginia
Died: July 4, 1826, Monticello, Virginia
Term of office: March 4, 1801—March 3, 1809
Age at inauguration: 57
Party: Democratic Republican
Vice President: Aaron Burr, George Clinton
First Lady: Martha Skelton Jefferson

4. James Madison
Born: March 16, 1751, Port Conway, Virginia
Died: June 28, 1836, Montpelier, Virginia
Term of office: March 4, 1809—March 3, 1817
Age at inauguration: 57
Party: Democratic Republican
Vice President: George Clinton, Elbridge Gerry
First Lady: Dolley Todd Madison

FUN FACT

George Washington is the only president who was unanimously elected. He received every single vote!

5. James Monroe

Born: April 28, 1758, Westmoreland County, Virginia
Died: July 4, 1831, New York, New York
Term of office: March 4, 1817–March 3, 1825
Age at inauguration: 58
Party: Democratic Republican
Vice President: Daniel D. Tompkins
First Lady: Elizabeth Kortright Monroe

6. John Quincy Adams

Born: July 11, 1767, Braintree, Massachusetts
Died: Feb. 23, 1848, Washington, DC
Term of office: March 4, 1825–March 3, 1829
Age at inauguration: 57
Party: Democratic Republican
Vice President: John C. Calhoun
First Lady: Louisa Johnson Adams

7. Andrew Jackson

Born: March 15, 1767, Waxhaw, North Carolina
Died: June 8, 1845, Nashville, Tennessee
Term of office: March 4, 1829–March 3, 1837
Age at inauguration: 61
Party: Democrat
Vice President: John C. Calhoun, Martin Van Buren
First Lady: Rachel Robards Jackson

8. Martin Van Buren

Born: Dec. 5, 1782, Kinderhook, New York
Died: July 24, 1862, Kinderhook, New York
Term of office: March 4, 1837–March 3, 1841
Age at inauguration: 54
Party: Democrat
Vice President: Richard M. Johnson
First Lady: Hannah Hoes Van Buren

9. William Henry Harrison

Born: Feb. 9, 1773, Berkeley, Virginia
Died: April 4, 1841, Washington, DC*
Term of office: March 4, 1841—April 4, 1841
Age at inauguration: 68
Party: Whig
Vice President: John Tyler
First Lady: Anna Symmes Harrison

10. John Tyler

Born: March 29, 1790, Greenway, Virginia
Died: Jan. 18, 1862, Richmond, Virginia
Term of office: April 6, 1841—March 3, 1845
Age at inauguration: 51
Party: Whig
Vice President: (none)**
First Lady: Letitia Christian Tyler, Julia Gardiner Tyler†

11. James Knox Polk

Born: Nov. 2, 1795, Mecklenburg, North Carolina
Died: June 15, 1849, Nashville, Tennessee
Term of office: March 4, 1845—March 3, 1849
Age at inauguration: 49
Party: Democrat
Vice President: George M. Dallas
First Lady: Sarah Childress Polk

12. Zachary Taylor

Born: Nov. 24, 1784, Orange County, Virginia
Died: July 9, 1850, Washington, DC*
Term of office: March 5, 1849—July 9, 1850
Age at inauguration: 64
Party: Whig
Vice President: Millard Fillmore
First Lady: Margaret (Peggy) Smith Taylor

FUN FACT

William Henry Harrison had the longest inauguration speech and the shortest term of any president. After giving a speech lasting 105 minutes in the cold rain, he developed pneumonia and died 32 days later.

* Died in office, natural causes
** Vice President Tyler took over the duties of the president when William Henry Harrison died in office, leaving the vice presidency vacant.
† President Tyler's first wife died in 1842. He remarried in 1844.

13. Millard Fillmore

Born: Jan. 7, 1800, Cayuga County, New York
Died: March 8, 1874, Buffalo, New York
Term of office: July 10, 1850—March 3, 1853
Age at inauguration: 50
Party: Whig
Vice President: (none)*
First Lady: Abigail Powers Fillmore

14. Franklin Pierce

Born: Nov. 23, 1804, Hillsboro, New Hampshire
Died: Oct. 8, 1869, Concord, New Hampshire
Term of office: March 4, 1853—March 3, 1857
Age at inauguration: 48
Party: Democrat
Vice President: William R. King
First Lady: Jane Appleton Pierce

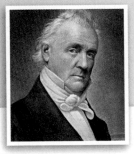

15. James Buchanan

Born: April 23, 1791, Mercersburg, Pennsylvania
Died: June 1, 1868, Lancaster, Pennsylvania
Term of office: March 4, 1857—March 3, 1861
Age at inauguration: 65
Party: Democrat
Vice President: John C. Breckenridge
First Lady: (none)**

16. Abraham Lincoln

Born: Feb. 12, 1809, Hardin, Kentucky
Died: April 15, 1865, Washington, DC†
Term of office: March 4, 1861—April 15, 1865
Age at inauguration: 52
Party: Republican
Vice President: Hannibal Hamlin,
Andrew Johnson
First Lady: Mary Todd Lincoln

* When Zachary Taylor died, Millard Fillmore became the second vice president to inherit the presidency, leaving the vice presidency vacant.
** Buchanan was the only president who never married. A favorite niece, Harriet Lane, acted as White House hostess during his administration.
† Assassinated

17. Andrew Johnson

Born: Dec. 29, 1808, Raleigh, North Carolina
Died: July 31, 1875, Carter Station, Tennessee
Term of office: April 15, 1865—March 3, 1869
Age at inauguration: 56
Party: Democrat (nominated by Republican Party)
Vice President: (none)*
First Lady: Eliza McCardle Johnson

18. Ulysses S. Grant

Born: April 27, 1822, Point Pleasant, Ohio
Died: July 23, 1885, Mt. McGregor, New York
Term of office: March 4, 1869—March 3, 1877
Age at inauguration: 46
Party: Republican
Vice President: Schuyler Colfax, Henry Wilson
First Lady: Julia Dent Grant

19. Rutherford Birchard Hayes

Born: Oct. 4, 1822, Delaware, Ohio
Died: Jan. 17, 1893, Fremont, Ohio
Term of office: March 4, 1877—March 3, 1881
Age at inauguration: 54
Party: Republican
Vice President: William A. Wheeler
First Lady: Lucy Webb Hayes

20. James Abram Garfield

Born: Nov. 19, 1831, Orange, Ohio
Died: Sept. 19, 1881, Elberon, New Jersey**
Term of office: March 4, 1881—Sept. 19, 1881
Age at inauguration: 49
Party: Republican
Vice President: Chester A. Arthur
First Lady: Lucretia Rudolph Garfield

FUN FACT

On March 1, 1872, Ulysses S. Grant established Yellowstone as the country's first national park.

* Andrew Johnson became president when Abraham Lincoln was assassinated, leaving the vice presidency vacant.
** Assassinated

21. Chester Alan Arthur

Born: Oct. 5, 1829, Fairfield, Vermont
Died: Nov. 18, 1886, New York City, New York
Term of office: Sept. 20, 1881—March 3, 1885
Age at inauguration: 51
Party: Republican
Vice President: (none)*
First Lady: Ellen Herndon Arthur

22. Grover Cleveland

Born: March 18, 1837, Caldwell, New Jersey
Died: June 24, 1908, Princeton, New Jersey
Term of office: March 4, 1885—March 3, 1889
Age at inauguration: 47
Party: Democrat
Vice President: Thomas A. Hendricks
First Lady: Frances Folsom Cleveland

23. Benjamin Harrison

Born: Aug. 20, 1833, North Bend, Ohio
Died: March 13, 1901, Indianapolis, Indiana
Term of office: March 4, 1889—March 3, 1893
Age at inauguration: 55
Party: Republican
Vice President: Levi P. Morton
First Lady: Caroline Scott Harrison

24. Grover Cleveland

Born: March 18, 1837, Caldwell, New Jersey
Died: June 24, 1908, Princeton, New Jersey
Term of office: March 4, 1893—March 3, 1897
Age at inauguration: 55
Party: Democrat
Vice President: Adlai E. Stevenson
First Lady: Frances Folsom Cleveland

Grover Cleveland is the only president elected
to two nonconsecutive terms.

*Chester Alan Arthur became president when James Garfield was assassinated, leaving the vice presidency vacant.

25. William McKinley
Born: Jan. 29, 1843, Niles, Ohio
Died: Sept. 14, 1901, Buffalo, New York*
Term of office: March 4, 1897—Sept. 14, 1901
Age at inauguration: 54
Party: Republican
Vice President: Garret A. Hobart,
Theodore Roosevelt
First Lady: Ida Saxton McKinley

26. Theodore Roosevelt
Born: Oct. 27, 1858, New York, New York
Died: Jan. 6, 1919, Oyster Bay, New York
Term of office: Sept. 14, 1901—March 3, 1909
Age at inauguration: 42
Party: Republican
Vice President: Charles W. Fairbanks
First Lady: Edith Carow Roosevelt

27. William Howard Taft
Born: Sept. 15, 1857, Cincinnati, Ohio
Died: March 8, 1930, Washington, DC
Term of office: March 4, 1909—March 3, 1913
Age at inauguration: 51
Party: Republican
Vice President: James S. Sherman
First Lady: Helen Herron Taft

28. Woodrow Wilson
Born: Dec. 28, 1856, Staunton, Virginia
Died: Feb. 3, 1924, Washington, DC
Term of office: March 4, 1913—March 3, 1921
Age at inauguration: 56
Party: Democrat
Vice President: Thomas R. Marshall
First Lady: Ellen Axson Wilson, Edith
Galt Wilson**

*Assassinated
**Wilson's first wife died early in his administration and he remarried before leaving the White House.

29. Warren Gamaliel Harding

Born: Nov. 2, 1865, Corsica (now Blooming Grove), Ohio
Died: Aug. 2, 1923, San Francisco, California*
Term of office: March 4, 1921—Aug. 2, 1923
Age at inauguration: 55
Party: Republican
Vice President: Calvin Coolidge
First Lady: Florence Kling DeWolfe Harding

30. Calvin Coolidge

Born: July 4, 1872, Plymouth Notch, Vermont
Died: Jan. 5, 1933, Northampton, Massachusetts
Term of office: Aug. 3, 1923—March 3, 1929
Age at inauguration: 51
Party: Republican
Vice President: Charles G. Dawes
First Lady: Grace Goodhue Coolidge

31. Herbert Clark Hoover

Born: Aug. 10, 1874, West Branch, Iowa
Died: Oct. 20, 1964, New York, New York
Term of office: March 4, 1929—March 3, 1933
Age at inauguration: 54
Party: Republican
Vice President: Charles Curtis
First Lady: Lou Henry Hoover

32. Franklin Delano Roosevelt

Born: Jan. 30, 1882, Hyde Park, New York
Died: April 12, 1945, Warm Springs, Georgia*
Term of office: March 4, 1933—April 12, 1945
Age at inauguration: 51
Party: Democrat
Vice President: John N. Garner, Henry A. Wallace, Harry S. Truman
First Lady: Anna Eleanor Roosevelt

Two presidents, John Adams and Thomas Jefferson, died on the same day—July 4, 1826. Another president, James Monroe, died on July 4, 1831. A fourth, Calvin Coolidge, was born on July 4, 1872.

*Died in office, natural causes

33. Harry S. Truman

Born: May 8, 1884, Lamar, Missouri
Died: Dec. 26, 1972, Kansas City, Missouri
Term of office: April 12, 1945–Jan. 20, 1953
Age at inauguration: 60
Party: Democrat
Vice President: Alben W. Barkley
First Lady: Elizabeth (Bess) Wallace Truman

34. Dwight David Eisenhower

Born: Oct. 14, 1890, Denison, Texas
Died: March 28, 1969, Washington, DC
Term of office: Jan. 20, 1953–Jan. 20, 1961
Age at inauguration: 62
Party: Republican
Vice President: Richard M. Nixon
First Lady: Mamie Doud Eisenhower

35. John Fitzgerald Kennedy

Born: May 29, 1917, Brookline, Massachusetts
Died: Nov. 22, 1963, Dallas, Texas*
Term of office: Jan. 20, 1961–Nov. 22, 1963
Age at inauguration: 43
Party: Democrat
Vice President: Lyndon B. Johnson
First Lady: Jacqueline Bouvier Kennedy

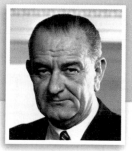

36. Lyndon Baines Johnson

Born: Aug. 27, 1908, Stonewall, Texas
Died: Jan. 22, 1973, San Antonio, Texas
Term of office: Nov. 22, 1963–Jan. 20, 1969
Age at inauguration: 55
Party: Democrat
Vice President: Hubert H. Humphrey
First Lady: Claudia (Lady Bird) Taylor Johnson

*Assassinated

37. Richard Milhous Nixon

Born: Jan. 9, 1913, Yorba Linda, California
Died: April 22, 1994, New York, New York
Term of office: Jan. 20, 1969–Aug. 9, 1974*
Age at inauguration: 56
Party: Republican
Vice President: Spiro T. Agnew (resigned), Gerald R. Ford
First Lady: Thelma (Pat) Ryan Nixon

38. Gerald Rudolph Ford

Born: July 14, 1913, Omaha, Nebraska
Died: Dec. 26, 2006, Rancho Mirage, California
Term of office: Aug. 9, 1974–Jan. 20, 1977
Age at inauguration: 61
Party: Republican
Vice President: Nelson A. Rockefeller
First Lady: Elizabeth (Betty) Bloomer Warren Ford

39. James Earl (Jimmy) Carter

Born: Oct. 1, 1924, Plains, Georgia
Term of office: Jan. 20, 1977–Jan. 20, 1981
Age at inauguration: 52
Party: Democrat
Vice President: Walter F. Mondale
First Lady: Rosalynn Smith Carter

40. Ronald Wilson Reagan

Born: Feb. 6, 1911, Tampico, Illinois
Died: June 5, 2004, Los Angeles, California
Term of office: Jan. 20, 1981–Jan. 20, 1989
Age at inauguration: 69
Party: Republican
Vice President: George H. W. Bush
First Lady: Nancy Davis Reagan

41. George Herbert Walker Bush

Born: June 12, 1924, Milton, Massachusetts
Term of office: Jan. 20, 1989–Jan. 20, 1993
Age at inauguration: 64
Party: Republican
Vice President: James Danforth (Dan) Quayle
First Lady: Barbara Pierce Bush

FUN FACT

There have been two father-son presidential combinations: John Adams and John Quincy Adams, and George H. W. Bush and George W. Bush. In addition, President William Henry Harrison was the grandfather of President Benjamin Harrison.

42. William Jefferson (Bill) Clinton

Born: Aug. 19, 1946, Hope, Arkansas
Term of office: Jan. 20, 1993—Jan. 20, 2001
Age at inauguration: 46
Party: Democrat
Vice President: Albert (Al) Gore Jr.
First Lady: Hillary Rodham Clinton

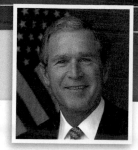

43. George Walker Bush

Born: July 6, 1946, New Haven, Connecticut
Term of office: Jan. 20, 2001—Jan. 20, 2009
Age at inauguration: 54
Party: Republican
Vice President: Richard B. (Dick) Cheney
First Lady: Laura Welch Bush

44. Barack Hussein Obama Jr.

Born: Aug. 4, 1961, Honolulu, Hawaii
Term of office: Jan. 20, 2009—
Age at inauguration: 47
Party: Democrat
Vice President: Joseph R. (Joe) Biden Jr.
First Lady: Michelle Robinson Obama

President Barack Obama was born in Honolulu, Hawaii, to a white mother who had grown up in Kansas and a black father from Kenya, Africa. As a young child, Obama was one of only a few black students at his school. He became an outstanding student at college and at Harvard Law School. After law school, he worked to help poor families in Chicago, Illinois, get better health care and more educational programs. In 1996, he became an Illinois state senator, and in 2004, he was elected to the US Senate. In 2008, Obama won the Democratic nomination for president and became the first African American to be elected to the highest office in the country. In 2012, President Obama defeated Republican candidate Mitt Romney to win reelection.

GEOGRAPHY

244

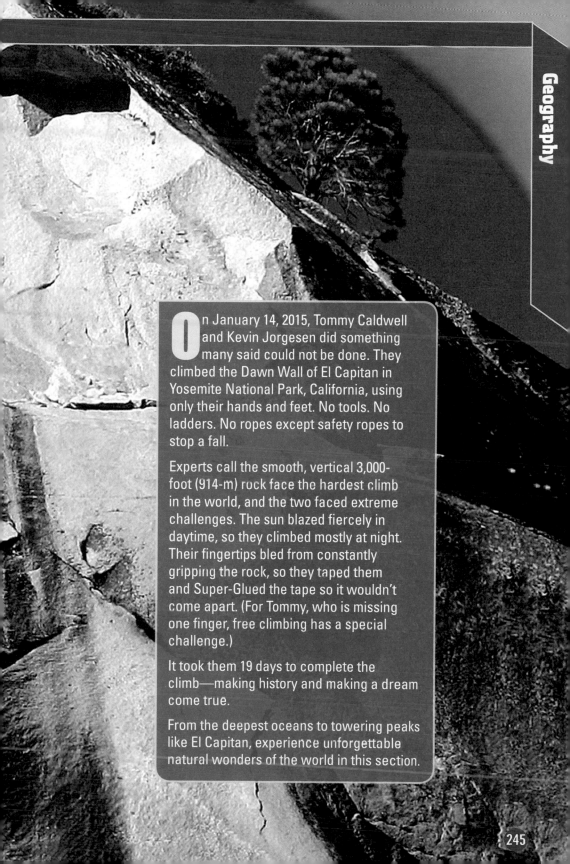

On January 14, 2015, Tommy Caldwell and Kevin Jorgesen did something many said could not be done. They climbed the Dawn Wall of El Capitan in Yosemite National Park, California, using only their hands and feet. No tools. No ladders. No ropes except safety ropes to stop a fall.

Experts call the smooth, vertical 3,000-foot (914-m) rock face the hardest climb in the world, and the two faced extreme challenges. The sun blazed fiercely in daytime, so they climbed mostly at night. Their fingertips bled from constantly gripping the rock, so they taped them and Super-Glued the tape so it wouldn't come apart. (For Tommy, who is missing one finger, free climbing has a special challenge.)

It took them 19 days to complete the climb—making history and making a dream come true.

From the deepest oceans to towering peaks like El Capitan, experience unforgettable natural wonders of the world in this section.

World/US Geography

How to Read a Map

Directions

When you're reading a map, how do you figure out which way is which? On most—but not all—maps:

 Up means north

 Down means south

 Left means west

 Right means east

Some maps are turned or angled so that north is not straight up. Always look for a symbol called a compass rose to show you exactly where north is on the map you're reading.

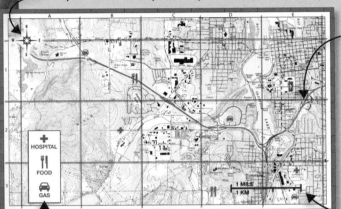

Location

Maps that show large areas, such as countries and continents, include lines of longitude and latitude. Maps of cities and streets are divided into blocks called grids. Grid maps have numbers along one border and letters along a perpendicular border. They also have an index that gives a number-letter combination for every location on the map.

Shapes and Symbols

Every picture, object, shape, and line on a map stands for something. A tiny red airplane stands for an airport. A thick line is one kind of road and a dotted line is another. A map's legend, or key, shows these symbols and explains what they stand for.

Distance

You can look at a map and think it's a hop, skip, and a jump from Maine to Maryland, but it's really a few million hops. The map scale shows you how many miles (or km) a certain length of map represents.

A Map is a Map is a Map . . .

All maps are not created equal. There are different maps for different purposes:
- A bathymetric map shows the depths and contours of the bottom of a body of water.
- A geological map shows earthquake faults, volcanoes, minerals, rock types, underground water, and landslide areas.
- A physical map shows mountains, lakes, and rivers.
- A planimetric map shows only horizontal features, such as roads and rivers.
- A political map shows boundaries of cities, states, countries, and provinces.
- A relief map uses different colors to show different elevations.
- A road map shows roads, highways, cities, and towns.
- A topographic map shows the contours and elevations of a land area in detail.
- A weather map shows temperatures, fronts, rain, snow, sleet, storms, fog, and other weather conditions.

Geographical Terms

Term	Definition
Altitude	the distance above sea level
Archipelago	a group or chain of islands clustered together in an ocean or sea
Atlas	a book of maps
Atoll	an ocean island made out of an underwater ring of coral
Bay	a body of water protected and partly surrounded by land
Cartographer	a mapmaker
Compass rose	a four-pointed design on a map that shows north, south, east, and west
Continent	one of Earth's seven largest landmasses
Degree	a unit of measurement used to calculate longitude and latitude
Delta	a flat, triangular piece of land that fans out at the mouth of a river
Elevation	the height of a point on Earth's surface above sea level
Equator	an imaginary circle around Earth halfway between the North Pole and the South Pole
Globe	a 3-D spherical map of Earth
GPS	short for Global Positioning System; finds longitude and latitude by bouncing information off satellites in space
Grid	a crisscross pattern of lines forming squares on a map
Hemisphere	one-half of the world
Island	land that is surrounded by water on all sides
Isthmus	a narrow strip of land (with water on both sides) that connects two larger land areas
Latitude	distance north or south of the equator
Legend	a key to the symbols on a map
Longitude	distance east or west of the prime meridian
Map	a flat picture of a place, drawn to scale
Meridian	an imaginary line running north and south and looping around the poles, used to measure longitude
North Pole	the most northerly point on Earth
Ocean	the body of salt water surrounding the great landmasses and divided by the landmasses into several distinct portions
Parallel	an imaginary line parallel to the equator, used to measure latitude
Peninsula	a body of land surrounded by water on three sides
Scale	a tool on a map that helps calculate real distance
Sea level	the surface of the ocean
South Pole	the most southerly point on Earth
Strait	a narrow body of water that connects two larger bodies of water
Topography	the physical features of a place, such as mountains

247

Continental Drift

Maps are all well and good if things don't change. "Go east one mile and turn south and find Mount Crumpet" works only if Mount Crumpet doesn't decide to walk a few miles north. Sound ridiculous? Actually, Earth didn't always look like it does today. About 250 million years ago, all the continents were scrunched together in one lump called Pangaea.

Gradually the land drifted and changed into the seven continents we know today in a process called continental drift. And the land is still moving. North America and Europe are moving away from each other at the rate of about one inch (2.5 cm) a year.

Pangaea

Journey to the Center of the Earth

Earth isn't just one big blue ball with the same stuff all the way through. It's made up of layers.

The part we walk around on is the crust, or lithosphere. It's only about 60 miles (100 km) deep.

Beneath the lithosphere is the mantle. It's a layer about 1,800 miles (2,897 km) deep.

Beneath that is the core, which is made of two parts:

The outer core (1,375 miles, or 2,200 km, thick) is almost as big as the moon, slightly bigger around than the planet Mars and made up of soupy molten iron.

The inner core is about 781 miles (1,250 km) thick and about as hot as the surface of the sun.

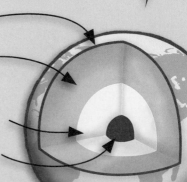

Earth's Layers

The Continents Today

North America

Europe

Asia

Africa

South America

Australia

Antarctica

30% LAND

70% WATER

Our Watery Earth

The total surface area of our planet is 196,937,583 square miles (510,066,000 sq km). However, about 70 percent of that is water. Turn the page to read about each of the seven continents in detail. Turn to pages 170—171 to read about the world's major oceans.

ASIA

Scale 1:48,000,000

Azimuthal Equal-Area Projection

0   800 Kilometers

0   800 Miles

Boundary representation is
not necessarily authoritative.

250

Map labels:

North Sea · NORWAY · Oslo · SWEDEN · Murmansk · Barents Sea · NOVAYA ZEMLYA · Kara Sea · SEVERNAYA ZEMLYA · NEW SIBERIAN ISLANDS · Laptev Sea · East Siberian Sea · Cherskiy · UKRAINE · Kharkiv · Voronezh · Kazan · Perm · Yekaterinburg · Omsk · Irtysh · Krasnoyarsk · SIBERIA · RUSSIA · Yakutsk · Tiksi · Donets'k · Saratov · Samara · Ufa · Chelyabinsk · Novosibirsk · Irkutsk · Chita · Rostov · Volgograd · URAL MOUNTAINS · Atryaū (Atyrau) · Astana · Qaraghandy (Karaganda) · Ulaanbaatar · GEO. · Tbilisi · ARM. · Yerevan · AZERBAIJAN · Baku · Caspian Sea · Aral Sea · KAZAKHSTAN · Lake Balkhash · MONGOLIA · GOBI DESERT · Shenyang · Tabrīz · Tehran · TURKMENISTAN · UZBEKISTAN · Ashgabat · Tashkent · Almaty · Bishkek · KYRGYZSTAN · Ürümqi · Beijing · Baotou · Tianjin · Dalian · Mashhad · Dushanbe · Kashi · TAKLA MAKAN DESERT · TIEN SHAN · Taiyuan · Qingdao · Jinan · IRAN · Esfahān · AFGHANISTAN · TAJIKISTAN · Lanzhou · Zhengzhou · Nanjing · Shanghai · Shīrāz · Kabul · CHINA · Xi'an · Wuhan · Hangzhou · Bandar 'Abbās · Kandahār · Islamabad · Faisalābād · Lahore · QING ZANG GAOYUAN · Chengde · Chongqing · Changsha · Nanchang · Doha · QATAR · Abu Dhabi · Quetta · PAKISTAN · Ludhiāna · Mt. Everest (highest point in the world) 8850 m · Guiyang · Muscat · U.A.E. · New Delhi · Lhasa · Kunming · Guangzhou · SAUDI ARABIA · OMAN · Karāchi · Jaipur · NEPAL · Kathmandu · BHUTAN · Thimphu · Nanning · Hong Kong S.A.R. · Macau S.A.R. · Ahmadābād · Lucknow · Kānpur · Patna · Thimphu · Dhaka · BANGLADESH · Mandalay · Hanoi · Haiphong · Hainan Dao · Indore · Mumbai · Pune · DECCAN · Hyderābād · INDIA · Nāgpur · Kolkata · Chittagong · BURMA · Nay Pyi Taw · LAOS · Vientiane · Da Nang · South China Sea · Surat · WESTERN GHATS · EASTERN GHATS · Vishākhapatnam · Rangoon · THAILAND · VIETNAM · Bengaluru · Chennai · Bay of Bengal · Bangkok · CAMBODIA · SPRATLY ISLANDS · Cochin · Jaffna · ANDAMAN ISLANDS (INDIA) · Andaman Sea · Phnom Penh · Ho Chi Minh City · SRI LANKA · Colombo · NICOBAR ISLANDS (INDIA) · Gulf of Thailand · Bandar Seri Begawan · BRUNEI · Male · Medan · MALAYSIA · Kuala Lumpur · MALAYSIA · Borneo · SINGAPORE · Singapore · Pontianak · Sumatra · INDON · Palembang · Jakarta · Semarang · Surabaya · Java · Bandung · Christmas Island (AUSTL.) · Arabian Sea · Persian Gulf · ZAGROS MTS. · CAUCASUS · QIZIL QUM · KARAKUM · Kyiv · Laccadive Sea

ASIA can be described best in one word: BIG. It's the biggest continent in size, covering about 30 percent of Earth's land area. It's also the biggest in population, with about 60 percent of all the people in the world living there. And in terms of contributions to the world, it's enormous. Asians founded the first cities; set up the first legal system; invented writing paper, printing, the magnetic compass, and gunpowder; and much more. All of the world's major religions began in Asia.

Asia rules in world-class geographical features, too. It has:

- The highest mountain range, the Himalayas, as well as the most mountains of any continent
- The highest point on Earth, Mount Everest, and the lowest, the Dead Sea

Asia at a Glance

Area
17,226,200 sq. mi. (44,614,000 sq km)

Population
4,388,026,000

Number of countries
50

Largest country
China
3,705,407 sq. mi. (9,596,960 sq km)

Most populated urban area
Tokyo, Japan

Longest river
Yangtze Kiang, China
3,915 mi. (6,300 km)

Largest lake
Lake Baikal, Russia
12,200 sq. mi. (31,500 sq km)

Highest point
Mt. Everest, Nepal/China
29,035 ft. (8,850 m) above sea level

Lowest point
Dead Sea, Israel/Jordan
1,380 ft. (421 m) below sea level

Asia has some of the world's largest international business centers, such as Tokyo, Singapore, and Hong Kong. At the same time, about half of all Asians are farmers.

North
Atlantic
Ocean

AZORES
(PORTUGAL)

LONDON
Brussels
BEL.
Prague
CZ. REP.
GERMANY
POLAND
LUX.
Paris
SWITZ.
FRANCE
Vienna
AUS.
Budapest
HUNG.
SLO.
CRO.
BOS. &
HER.
ITALY
Rome
Corsica
MONT.
SER.
MACE.
ALB.
Sardinia
Belgrade
Sofia
BULG.
GREECE
Athens
ROM.
MOL.
Bucharest
Black Sea
UKRAINE
Kyiv
GEO.
ARM.
AZER.
Caspian
Sea
KAZAKH

PORTUGAL
Lisbon
Madrid
SPAIN
AND.

MADEIRA ISLANDS
(PORTUGAL)
Rabat
Casablanca
Fès
Marrakech
MOROCCO
Oran
Constantine
Algiers
Tunis
TUNISIA
MALTA
Tripoli
Banghāzi
Alexandria
ISRAEL
Jerusalem
Cairo
Al Jīzah
CYPRUS
LEB.
Beirut
Damascus
SYRIA
Amman
JORDAN
IRAQ
Baghdad
KUW.
Riyadh
SA
AR

Mediterranean Sea

CANARY ISLANDS
(SPAIN)
Western
Sahara
Laayoune
(El Aaiún)
Nouadhibou

ALGERIA
LIBYA
EGYPT
Aswān
Al Jawf
Admin.
Boundary
Port
Sudan
Red
Sea

S A H A R A

CAPE VERDE
Praia
Dakar
Nouakchott
MAURITANIA
SENEGAL
Banjul
THE GAMBIA
Bissau
GUINEA-BISSAU
Conakry
Freetown
SIERRA LEONE
Monrovia
LIBERIA
GUINEA
Bamako
Tombouctou
Agadez
NIGER
Niamey
BURKINA
FASO
Ouagadougou
Zinder
Kano
CHAD
N'Djamena
Omdurman
Khartoum
SUDAN
ERITREA
Asmara
Sanaa
Lac 'Assal
(lowest point in
Africa, -155 m)
Djibouti
DJIBOUTI
Hargeysa
MALI

CÔTE
D'IVOIRE
GHANA
TOGO
BENIN
NIGERIA
Abuja
Ogbomoso
Ibadan
Lagos
Accra
Lomé
Porto-
Novo
Yamoussoukro
Abidjan
Moundou
CENTRAL AFRICAN
REPUBLIC
Bangui
SOUTH
SUDAN
Juba
Addis
Ababa
ETHIOPIA
Prov.
Admin.
Line
SOM

CAMEROON
Douala
Malabo
EQUATORIAL GUINEA
Yaoundé
Libreville
GABON
São Tomé
SAO TOME
AND PRINCIPE
Annobón
(EQUA. GUI.)
Equator
Gulf of Guinea
CONGO
BASIN
Congo
REP.
OF THE
CONGO
Kisangani
DEM. REP.
OF THE CONGO
UGANDA
Kampala
RWANDA
Kigali
Bukavu
BURUNDI
Bujumbura
KENYA
Nairobi
Mombasa
Mogadis
India
Ocea

Ascension
(St. Helena)
Brazzaville
Kinshasa
Pointe-Noire
ANGOLA
(Cabinda)
Luanda
Mbuji-Mayi
Lubumbashi
Dodoma
Zanzibar
TANZANIA
Dar es
Salaam
Mt. Kilimanjaro
(highest point in
Africa, 5895 m)

ANGOLA
Namibe
Lubango
Kitwe
Kitwe
ZAMBIA
Lusaka
MALAWI
Lilongwe
Blantyre
Cidade
de Nacala
COMOROS
Moroni
Glorio
(FR
Mayotte
(admin. by France,
claimed by Comoros)
Juan de Nova
Island
(FRANCE)
Mahajang

Walvis Bay
Windhoek
NAMIBIA
KALAHARI
DESERT
BOTSWANA
Gaborone
Harare
ZIMBABWE
Beira
MOZAMBIQUE
Mozambique
Channel
Bassas
da India
(FRANCE)
Europa
Island
(FRANCE)
MADAGASC
Toamasina
Antar

Cape Town
Port Elizabeth
SOUTH
AFRICA
Johannesburg
Pretoria
Mbabane
SWAZILAND
Maseru
LESOTHO
Durban
Maputo

Indian Ocean

SOUTHWEST INDIAN

Scale 1:51,
Azimuthal Equal-
0   80
0

Boundary rep
not necessaril

AFRICA is second to Asia in area and population, but it tops all continents in other categories:

- Biggest desert: The Sahara, covering about 3.5 million square miles (9 million sq km), or about one-third of the continent
- Longest freshwater lake: Lake Tanganyika, 420 miles (680 km)
- Most independent countries: 54

Africa is a land of treasures, from the lions, giraffes, rhinos, and other spectacular wildlife that inhabit its rain forests and grasslands to its rich supplies of gold and diamonds. However, most Africans remain poor because of drought, famine, disease, and other ongoing serious problems.

Africa at a Glance

Area
11,684,000 sq. mi. (30,262,000 sq km)

Population
1,177,263,000

Largest country
Algeria
919,595 sq. mi. (2,381,740 sq km)

Most populated urban area
Cairo, Egypt

Longest river
Nile
4,132 mi. (6,650 km)

Largest lake
Lake Victoria, Tanzania/Uganda/Kenya
26,828 sq. mi. (69,484 sq km)

Highest point
Mount Kilimanjaro, Tanzania
19,340 ft. (5,895 m) above sea level

Lowest point
Lake Assal, Djibouti
509 ft. (155 m) below sea level

From fossils found in Africa, scientists say that the earliest human beings lived there about 2 million years ago.

NORTH AMERICA

NORTH AMERICA, the third-largest continent in area and the fourth-largest in population, is all about variety. The continent has an enormous mix of climates and habitats, from the frozen Arctic to warm, humid Central American rain forests, which support an amazing number of plants and animals. North American human inhabitants live in a variety of environments, too, from rural farms to such bustling, densely populated urban centers as Mexico City. Many—but not all—North Americans enjoy a high standard of living compared to inhabitants of the rest of the world.

Of all the continents, North America has:
- The world's largest island: Greenland,* 836,330 square miles (2,166,086, sq km)
- The world's largest freshwater lake: Lake Superior
- The longest coastline: 190,000 miles (300,000 km), or more than 60,000 times the distance across the Atlantic Ocean

*Except for Australia, which is classified as a continent as well as an island

North America at a Glance

Area
9,352,000 sq. mi. (24,220,000 sq km)

Population
569,096,000

Number of countries
23

Largest country
Canada
3,855,101 sq. mi. (9,984,670 sq km)

Most populated urban area
Mexico City, Mexico

Longest river
Mississippi-Missouri, United States
3,710 mi. (5,971 km) long

Largest lake
Lake Superior, United States/Canada
31,700 sq. mi. (82,100 sq km)

Highest point
Mt. McKinley, Alaska
20,320 ft. (6,194 m) above sea level

Lowest point
Death Valley, California
282 ft. (86 m) below sea level

Nearly half of all Canadians and about a third of Americans come from English, Irish, Scottish, or Welsh ancestors. However, North America's first settlers were from Asia. Scientists say that these Native Americans, now sometimes called Indians, walked across the Bering Strait, which was dry land between 15,000 and 35,000 years ago. Before they came, there were no people on the continent.

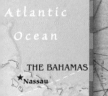

SOUTH AMERICA

Tegucigalpa
Providencia (COLOMBIA)
Aruba (NETH.)
(NETH.)
THE GRENADINES
GRENADA

NICARAGUA
Managua
Isla de San Andrés (COLOMBIA)
Barranquilla
Maracaibo
Caracas
Port-of-Spain
TRINIDAD AND TOBAGO

San José
Panama
Cartagena
Barquisimeto
Valencia
Barcelona

COSTA RICA
PANAMA
Cúcuta
San Cristobal
Ciudad Guayana
Georgetown
Paramaribo

Medellín
Bucaramanga
VENEZUELA
GUYANA
SURINAME
Cayenne

Pereira
Ibagué
Bogotá
GUIANA HIGHLANDS
French Guiana (FRANCE)

Isla de Malpelo (COLOMBIA)
COLOMBIA
Cali
Boa Vista

Macapá
Equator

Quito
ECUADOR
Guayaquil
A M A Z O N
Río Negro
Amazon
Belém
São L

Cuenca
Iquitos
Manaus
Santarém

Piura
B A S I N
Teresina

Chiclayo
Pucallpa
Río Madeira
Río Tocantins

Trujillo
Huánuco
Río Branco
Pôrto Velho
B R A Z I L
BRAZILIA

PERU
Huancayo
MATO GROSSO PLATEAU
Cuiabá
Brasília

Lima
Cusco
Ica
ANDES
Trinidad
Goiânia
H I G H L A N D

South Pacific
Arequipa
PERU-CHILE TRENCH
Lago Titicaca
La Paz
BOLIVIA
Uberlândia
Conta
Belo Horizonte

Cochabamba
Sucre
Santa Cruz
Campo Grande
Vitór

Arica
ALTIPLANO
Potosí
Londrina
Campinas
Campos

Iquique
ATACAMA DESERT
PARAGUAY
São Paulo
Santos
Rio de

Antofagasta
Asunción
Ciudad del Este
Curitiba
Joinvile

Salta
San Miguel de Tucumán
Resistencia
Florianópolis

CHILE
Cerro Aconcagua (highest point in South America; 6962 m)
Córdoba
Santa Fe
Porto Alegre

Rosario
Salto
URUGUAY

Valparaíso
Mendoza
PAMPAS
Buenos Aires
La Plata
Montevideo
South Atlan Ocea

Santiago
ARGENTINA

Concepcion
Bahía Blanca

Temuco
San Carlos de Bariloche

Puerto Montt
PATAGONIA
ANDES

Laguna del C (lowest point in Sout the Western Hemis

Comodoro Rivadavia

Río Gallegos
Punta Arenas
Strait of Magellan
Ushuaia
Cape Horn

North Atlant Ocea

Equator

SOUTH AMERICA is dotted with some of the world's most spectacular physical features:

- The longest mountain range, the Andes, stretching 4,500 miles (7,200 km) from Chile in the south, to Venezuela and Panama in the north
- The largest rain forest, the Amazon, covering about 2 million square miles (5.2 million sq km), or two-fifths of the continent
- The highest waterfall, Angel Falls in Venezuela, plunging 3,212 feet (979 m)

South America is the fourth-largest continent, but only Australia and Antarctica have fewer people. About 80 percent of the people live in urban areas such as São Paulo, Brazil. South America's economy is growing fast, led by Brazil, Argentina, Colombia, and Chile.

Fortaleza
Natal
João
Pessoa
Recife
Maceió
Aracajú
Salvador

RIO
GRANDE
RISE

South America at a Glance

Area
6,887,000 sq. mi. (17,836,000 sq km)

Population
413,535,000

Number of countries
12

Largest country
Brazil
3,287,613 sq. mi. (8,514,877 sq km)

Most populated urban area
São Paulo, Brazil

Longest river
Amazon, Brazil
4,000 mi. (6,437 km)

Largest lake
Lake Maracaibo, Venezuela
5,217 sq. mi. (13,512 sq km)

Highest point
Aconcagua, Argentina
22,835 ft. (6,960 m) above sea level

Lowest point
Laguna del Carbón, Argentina
344 ft. (105 m) below sea level

The Amazon rain forest is home to an estimated ten percent of all plant and animal species on Earth.

EUROPE

EUROPE is a small continent divided into many individual countries, with at least 50 different languages and up to 100 different dialects spoken. With the third-largest population and the second-smallest area of any continent, Europe is densely populated. In fact, it is home to the most densely populated country in the world, tiny Monaco. Still, there's plenty of natural beauty in its rivers, lakes, canals, and towering mountain ranges, such as the Urals and the Alps. European contributions in art, music, philosophy, and culture formed the basis for Western civilization.

Europe at a Glance

Area
4,033,000 sq. mi. (10,445,000 sq km)

Population
743,852,000

Number of countries
49

Largest country (entirely in Europe)
Ukraine
233,090 sq. mi. (603,628 sq km)

Most populated urban area
Moscow, Russia

Longest river
Volga, Russia
2,194 mi. (3,531 km) long

Largest lake
Lake Ladoga, Russia
6,835 sq. mi. (17,702 sq km)

Highest point
Mt. Elbrus, Russia
18,510 ft. (5,642 m) above sea level

Lowest point
Shore of the Caspian Sea
92 ft. (28 m) below sea level

Europe has some of the world's longest railroad tunnels, including the Channel Tunnel, or Chunnel, which runs 31.1 miles (50 km) under the English Channel and connects the United Kingdom and France.

Arkhangel'sk

Lake Onega

Petersburg

RUSSIA

Moscow★

Smolensk

ilyow
nsk

RUS
Homyel
Chernihiv

Kyiv

tomyr
UKRAINE
Vinnytsya

Mykolayiv
Chisinau★
Iaşi★
MOLDOVA
Odesa

NIA
rest
Constanţa

Varna
Black Sea

LGARIA
a
Istanbul

salónikP
Bursa

TURKEY
İzmir

Aegean Sea

ns★

Rhodes

Crete

tion,
8°N

South Atlantic
Ocean

60

70

area of
enlargement

Queen Maud Land

Enderby
Land

Halley

Weddell Sea

80

Mac. Robertson
Land

Palmer
Land

Ronne
Ice Shelf

Ar

Bellingshausen
Sea

Ellsworth

Vinson Massif
(highest point in Antarctica, 4892 m)

South Pole
2800 m.

Peter I Island

Land

▽

Bentley Subglacial Trench
(lowest point in Antarctica, -2540 m)

Wilkes Land

Marie Byrd
Land

Ross
Ice Shelf

Amundsen
Sea

80

Ross Sea

average minimum
extent of sea ice

Victoria Land

70

Antarctic   Circle

Scott
Island

**BALLENY
ISLANDS**

60

ANTARCTICA is the southernmost continent and the coldest place on Earth. It's almost entirely covered with ice that in some places is ten times as high as New York's One World Trade Center, the tallest building in the United States. Gusts of wind up to 120 miles per hour (190 kph) make it feel even colder.

Antarctica is so cold, windy, and dry that humans never settled there. There are no countries, cities, or towns. However, researchers and scientists from different countries come to study earthquakes, the environment, weather, and more at scientific stations established by 19 countries. Some of these nations have claimed parts of Antarctica as their national territory, although other countries do not recognize the claims.

Few land animals can survive the continent's harsh conditions. The smallest one is a wingless insect called a midge, which is only one-half inch long. However, a great variety of whales, seals, penguins, and fish live in and near the surrounding ocean.

Ice Shelf

Shackleton
Ice Shelf

ic Convergence

Antarctica at a Glance

Area
About 5,400,000 sq. mi. (14,000,000 sq km)

Population
No native people, but researchers come for various periods

Number of countries claiming territory
7

Number of research stations
60

Longest river
Onyx River 19 mi. (31 km) long

Highest point
Vinson Massif
16,050 ft. (4,892 m) above sea level

Lowest point
Bentley Subglacial Trench
8,383 ft. (2,555 m) below sea level

The ice sheets covering Antarctica form the largest body of freshwater or ice in the world, or about 70 percent of the world's fresh water.

Oceania
(Including Australia)

Samarinda • Palu • Ternate
Balikpapan • Moncca Sea
Banjarmasin • Sorong • Biak
Kendari • Jayapura • Wewak • New Ireland
Makassar • Ambon • Madang • PAPUA NEW GUINEA
Jaya Sea • Banda Sea • Mount Hagen • Lae • New Britain • Bougainville • SOLOMON ISL
Surabaya • Bali • I N D O N E S I A • Awara • Solomon Sea • Honiar
Java • Sumbawa • Flores • Dili • Port Moresby • Guadalcanal
Denpasar • Lombok • TIMOR-LESTE
Sumba • Kupang • Timor • Timor Sea • Arafura Sea • Torres Strait

Yaren Dis
NA

SOLOMO
ISL
Honiar

Indian Ocean

Ashmore and Cartier Island (AUSTRALIA)
Darwin
Gulf of Carpentaria
Cairns
Coral Islands
Coral Sea

KING LEOPOLD RANGE
Townsville
MACDONNELL RANGE
Mount Isa
Mackay
Port Hedland
GREAT SANDY DESERT
Rockhampton
HAMMERSLEY RANGE
Alice Springs
Gladstone
GIBSON DESERT
A U S T R A L I A
SIMPSON DESERT
Toowoomba • Brisbane
Geraldton
GREAT VICTORIA DESERT
Lake Eyre (lowest point in Australia, -15 m)
Gold Coast
DARLING RANGE
Kalgoorlie
FLINDERS RANGE
Perth
Rockingham
Bunbury
Broken Hill
Newcastle
Sydney
Wollongong
Esperance
Whyalla
Adelaide
Canberra
Mount Kosciuszko (highest point in Australia, 2229 m)
Great Australian Bight
Geelong • Melbourne
Bass Strait

GREAT DIVIDING RANGE

LORD HOWE RISE

Tasman Sea

20
40

Pacific Islands

Johnston Atoll (U.S.)

North Pacific Ocean

CLARION FRACTURE

Ebeye
MARSHALL ISLANDS
Kwajalein
Majuro
Kingman Reef (U.S.)
Palmyra Atoll (U.S.)
CLIPPERTON FRACTURE ZONE

Pohnpei
Palikir
Tarawa
KIRIBATI (GILBERT ISLANDS)
Banaba
Howland Island (U.S.)
Baker Island (U.S.)
Jarvis Island (U.S.)
Kiritimati (Christmas Island) (KIRIBATI)
LINE ISLANDS
ÎLES MARQUISES

Yaren District
NAURU
K I R I B A T I
RAWAKI (PHOENIX ISLANDS)
K I R I B A T I

Bougainville
SOLOMON ISLANDS
Honiara
SANTA CRUZ ISLANDS
TUVALU
Funafuti
Rotuma
Tokelau (N.Z.)
Swains Island
Wallis and Futuna (FRANCE)
SAMOA
Mata-Utu
Apia
Pago Pago
American Samoa (U.S.)
Cook Islands (N.Z.)
SOCIETY ISLANDS
Papeete
Tahiti
ARCHIPEL DES TUAMOTU

Guadalcanal
VANUATU
Port-Vila
FIJI
Suva
Viti Levu
Vanua Levu
TONGA
Alofi • Niue (N.Z.)
Avarua
French Polynesia (FRANCE)
Mururoa
Adamstown

New Caledonia (FRANCE)
Noumea
Ceva-i-Ra
Nuku'Alofa
Minerva Reefs
ÎLES TUBUAI

Coral Sea

LORD HOWE

Kingston
Norfolk Island (AUSTRALIA)
KERMADEC ISLANDS (N.Z.)

OCEANIA is a large geographical area that includes Australia, New Zealand, Papua New Guinea, 11 other independent countries, and thousands of smaller islands. Australia is the world's smallest continent and the only continent that is also a country. Because Australia is surrounded by water, it is also technically an island.

Most of Australia is low and flat, with deserts covering about one-third of the continent. The world's largest coral reef, the Great Barrier Reef, is in the Coral Sea off the coast of Queensland in northeast Australia. Huge cattle and sheep ranches make Australia a leading producer of beef, mutton, and wool. Still, 90 percent of Australians live in cities and towns.

Oceania at a Glance

Area
3,300,000 sq. mi. (8,600,000 sq km)

Population
37,575,000

Number of countries
14

Most populated urban area
Sydney, Australia

Longest river system
Murray-Darling, Australia
2,254.6 mi. (3,672 km) long

Largest lake
Lake Eyre, Australia
3,708 sq. mi. (9,399 sq km)

Highest point
Mt. Wilhelm, Papua New Guinea
14,793 ft. (4,509 m)

Lowest point
Lake Eyre
–52 ft. (–16 m)

All of Australia is located below the equator. This is why the continent is called "the Land Down Under."

The Continents and Major Oceans

HOW MANY oceans are there? Actually, there's only one. Although the seven continents split the ocean into five major parts, the ocean is one huge connected body of water. This *world ocean* has an average depth of 13,000 feet (4,000 m), with parts plunging almost three times that deep. On the ocean floor is a landscape of valleys and ridges that is constantly changing, as magma from underwater volcanoes seeps out and forms new land.

The ocean provides food, energy, medicines, minerals, and most of the precipitation that falls to Earth's surface. It regulates the world's climate by storing and releasing heat from the sun. Without the ocean, there could be no life on our planet.

In the darkest ocean depths, tubeworms and giant mussels live on chemicals gushing from openings in the sea floor call hydrothermal vents.

North America

Atlantic Ocean

South America

Pacific Ocean

Area
About 66 million sq. mi. (171 million sq km)
Greatest depth
35,840 ft. (10,924 m), in the Challenger Deep
Surface temperature
Highest: 82°F (28°C), near the equator in August
Lowest: 30°F (–1°C), in the polar region in winter

Area
About 34 million sq. mi. (88 million sq km)
Greatest depth
28,232 ft. (8,605 m) in the Puerto Rico Trench
Surface temperature
Highest: About 86°F (30°C), near the equator in summer
Lowest: 28°F (–2°C), at and near the boundary with the Southern Ocean in winter

Arctic Ocean

Area
About 3,680,000 sq. mi. (9,530,000 sq km)
Greatest depth
18,399 ft. (5,608 m), in Molloy Hole, northwest of Svalbard
Surface temperature
Highest: 29°F (-1.5°C), in July
Lowest: 28°F (-2°C), in January

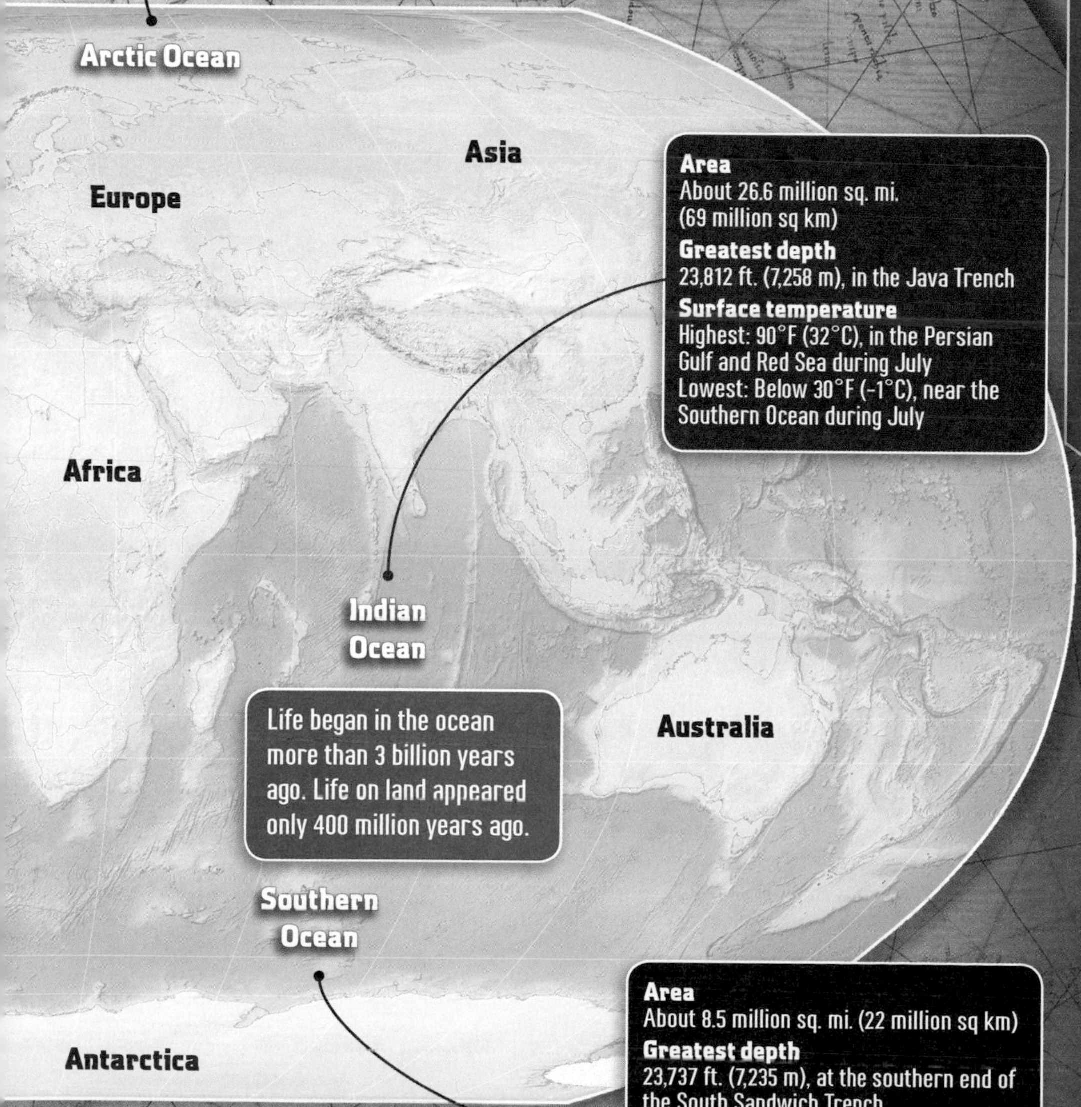

Europe

Asia

Africa

Indian Ocean

Area
About 26.6 million sq. mi.
(69 million sq km)
Greatest depth
23,812 ft. (7,258 m), in the Java Trench
Surface temperature
Highest: 90°F (32°C), in the Persian Gulf and Red Sea during July
Lowest: Below 30°F (-1°C), near the Southern Ocean during July

Australia

Life began in the ocean more than 3 billion years ago. Life on land appeared only 400 million years ago.

Southern Ocean

Antarctica

Area
About 8.5 million sq. mi. (22 million sq km)
Greatest depth
23,737 ft. (7,235 m), at the southern end of the South Sandwich Trench
Surface temperature
Highest: 30 to 43°F (-1 to 6°C), near 60° south latitude in February
Lowest: 28 to 30°F (-2 to-1°C), near Antarctica in August

World's **5** Deepest Oceans and Seas

(Ranked by average depth)

Pacific Ocean
14,040 ft. (4,279 m)

Indian Ocean
12,800 ft. (3,900 m)

Atlantic Ocean
11,810 ft. (3,600 m)

Caribbean Sea
8,448 ft. (2,575 m)

Sea of Japan
5,468 ft. (1,666 m)

World's **5** Largest Lakes

Caspian Sea
Azerbaijan/Iran/Kazakhstan/
Russia/Turkmenistan
146,101 sq. mi.
(378,401 sq km)

Lake Superior
Canada/United States
31,699 sq. mi.
(82,000 sq km)

Lake Victoria
Kenya/Tanzania/Uganda
26,828 sq. mi.
(69,485 sq km)

Lake Huron
Canada/United States
23,004 sq. mi.
(59,580 sq km)

Lake Michigan
United States
22,278 sq. mi.
(57,700 sq km)

World's **5** Tallest Waterfalls

Angel
Venezuela
Tributary of Caroni River
3,212 ft. (979 m)

Tugela
South Africa
Tugela River
3,110 ft. (948 m)

Tres Hermanas
Peru
Cutivireni River
3,000 ft. (914 m)

Olo'upena
United States
2,953 ft. (900 m)

Yumbilla
Peru
2,938 ft. (896 m)

World's **5** Longest River Systems

Nile
Tanzania/Uganda/Sudan/Egypt
4,145 mi.
(6,670 km)

Amazon
Peru/Brazil
4,007 mi.
(6,448 km)

Yangtze Kiang
China
3,915 mi.
(6,300 km)

Mississippi-Missouri
United States
3,710 mi.
(5,971 km)

Yenisey-Angara-Selenga
Mongolia/Russia
2,500 mi.
(4,000 km)

World's **5** Highest Mountains

(Height of principal peak; lower peaks of same mountain excluded)

Mt. Everest
Nepal/Tibet
29,035 ft. (8,850 m)

K2
Pakistan/China
28,250 ft. (8,611 m)

Kanchenjunga
Nepal/India
28,208 ft. (8,598 m)

Lhotse
Tibet
27,923 ft. (8,511 m)

Makalu
Nepal/Tibet
27,824 ft. (8,480 m)

Natural Wonders of the United States

Bryce Canyon
Location: Utah

Yellowstone
Location: Wyoming

Big Sur
Location: California

Crater Lake
Location: Oregon

10 Largest States in Total Area

1.	Alaska	663,267 sq. mi. (1,717,854 sq km)
2.	Texas	268,581 sq. mi. (695,622 sq km)
3.	California	163,696 sq. mi. (423,971 sq km)
4.	Montana	147,042 sq. mi. (380,837 sq km)
5.	New Mexico	121,589 sq. mi. (314,914 sq km)
6.	Arizona	113,998 sq. mi. (295,253 sq km)
7.	Nevada	110,561 sq. mi. (286,352 sq km)
8.	Colorado	104,094 sq. mi. (269,602 sq km)
9.	Oregon	98,381 sq. mi. (254,806 sq km)
10.	Wyoming	97,814 sq. mi. (253,337 sq km)

10 Smallest States in Total Area

1.	Rhode Island	1,545 sq. mi. (4,002 sq km)
2.	Delaware	2,489 sq. mi. (6,446 sq km)
3.	Connecticut	5,543 sq. mi. (14,356 sq km)
4.	New Jersey	8,721 sq. mi. (22,587 sq km)
5.	New Hampshire	9,350 sq. mi. (24,216 sq km)
6.	Vermont	9,614 sq. mi. (24,900 sq km)
7.	Massachusetts	10,555 sq. mi. (27,337 sq km)
8.	Hawaii	10,931 sq. mi. (28,311 sq km)
9.	Maryland	12,407 sq. mi. (32,134 sq km)
10.	West Virginia	24,230 sq. mi. (62,755 sq km)

5 Highest US Mountains

Mt. McKinley
Alaska
20,320 ft. (6,194 m)

Mt. St. Elias
Alaska–Yukon
18,008 ft. (5,489 m)

Mt. Foraker
Alaska
17,400 ft. (5,304 m)

Mt. Bona
Alaska
16,550 ft. (5,044 m)

Mt. Blackburn
Alaska
16,390 ft. (4,996 m)

10 Longest US Rivers

Mississippi
2,348 mi. (3,779 km)

Missouri
2,315 mi. (3,726 km)

Yukon
1,979 mi. (3,186 km)

Rio Grande
1,900 mi. (3,058 km)

Arkansas
1,459 mi. (2,348 km)

Red
1,290 mi. (2,076 km)

Columbia
1,243 mi. (2,000 km)

Snake
1,038 mi. (1,670 km)

Ohio
981 mi. (1,579 km)

St. Lawrence
800 mi. (1,287 km)

10 Largest US National Historical Parks

(By total acreage and hectares)

Chaco Culture
New Mexico
33,960 acres (13,743 h)

Cumberland Gap
Kentucky/Tennessee/Virginia
22,365 acres (9,050 h)

Jean Lafitte
Louisiana
20,001 acres (8,094 h)

Chesapeake & Ohio Canal
Maryland/West Virginia/
Washington, DC
19,615 acres (7,938 h)

Klondike Gold Rush
Alaska/Washington
12,996 acres (5,259 h)

Colonial
Virginia
8,676 acres (3,511 h)

Pecos
New Mexico
6,669 acres (2,699 h)

Nez Perce
Idaho/Montana/
Oregon/Washington
4,569 acres (1,849 h)

Harpers Ferry
West Virginia/Maryland/Virginia
3,645 acres (1,475 h)

Cedar Creek & Belle Grove
Virginia
3,712 acres (1,502 h)

The Great Lakes—Facts and Figures

Lake Superior

Area	31,700 sq. mi. (82,103 sq km)
Borders	Minnesota, Wisconsin, Michigan (United States); Ontario (Canada)
Major Ports	Duluth, Superior, Sault Ste. Marie (United States); Sault Ste. Marie, Thunder Bay (Canada)

Lake Huron

Area	23,000 sq. mi. (59,570 sq km)
Borders	Michigan (United States); Ontario (Canada)
Major Ports	Port Huron (United States); Sarnia (Canada)

Lake Michigan

Area	22,300 sq. mi. (57,570 sq km)
Borders	Illinois, Indiana, Michigan, Wisconsin (United States)
Major Ports	Milwaukee, Racine, Kenosha, Chicago, Gary, Muskegon (United States)

Lake Erie

Area	9,940 sq. mi. (25,745 sq km)
Borders	Michigan, New York, Ohio, Pennsylvania (United States); Ontario (Canada)
Major Ports	Toledo, Sandusky, Lorain, Cleveland, Erie, Buffalo (United States)

Lake Ontario

Area	7,340 sq. mi. (19,011 sq km)
Borders	New York (United States); Ontario (Canada)
Major Ports	Rochester, Uswego (United States); Toronto, Hamilton (Canada)

The Great Lakes from Space

An easy way to remember the names of the Great Lakes is the mnemonic *HOMES*:

HURON
ONTARIO
MICHIGAN
ERIE
SUPERIOR

271

National Parks by State

Alaska
Denali
Gates of the Arctic
Glacier Bay
Katmai
Kenai Fjords
Kobuk Valley
Lake Clark
Wrangell–St. Elias

Arizona
Grand Canyon
Petrified Forest
Saguaro

Arkansas
Hot Springs

California
Channel Islands
Death Valley
Joshua Tree
Kings Canyon
Lassen Volcanic
Redwood
Sequoia
Yosemite

Colorado
Black Canyon of the Gunnison
Great Sand Dunes
Mesa Verde
Rocky Mountain

Florida
Biscayne
Dry Tortugas
Everglades

Hawaii
Haleakala
Hawaii Volcanoes

Idaho
Yellowstone

Kentucky
Mammoth Cave

Maine
Acadia

Michigan
Isle Royale

Minnesota
Voyageurs

Montana
Glacier
Yellowstone

Nevada
Death Valley
Great Basin

New Mexico
Carlsbad Caverns

North Carolina
Great Smoky Mountains

North Dakota
Theodore Roosevelt

Ohio
Cuyahoga Valley

Oregon
Crater Lake

South Carolina
Congaree

South Dakota
Badlands
Wind Cave

Tennessee
Great Smoky Mountains

Texas
Big Bend
Guadalupe Mountains

Utah
Arches
Bryce Canyon
Canyonlands
Capitol Reef
Zion

Virginia
Shenandoah

Washington
Mount Rainier
North Cascades
Olympic

Wyoming
Grand Teton
Yellowstone

10 Most Visited US National Parks

A total of 68,928,098 people visited US national parks in 2014.

Park (Location)	Visitors in 2014
Great Smoky Mountains (Tennessee/North Carolina)	10,099,276
Grand Canyon (Arizona)	4,756,771
Yosemite (California)	3,882,642
Yellowstone (Wyoming)	3,513,484
Rocky Mountain (Colorado)	3,434,751
Olympic (Washington)	3,243,872
Zion (Utah)	3,189,696
Grand Teton (Wyoming)	2,791,391
Acadia (Maine)	2,563,129
Glacier (Montana)	2,338,528

Selected US National Memorials

Memorial	State	Description
Arkansas Post	Arkansas	First permanent French settlement in the lower Mississippi River valley
Arlington House (Robert E. Lee Memorial)	Virginia	Lee's home overlooking the Potomac
Chamizal	Texas	Commemorates 1963 settlement of 99-year border dispute with Mexico
Coronado	Arizona	Commemorates first European exploration of the Southwest
De Soto	Florida	Commemorates 16th-century Spanish explorations
Father Marquette	Michigan	Commemorates Father Jacques Marquette, a French Jesuit missionary who helped establish Michigan's first European settlement at Sault Ste. Marie in 1668
Federal Hall	New York	First seat of US government under the Constitution
Flight 93	Pennsylvania	Commemorates the passengers and crew of Flight 93, who lost their lives to bring down a plane headed to attack the nation's capital on September 11, 2001
Fort Caroline	Florida	On St. Johns River; overlooks site of a French Huguenot colony
Fort Clatsop	Oregon	Lewis and Clark encampment, 1805–1806
Franklin Delano Roosevelt	DC	Statues of President Roosevelt and First Lady Eleanor Roosevelt, as well as waterfalls and gardens; dedicated May 2, 1997
General Grant	New York	Grant's Tomb
Hamilton Grange	New York	Home of Alexander Hamilton
Jefferson National Expansion Memorial	Missouri	Commemorates westward expansion
Johnstown Flood	Pennsylvania	Commemorates tragic flood of 1889
Korean War Veterans	DC	Dedicated in 1995; honors those who served in the Korean War
Lincoln Boyhood	Indiana	Site of Lincoln cabin, boyhood home, and grave of Lincoln's mother
Lincoln Memorial	DC	Marble statue of the 16th US president
Lyndon B. Johnson Memorial Grove on the Potomac	DC	Honors the 36th president; overlooks the Potomac River vista of the capital
Martin Luther King Jr. Memorial	DC	Dedicated October 16, 2011; honors the civil rights leader with a sculpture, the "Stone of Hope"
Mount Rushmore	South Dakota	World-famous sculpture of four presidents
Oklahoma City	Oklahoma	Commemorates the April 19, 1995, bombing of the Alfred P. Murrah Federal Building
Perry's Victory and International Peace Memorial	Ohio	The world's largest Doric column, constructed 1912–1915, promotes pursuit of international peace through arbitration and disarmament
Roger Williams	Rhode Island	Memorial to founder of Rhode Island
Thaddeus Kosciuszko	Pennsylvania	Memorial to Polish hero of the American Revolution
Theodore Roosevelt Island	DC	Statue of the 26th president in wooded island sanctuary
Thomas Jefferson Memorial	DC	Statue of the 3rd president in a circular, colonnaded structure
USS *Arizona*	Hawaii	Memorializes American losses at Pearl Harbor
Vietnam Veterans	DC	Black granite wall inscribed with names of those missing or killed in action in the Vietnam War
Washington Monument	DC	Obelisk honoring the 1st US president
World War II	DC	Oval plaza with central pool commemorating those who fought and died in World War II
Wright Brothers	North Carolina	Site of first airplane flight, December 17, 1903

US National Battlefields

Big Hole, Montana
Site of major battle between Nez Perce and US Army

Stones River, Tennessee
Scene of battle that began Union offensive to trisect Confederacy

Fort Donelson, Tennessee
Site of first major Union victory

Petersburg, Virginia
Scene of 10-month Union campaign, 1864–1865

Antietam, Maryland
Battle here ended first Confederate invasion of North, September 17, 1862

Fort Necessity, Pennsylvania
Some of the first battles of French and Indian War

Wilson's Creek, Missouri
Scene of Civil War battle for control of Missouri

Tupelo, Mississippi
Site of crucial Civil War battle over Sherman's supply line

Moores Creek, North Carolina
1776 battle between Patriots and Loyalists commemorated here

Monocacy, Maryland
Civil War battle in defense of Washington, DC, fought here July 9, 1864

Cowpens, South Carolina
American Revolution battlefield

Stats on the Statue of Liberty

The Statue of Liberty was designed by French sculptor Frédéric-Auguste Bartholdi and arrived in 214 packing cases from Rouen, France, in June 1885. The completed statue was dedicated on October 28, 1886, by President Grover Cleveland. It was designated a National Monument in 1924 and is one of America's most famous symbols of freedom.

Part of Statue	Measurement
Height from heel to torch	151 ft. 1 in. (45.3 m)
Height from base of pedestal to torch	305 ft. 1 in. (91.5 m)
Length of hand	16 ft. 5 in. (5 m)
Length of index finger	8 ft. 0 in. (2.4 m)
Circumference at second finger joint	3 ft. 6 in. (1 m)
Size of fingernail	13 x 10 in. (33 x 25 cm)
Height of head from chin to cranium	17 ft. 3 in. (5 m)
Thickness of head from ear to ear	10 ft. 0 in. (3 m)
Distance across each eye	2 ft. 6 in. (0.76 m)
Length of nose	4 ft. 6 in. (1.4 m)
Length of right arm	42 ft. 0 in. (12.8 m)
Thickness of right arm at thickest point	12 ft. 0 in. (3.7 m)
Thickness of waist	35 ft. 0 in. (10.7 m)
Width of mouth	3 ft. 0 in. (1 m)
Length of tablet	23 ft. 7 in. (7.2 m)
Width of tablet	13 ft. 7 in. (4.1 m)
Thickness of tablet	2 ft. 0 in. (0.6 m)

Select National Sites of Washington, DC

WASHINGTON MONUMENT

VIETNAM VETERANS MEMORIAL

LINCOLN MEMORIAL

KOREAN WAR MEMORIAL

MARTIN LUTHER KING JR. MEMORIAL

HOLOCAUST MEMORIAL MUSEUM

WHITE HOUSE

US CAPITOL

JEFFERSON MEMORIAL

Independence Ave

MacArthur Boulevard

Ave

Connecticut Ave

Street

Ave

Rhode Isl

New York Ave

Florida Ave

Constitution Ave

Pennsylvania Ave

Potomac River

Anacostia River

VIRGINIA

WASHINGTON, DC

AND

US Capitol
The Capitol is open to the public for guided tours 8:50 AM to 3:20 PM, Monday through Saturday. Tickets are available at tour kiosks at the east and west fronts of the Capitol.
Phone: (202) 226-8000

Holocaust Memorial Museum
The museum is open daily, beginning at 10:00 AM, except on Yom Kippur and December 25. 100 Raoul Wallenburg Pl., SW (formerly 15th St., SW) near Independence Ave.
Phone: (202) 488 0400

Jefferson Memorial
The memorial, which is located on the south edge of the Tidal Basin, is open 8:00 AM to 11:45 PM every day except Christmas Day. An elevator and curb ramps for the disabled are in service.
Phone: (202) 426-6841

Korean War Memorial
The $18 million military memorial, which was funded by private donations, is open 24 hours a day.
Phone: (202) 426-6841

Lincoln Memorial
The memorial, which is located in West Potomac Park, is open 8:00 AM to 11:45 PM every day except Christmas Day. An elevator and curb ramps for the disabled are in service.
Phone: (202) 426-6841

Martin Luther King Jr. Memorial
This memorial features a sculpture of the late civil rights leader that seems to be rising from a mountain of granite and a wall inscribed with some of his famous quotes. It is open 24 hours a day throughout the year.
Phone: (202) 426-6841

Vietnam Veterans Memorial
The memorial is open 24 hours a day throughout the year.
Phone: (202) 426-6841

Washington Monument
The memorial is open 9:00 AM to 4:45 PM daily, except on July 4 and December 25. Tickets are required for entry and can be either reserved ahead of time or picked up same day. The monument was closed in 2011 for repairs of damages caused by an earthquake, but it reopened on May 12, 2014.
Phone: (202) 426-6841

The White House
Free reserved tickets for guided tours can be obtained up to six months in advance. Contact your senators or representatives for tickets.
Phone: (202) 456-7041

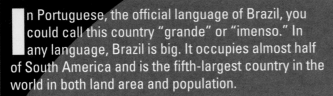

In Portuguese, the official language of Brazil, you could call this country "grande" or "imenso." In any language, Brazil is big. It occupies almost half of South America and is the fifth-largest country in the world in both land area and population.

Almost 60 percent of Brazil is covered with rain forests, making it home to one-third of the wildlife in the world. It has more species of monkeys than any other country. Millions of rain forest plants and trees convert carbon dioxide into oxygen, providing clean air for the planet. However, most Brazilians live in big cities.

The country's second-largest city, Rio de Janeiro, will host the Summer Olympics and Paralympics in August and September, 2016. It will be the first South American city ever to host the Olympics. You can learn facts about Brazil and see its country flag on p. 283.

Windsurfers get ready to race in Rio de Janeiro, Brazil, while the city's famous Christ the Redeemer statue towers 2,300 feet (700 m) above on Mount Corcovado.

FLAGS & FACTS
COUNTRIES OF THE WORLD

Countries of the World

ARCTIC OCEAN

75°N

GREENLAND
(Denmark)

Prime Meridian

Arctic Circle

ICELAND

IRELAND
UNITED
KINGDOM
NE

CANADA

BELGI
L
FRANC

ANDORRA

45°N

UNITED STATES

ATLANTIC OCEAN

AZORES
(Portugal)
PORTUGAL
SPAIN

MOROCCO

30°N

MEXICO

BAHAMAS

Tropic of Cancer

CANARY ISLANDS
(Spain)
WESTERN
SAHARA
ALGERIA

CUBA
DOMINICAN
REPUBLIC

MAURITANIA
MALI

CAPE VERDE

HAITI

JAMAICA

15°N

BELIZE
HONDURAS

GUATEMALA
NICARAGUA

EL SALVADOR

COSTA RICA

PANAMA

SENEGAL
GAMBIA
BURKINA
FASO
BENI

GUINEA-BISSAU
GUINEA

COTE
D'IVOIRE

SIERRA LEONE

GAMBIA

LIBERIA

TOGO
EQ. GI

PACIFIC OCEAN

VENEZUELA
SURINAME

COLOMBIA
GUYANA
FRENCH
GUIANA
(France)

0°

Equator

ECUADOR

"Equator

SÃO TOMÉ & PRÍN

PERU

BRAZIL

FRENCH POLYNESIA
(France)

15°S

BOLIVIA

Tropic of Capricorn

PARAGUAY

30°S

CHILE

URUGUAY

ARGENTINA

ATLANTIC OCEAN

45°S

FALKLAND ISLANDS
(U.K.)

SOUTH GEORGIA
(U.K.)

Prime Meridian

0   1,000   2,000 Miles
0   1,000   2,000 Kilometers

60°S

Antarctic Circle

165°W   150°W   135°W   120°W   105°W   90°W   75°W   60°W   45°W   30°W   15°W   0°

ARCTIC OCEAN

ARCTIC OCEAN

SWEDEN
FINLAND

ESTONIA
LATVIA
LITHUANIA
RUS.
BELARUS
POLAND
CZECH REP.
SLOVAKIA
AUSTRIA HUNGARY
SLOVENIA MOLDOVA
CROATIA UKRAINE
ROMANIA
BOSNIA &
HERZ. BULGARIA
MONT.
ITALY ALBANIA
MALTA GREECE
CYPRUS
LEBANON
ISRAEL SYRIA
JORDAN
LIBYA
EGYPT
TURKEY
GEORGIA
ARMENIA AZERBAIJAN
IRAQ
KUWAIT
IRAN
BAHRAIN
QATAR
U.A.E.
SAUDI ARABIA
OMAN
YEMEN
ERITREA
DJIBOUTI
CHAD
SUDAN
CENTRAL
AFRICAN REP.
SOUTH
SUDAN
ETHIOPIA
SOMALIA
CAMEROON
DEMOCRATIC
REPUBLIC
OF THE
CONGO
UGANDA KENYA
RWANDA
BURUNDI
TANZANIA
ANGOLA
ZAMBIA
MALAWI
COMOROS
NAMIBIA
ZIMBABWE MOZAMBIQUE
BOTSWANA
MADAGASCAR
SWAZILAND
SOUTH
AFRICA
LESOTHO

RUSSIA

KAZAKHSTAN

MONGOLIA

UZBEKISTAN
KYRGYZSTAN
TURKMENISTAN
TAJIKISTAN
AFGHANISTAN
PAKISTAN
NEPAL
BHUTAN
INDIA
BANGLADESH
BURMA
LAOS
THAILAND
CAMBODIA
VIETNAM
MALDIVES
SRI
LANKA

CHINA

NORTH
KOREA
SOUTH
KOREA
JAPAN

PHILIPPINES

BRUNEI
MALAYSIA
SINGAPORE
BORNEO
INDONESIA
TIMOR-LESTE

PAPUA
NEW GUINEA

PACIFIC OCEAN

Tropic of Cancer

NORTHERN
MARIANA ISLANDS
(U.S.)

FEDERATED STATES
OF MICRONESIA

PALAU

MARSHALL
ISLANDS

Equator

SOLOMON
ISLANDS

KIRIBATI

TUVALU

SAMOA

INDIAN OCEAN

Tropic of Capricorn

AUSTRALIA

NEW CALEDONIA
(France)

VANUATU
FIJI

TONGA

NEW
ZEALAND

N
W   E
S

ANTARCTICA

15°E   30°E   45°E   60°E   75°E   90°E   105°E   120°E   135°E   150°E   165°E   180°

AFGHANISTAN

Capital: Kabul
Population: 33,332, 025
Area: 250,001 sq. mi. (647,500 sq km)
Language: Dari (Afghan Persian), Pashto
Money: Afghani
Government: Islamic republic

ALBANIA

Capital: Tirana
Population: 3,039,000
Area: 11,100 sq. mi. (28,748 sq km)
Language: Albanian, Greek
Money: Lek
Government: Republic

ALGERIA

Capital: Algiers
Population: 40,264,000
Area: 919,595 sq. mi. (2,381,740 sq km)
Language: Arabic, Berber, French
Money: Dinar
Government: Republic

> Thousands of frigate birds live in a sanctuary on Barbuda. A frigate bird's wingspan can reach nearly eight feet (2.4 m).

ANDORRA

Capital: Andorra la Vella
Population: 86,000
Area: 180 sq. mi. (468 sq km)
Language: Catalan, French, Castillan, Portuguese
Money: Euro
Government: Parliamentary democracy

ANGOLA

Capital: Luanda
Population: 20,172,000
Area: 481,400 sq. mi. (1,246,700 sq km)
Language: Portuguese, Bantu, others
Money: Kwanza
Government: Republic

ANTIGUA AND BARBUDA

Capital: St. John's
Population: 94,000
Area: 171 sq. mi. (443 sq km)
Language: English
Money: Dollar
Government: Parliamentary democracy; independent sovereign state within the Commonwealth

Population figures from the US Census Bureau International Database, 2016 projections

ARGENTINA

Capital: Buenos Aires
Population: 43,833,000
Area: 1,068,302 sq. mi. (2,766,890 sq km)
Language: Spanish, Italian, English, German, French
Money: Peso
Government: Republic

ARMENIA

Capital: Yerevan
Population: 3,052,000
Area: 11,484 sq. mi. (29,743 sq km)
Language: Armenian, Kurdish, Russian
Money: Dram
Government: Republic

AUSTRALIA

Capital: Canberra
Population: 22,993,000
Area: 2,967,909 sq. mi. (7,686,850 sq km)
Language: English, Chinese, Italian, aboriginal languages
Money: Dollar
Government: Constitutional monarchy; democratic, federal-state system recognizing British monarchy as sovereign

AUSTRIA

Capital: Vienna
Population: 8,225,000
Area: 32,382 sq. mi. (83,870 sq km)
Language: German
Money: Euro
Government: Federal parliamentary democracy

The Andes mountains run along the western edge of Argentina, on the border with Chile.

AZERBAIJAN

Capital: Baku
Population: 9,873,000
Area: 33,436 sq. mi. (86,600 sq km)
Language: Azerbaijani, Russian, Armenian, others
Money: Manat
Government: Republic

THE BAHAMAS

Capital: Nassau
Population: 327,000
Area: 5,382 sq. mi. (13,940 sq km)
Language: English, Creole
Money: Dollar
Government: Constitutional parliamentary democracy

BAHRAIN

Capital: Manama
Population: 1,379,000
Area: 257 sq. mi. (665 sq km)
Language: Arabic, English, Farsi, Urdu
Money: Dinar
Government: Constitutional monarchy

BANGLADESH

Capital: Dhaka
Population: 171,697,000
Area: 55,599 sq. mi. (144,000 sq km)
Language: Bengali, Chakma, Bagh
Money: Taka
Government: Parliamentary democracy

BARBADOS

Capital: Bridgetown
Population: 291,000
Area: 166 sq. mi. (431 sq km)
Language: English
Money: Dollar
Government: Parliamentary democracy

BELARUS

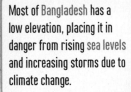

Capital: Minsk
Population: 9,570,000
Area: 80,155 sq. mi. (207,600 sq km)
Language: Belarusian, Russian
Money: Ruble
Government: Republic

BELGIUM

Capital: Brussels
Population: 10,457,000
Area: 11,787 sq. mi. (30,528 sq km)
Language: Dutch, French, German
Money: Euro
Government: Parliamentary democracy under a constitutional monarchy

Most of Bangladesh has a low elevation, placing it in danger from rising sea levels and increasing storms due to climate change.

BELIZE

Capital: Belmopan
Population: 354,000
Area: 8,867 sq. mi. (22,966 sq km)
Language: English, Creole, Spanish, Mayan dialects
Money: Dollar
Government: Parliamentary democracy

BENIN

Capital: Porto-Novo
Population: 10,741,000
Area: 43,483 sq. mi.
(112,620 sq km)
Language: French, Fon, Yoruba
in the south; Nagot, Bariba, Dendi
in the north
Money: West African CFA franc
Government: Republic under
multiparty democratic rule

BHUTAN

Capital: Thimphu
Population: 750,000
Area: 18,147 sq. mi. (47,000 sq km)
Language: Dzongkha, Nepali,
Tibetan
Money: Ngultrum
Government: Constitutional
monarchy

BOLIVIA

Capital: La Paz
Population: 10,970,000
Area: 424,164 sq. mi.
(1,098,580 sq km)
Language: Spanish, Quecha,
Aymara, Guarani
Money: Boliviano
Government: Republic

BOSNIA AND HERZEGOVINA

Capital: Sarajevo
Population: 3,862,000
Area: 19,772 sq. mi. (51,209 sq km)
Language: Bosnian, Serbian,
Croatian
Money: Convertible marka
Government: Federal
democratic republic

BOTSWANA

Capital: Gaborone
Population: 2,209,000
Area: 231,804 sq. mi.
(600,370 sq km)
Language: English, Setswana,
Kalanga
Money: Pula
Government: Parliamentary
republic

Bolivia was named after
Símon Bolívar (1783–1830),
who led that country as
well as Venezuela, Colombia,
Ecuador, and Peru to
independence from Spain.

BRAZIL

Capital: Brasilia
Population: 205,824,000
Area: 3,286,488 sq. mi.
(8,511,965 sq km)
Language: Portuguese
Money: Real
Government: Federative
republic

283

BRUNEI

Capital: Bandar Seri Begawan
Population: 437,000
Area: 2,228 sq. mi. (5,770 sq km)
Language: Malay, English, Chinese
Money: Dollar
Government: Constitutional sultanate

BULGARIA

Capital: Sofia
Population: 6,809,000
Area: 42,823 sq. mi. (110,910 sq km)
Language: Bulgarian, Turkish, Roma
Money: Lev
Government: Parliamentary democracy

BURKINA FASO

Capital: Ouagadougou
Population: 19,513,000
Area: 105,869 sq. mi. (274,200 sq km)
Language: French
Money: West African CFA franc
Government: Republic

BURMA

Capital: Yangon (Rangoon)
Population: 56,890,000
Area: 261,970 sq. mi. (678,500 sq km)
Language: Burmese, many ethnic languages
Money: Kyat
Government: Military junta

BURUNDI

Capital: Bujumbura
Population: 11,099,000
Area: 10,745 sq. mi. (27,830 sq km)
Language: Kirundi, French, Swahili
Money: Franc
Government: Republic

Mandrill monkeys living in Cameroon and other central African countries live in extremely large groups known as hordes. Researchers say hordes can include as many as 845 members.

CAMBODIA

Capital: Phnom Penh
Population: 15,957,000
Area: 69,900 sq. mi. (181,040 sq km)
Language: Khmer, French, English
Money: Riel
Government: Multiparty democracy under a constitutional monarchy

CAMEROON

Capital: Yaoundé
Population: 24,361,000
Area: 183,568 sq. mi. (475,440 sq km)
Language: French, English, 24 major African language groups
Money: Central African CFA franc
Government: Republic

CANADA

Capital: Ottawa
Population: 35,363,000
Area: 3,855,103 sq. mi.
(9,984,670 sq km)
Language: English, French
Money: Dollar
Government: A parliamentary
democracy, a federation, and a
constitutional monarchy

CAPE VERDE

Capital: Praia
Population: 553,000
Area: 1,557 sq. mi. (4,033 sq km)
Language: Portuguese, Crioulo
Money: Escudo
Government: Republic

CENTRAL AFRICAN REPUBLIC

Capital: Bangui
Population: 5,507,000
Area: 240,535 sq. mi.
(622,984 sq km)
Language: Sangho, French,
tribal languages
Money: Central African CFA
franc
Government: Republic

CHAD

Capital: N'Djaména
Population: 11,852,000
Area: 495,755 sq. mi.
(1,284,000 sq km)
Language: French, Arabic,
more than 120 others
Money: Central African
CFA franc

CHILE

Capital: Santiago
Population: 17,650,000
Area: 292,260 sq. mi.
(756,950 sq km)
Language: Spanish
Money: Peso
Government:
Republic

CHINA

Capital: Beijing
Population: 1,366,994,000
Area: 3,705,407 sq. mi.
(9,596,960 sq km)
Language: Mandarin, Yue,
Wu, Minbei, Minnan, Xiang, Gan,
Hakka dialects, others
Money: Yuan
Government: Communist
Party led state

You won't find pork egg rolls, fortune cookies, General Tso's chicken and other Chinese foods popular with Americans on most restaurant menus in China. "Real" Chinese food includes Chow fun, Peking duck, and jellyfish.

The three islands that make up Comoros are sometimes called the Perfume Islands. The country is the world's leading producer of essence of ylang-ylang, a flower oil used to make perfumes and soaps.

COLOMBIA

Capital: Bogotá
Population: 47,221,000
Area: 439,736 sq. mi.
(1,138,910 sq km)
Language: Spanish
Money: Peso
Government: Republic

COMOROS

Capital: Moroni
Population: 795,000
Area: 838 sq. mi. (2,170 sq km)
Language: Arabic, French,
Shikomoro
Money: Franc
Government: Republic

CONGO, Democratic Republic of the

Capital: Kinshasa
Population: 81,331,000
Area: 905,588 sq. mi.
(2,345,410 sq km)
Language: French, Lingala,
Swahili, Kikongo, Tshiluba
Money: Congolese franc
Government: Republic

CONGO, Republic of the

Capital: Brazzaville
Population: 4,852,000
Area: 132,047 sq. mi. (342,000 sq km)
Language: French, Lingala,
Monokutuba, Kikongo
Money: Central African CFA franc
Government: Republic

COSTA RICA

Capital: San José
Population: 4,873,000
Area: 19,730 sq. mi. (51,100 sq km)
Language: Spanish, English
Money: Colón
Government: Democratic republic

CÔTE d'IVOIRE (Ivory Coast)

Capital: Yamoussoukro
Population: 23,740,000
Area: 124,503 sq. mi.
(322,460 sq km)
Language: French, Dioula, 59
other native dialects
Money: West African CFA franc
Government: Republic with
multiparty presidential regime

CROATIA

Capital: Zagreb
Population: 4,459,000
Area: 21,831 sq. mi. (56,542 sq km)
Language: Croatian, Serbian
Money: Kuna
Government: Parliamentary democracy

CUBA

Capital: Havana
Population: 11,014,000
Area: 42,803 sq. mi. (110,860 sq km)
Language: Spanish
Money: Peso
Government: Communist state

CYPRUS

Capital: Nicosia
Population: 1,206,000
Area: 3,571 sq. mi. (9,250 sq km)
Language: Greek, Turkish, English
Money: Euro
Government: Republic

CZECH REPUBLIC

Capital: Prague
Population: 10,661,000
Area: 30,450 sq. mi. (78,866 sq km)
Language: Czech, Slovak
Money: Koruna
Government: Parliamentary democracy

DENMARK

Capital: Copenhagen
Population: 5,594,000
Area: 16,639 sq. mi. (43,094 sq km)
Language: Danish, Faroese, Greenlandic, English
Money: Krone
Government: Constitutional monarchy

DJIBOUTI

Capital: Djibouti
Population: 847,000
Area: 8,880 sq. mi. (23,000 sq km)
Language: French, Arabic, Afar, Somali
Money: Franc
Government: Republic

LEGO blocks were invented in Denmark. The name comes from the Danish words *leg* and *godt*, which mean "play well." Legoland in Billund, Denmark, is the oldest Legoland. Yes, those buildings really are made of Legos!

287

The Galápagos Islands, off Ecuador's coast, are home to the Galápagos tortoise. These ancient creatures can weigh more than 475 pounds (215 kg) and live more than 100 years.

DOMINICA

Capital: Roseau
Population: 74,000
Area: 291 sq. mi. (754 sq km)
Language: English, French patois
Money: Dollar
Government: Parliamentary democracy

DOMINICAN REPUBLIC

Capital: Santo Domingo
Population: 10,607,000
Area: 18,815 sq. mi. (48,730 sq km)
Language: Spanish
Money: Peso
Government: Democratic republic

ECUADOR

Capital: Quito
Population: 16,081,000
Area: 109,483 sq. mi. (283,560 sq km)
Language: Spanish, Quechua, Jivaroan
Money: Dollar
Government: Republic

EGYPT

Capital: Cairo
Population: 90,068,000
Area: 386,662 sq. mi. (1,001,450 sq km)
Language: Arabic, English, French
Money: Pound
Government: Republic

EL SALVADOR

Capital: San Salvador
Population: 6,157,000
Area: 8,124 sq. mi. (21,040 sq km)
Language: Spanish, Nahua
Money: Colón
Government: Republic

EQUATORIAL GUINEA

Capital: Malabo
Population: 759,000
Area: 10,831 sq. mi. (28,051 sq km)
Language: Spanish, French, Fang, Bubi
Money: Central African CFA franc
Government: Republic

ERITREA

Capital: Asmara
Population: 6,674,000
Area: 46,842 sq. mi. (121,320 sq km)
Language: Afar, Arabic, English, Tigre, Kunama
Money: Nakfa
Government: In transition

ESTONIA

Capital: Tallinn
Population: 1,241,000
Area: 17,462 sq. mi. (45,226 sq km)
Language: Estonian, Russian, Latvian
Money: Kroon
Government: Parliamentary republic

ETHIOPIA

Capital: Addis Ababa
Population: 102,374,000
Area: 435,186 sq. mi. (1,127,127 sq km)
Language: Amarigna, Oromigna, Tigrigna, Somaligna, English
Money: Birr
Government: Federal republic

FIJI

Capital: Suva
Population: 915,000
Area: 7,054 sq. mi. (18,270 sq km)
Language: English, Fijian, Hindustani
Money: Dollar
Government: Republic

FINLAND

Capital: Helsinki
Population: 5,273,000
Area: 130,559 sq. mi. (338,145 sq km)
Language: Finnish, Swedish
Money: Euro
Government: Constitutional republic

Ethiopian runner Genzebe Dibaba is one of only three athletes ever to break three world records in three different events in two weeks. The other two are Jesse Owens and Usain Bolt.

FRANCE

Capital: Paris
Population: 66,836,000
Area: 248,429 sq. mi. (643,427 sq km)
Language: French
Money: Euro
Government: Republic

GABON

Capital: Libreville
Population: 1,739,000
Area: 103,347 sq. mi.
(267,667 sq km)
Language: French, Fang, others
Money: Central African CFA
franc
Government: Republic

THE GAMBIA

Capital: Banjul
Population: 2,010,000
Area: 4,363 sq. mi. (11,300 sq km)
Language: English, Mandinka,
Wolof, Fula, others
Money: Dalasi
Government: Republic

GEORGIA

Capital: Tbilisi
Population: 4,928,000
Area: 26,911 sq. mi. (69,700 sq km)
Language: Georgian, Russian,
Abkhaz
Money: Lari
Government: Republic

GERMANY

Capital: Berlin
Population: 80,723,000
Area: 137,847 sq. mi.
(357,021 sq km)
Language: German
Money: Euro
Government: Federal republic

GHANA

Capital: Accra
Population: 26,908,000
Area: 92,456 sq. mi. (239,460 sq km)
Language: English, Asante, Ewe,
Fante
Money: Cedi
Government: Constitutional
democracy

GREECE

Capital: Athens
Population: 10,773,000
Area: 50,942 sq. mi. (131,940 sq km)
Language: Greek, Turkish,
English
Money: Euro
Government: Parliamentary
republic

Germany generates nearly 20% of
its electricity from wind power
and solar power. It plans to use
only renewable energy by 2050.

GRENADA

Capital: St. George's
Population: 111,000
Area: 133 sq. mi. (344 sq km)
Language: English, French patois
Money: Dollar
Government: Parliamentary democracy

GUATEMALA

Capital: Guatemala City
Population: 15,190,000
Area: 42,043 sq. mi.
(108,890 sq km)
Language: Spanish, 23 Amerindian dialects
Money: Quetzal
Government: Constitutional democratic republic

GUINEA

Capital: Conakry
Population: 12,093,000
Area: 94,926 sq. mi.
(245,857 sq km)
Language: French, Peul, Malinke, Soussou
Money: Franc
Government: Republic

GUINEA-BISSAU

Capital: Bissau
Population: 1,759,000
Area: 13,946 sq. mi. (36,120 sq km)
Language: Portuguese, Creole, French, others
Money: West African CFA franc
Government: Republic

GUYANA

Capital: Georgetown
Population: 736,000
Area: 83,000 sq. mi. (214,970 sq km)
Language: English, Guyanese, Creole
Money: Dollar
Government: Republic

More than one-half of Guatemalans are descended from the Maya. The Mayan Indian civilization developed a calendar with a 365-day year, among many other achievements.

HAITI

Capital: Port-au-Prince
Population: 10,228,000
Area: 10,714 sq. mi. (27,750 sq km)
Language: French, Creole
Money: Gourde
Government: Republic

THE HOLY SEE
(VATICAN CITY)

Capital: Vatican City
Population: 842*
Area: 0.17 sq. mi.
(0.44 sq km)
Language: Italian, Latin,
French, various others
Money: Euro
Government: Ecclesiastical

*2014 estimate, *CIA World Factbook*

HONDURAS

Capital: Tegucigalpa
Population: 8,893,000
Area: 43,278 sq. mi.
(112,090 sq km)
Language: Spanish,
Amerindian dialects
Money: Lempira
Government: Democratic
constitutional republic

HUNGARY

Capital: Budapest
Population: 9,875,000
Area: 35,919 sq. mi.
(93,030 sq km)
Language: Hungarian
Money: Forint
Government: Parliamentary
democracy

ICELAND

Capital: Reykjavik
Population: 321,000
Area: 39,769 sq. mi.
(103,000 sq km)
Language: Icelandic
Money: Krona
Government:
Constitutional republic

INDIA

Capital: New Delhi
Population: 1,266,884,000
Area: 1,269,346 sq. mi.
(3,287,590 sq km)
Language: Hindi, English, 21 others
Money: Rupee
Government: Federal republic

Holi, the Hindu Festival of Colors,
is celebrated every March in
India and other places. Squirting
colored water on friends is a
popular activity.

INDONESIA

Capital: Jakarta
Population: 258,316,000
Area: 741,100 sq. mi.
(1,919,440 sq km)
Language: Bahasa Indonesia,
English, Dutch, Javanese
Money: Rupiah
Government: Republic

IRAN

Capital: Tehran
Population: 82,802,000
Area: 636,296 sq. mi.
(1,648,000 sq km)
Language: Persian, Turkic,
Kurdish, Arabic, others
Money: Rial
Government: Islamic republic

IRAQ

Capital: Baghdad
Population: 34,032,000
Area: 168,754 sq. mi.
(437,072 sq km)
Language: Arabic, Kurdish,
Turkoman, Assyrian, Armenian
Money: Dinar
Government: Parliamentary
democracy

IRELAND

Capital: Dublin
Population: 4,952,000
Area: 27,135 sq. mi. (70,280 sq km)
Language: English, Gaelic
Money: Euro
Government: Parliamentary
republic

ISRAEL

Capital: Jerusalem
Population: 8,047,000
Area: 8,019 sq. mi. (20,770 sq km)
Language: Hebrew, Arabic,
English
Money: New shekel
Government: Republic

Engineers successfully
stopped Italy's famous Leaning
Tower of Pisa from collapsing
through a 3-year construction
project completed in 2001.

ITALY

Capital: Rome
Population: 62,008,000
Area: 116,306 sq. mi.
(301,230 sq km)
Language: Italian, German,
French, Slovene
Money: Euro
Government: Republic

JAMAICA

Capital: Kingston
Population: 2,970,000
Area: 4,244 sq. mi. (10,991 sq km)
Language: English, English patois
Money: Dollar
Government: Constitutional
monarchy with parliamentary
system

JAPAN

Capital: Tokyo
Population: 126,702,000
Area: 145,883 sq. mi. (337,835 sq km)
Language: Japanese
Money: Yen
Government: Constitutional
monarchy with parliamentary
democracy

JORDAN

Capital: Amman
Population: 6,744,000
Area: 35,637 sq. mi. (92,300 sq km)
Language: Arabic, English
Money: Dinar
Government: Constitutional monarchy

KAZAKHSTAN

Capital: Astana
Population: 18,360,000
Area: 1,049,155 sq. mi. (2,717,300 sq km)
Language: Kazakh, Russian, German
Money: Tenge
Government: Republic

KENYA

Capital: Nairobi
Population: 46,791,000
Area: 224,962 sq. mi. (582,650 sq km)
Language: Kiswahili, English, numerous indigenous languages
Money: Shilling
Government: Republic

KIRIBATI

Capital: Tawara
Population: 107,000
Area: 313 sq. mi. (811 sq km)
Language: English, I-Kiribati
Money: Dollar
Government: Republic

Hunting with birds of prey such as eagles and falcons is a tradition in Kazakhstan that goes back to the time of the warrior known as Genghis Khan.

NORTH KOREA

Capital: Pyongyang
Population: 25,115,000
Area: 46,541 sq. mi. (120,540 sq km)
Language: Korean
Money: Won
Government: Communist state

SOUTH KOREA

Capital: Seoul
Population: 49,181,000
Area: 38,023 sq. mi. (98,480 sq km)
Language: Korean, English
Money: Won
Government: Republic

KOSOVO

Capital: Pristina
Population: 1,883,000
Area: 4,203 sq. mi.
(10,887 sq km)
Language: Albanian, Serbian,
Bosnian, Turkish, Roma
Money: Euro
Government: Republic

KUWAIT

Capital: Kuwait City
Population: 2,833,000
Area: 6,880 sq. mi. (17,820 sq km)
Language: Arabic, English
Money: Dinar
Government: Constitutional
emirate

KYRGYZSTAN

Capital: Bishkek
Population: 5,728,000
Area: 76,641 sq. mi.
(198,500 sq km)
Language: Kyrgyz, Russian, Uzbek
Money: Som
Government: Republic

LAOS

Capital: Vientiane
Population: 7,019,000
Area: 91,429 sq. mi.
(236,800 sq km)
Language: Lao, French,
English, other ethnic languages
Money: Kip
Government: Communist state

LATVIA

Capital: Riga
Population: 2,138,000
Area: 24,938 sq. mi.
(64,589 sq km)
Language: Latvian,
Lithuanian, Russian
Money: Euro
Government: Parliamentary
democracy

LEBANON

Capital: Beirut
Population: 4,170,000
Area: 4,015 sq. mi.
(10,400 sq km)
Language: Arabic, English,
French, Armenian
Money: Pound
Government: Republic

Elephants and
tigers must cope
with threats
from expanding
development along
the Mekong River,
the longest river in
Southeast Asia. It
runs through parts
of six countries,
including Laos.

LESOTHO

Capital: Maseru
Population: 1,953,000
Area: 11,720 sq. mi.
(30,355 sq km)
Language: Sesotho,
English, Zulu, Xhosa
Money: Loti
Government:
Parliamentary constitutional
monarchy

LIBERIA

Capital: Monrovia
Population: 4,300,000
Area: 43,000 sq. mi. (111,370 sq km)
Language: English, about 20 ethnic languages
Money: Dollar
Government: Republic

LIBYA

Capital: Tripoli
Population: 6,542,000
Area: 679,362 sq. mi. (1,759,540 sq km)
Language: Arabic, Italian, English
Money: Dinar
Government: In transition

LIECHTENSTEIN

Capital: Vaduz
Population: 38,000
Area: 62 sq. mi. (160 sq km)
Language: German, Alemannic dialect
Money: Swiss franc
Government: Constitutional monarchy

LITHUANIA

Capital: Vilnius
Population: 3,484,000
Area: 25,212 sq. mi. (65,300 sq km)
Language: Lithuanian, Russian, Polish
Money: Euro
Government: Parliamentary democracy

Madagascar is the world's fourth-largest island, after Greenland, New Guinea, and Borneo. It is home to a huge variety of unique plants and animals that evolved 165 million years ago. Recently, scientists discovered in a cave the remains of extinct lemurs the size of gorillas.

LUXEMBOURG

Capital: Luxembourg
Population: 532,000
Area: 998 sq. mi. (2,586 sq km)
Language: Luxembourgish, German, French
Money: Euro
Government: Constitutional monarchy

MACEDONIA

Capital: Skopje
Population: 2,100,000
Area: 9,781 sq. mi. (25,333 sq km)
Language: Macedonian, Albanian, Turkish
Money: Denar
Government: Parliamentary democracy

MADAGASCAR

Capital: Antananarivo
Population: 24,430,000
Area: 226,657 sq. mi.
(587,040 sq km)
Language: Malagasy, English, French
Money: Ariary
Government: Republic

MALAWI

Capital: Lilongwe
Population: 18,197,000
Area: 45,745 sq. mi. (118,480 sq km)
Language: Chichewa, Chinyan'ji, Chiyao, Chitumbka
Money: Kwacha
Government: Multiparty democracy

MALAYSIA

Capital: Kuala Lumpur
Population: 30,950,000
Area: 127,317 sq. mi. (329,750 sq km)
Language: Bahasa Malaysia, English, Chinese dialects, Panjabi, Thai
Money: Ringgit
Government: Constitutional monarchy

MALDIVES

Capital: Male
Population: 393,000
Area: 116 sq. mi. (300 sq km)
Language: Maldivian Dhivehi, English
Money: Rufiyaa
Government: Republic

MALI

Capital: Bamako
Population: 17,467,000
Area: 478,767 sq. mi.
(1,240,000 sq km)
Language: French, Bambara, numerous African languages
Money: Western African CFA franc
Government: Republic

MALTA

Capital: Valletta
Population: 415,000
Area: 122 sq. mi. (316 sq km)
Language: Maltese, English
Money: Euro
Government: Republic

MARSHALL ISLANDS

Capital: Majuro
Population: 73,000
Area: 70 sq. mi. (181 sq km)
Language: Marshallese, English
Money: US dollar
Government: Constitutional government in free association with the United States

MAURITANIA

Capital: Nouakchott
Population: 3,677,000
Area: 397,955 sq. mi. (1,030,700 sq km)
Language: Arabic, Pulaar, Soninke, Wolof, French
Money: Ouguiya
Government: Military junta

Mexico has dozens of bullfighting rings, including one that holds almost 42,000 people—about the entire population of Biloxi, Mississippi. In 2013, Sonora became the first Mexican state to ban bullfighting.

MAURITIUS

Capital: Port Louis
Population: 1,348,000
Area: 788 sq. mi. (2,040 sq km)
Language: Creole, Bhojpuri, French
Money: Rupee
Government: Parliamentary democracy

MEXICO

Capital: Mexico City
Population: 123,167,000
Area: 761,606 sq. mi. (1,972,550 sq km)
Language: Spanish, various Mayan, Nahuati, other regional indigenous dialects
Money: Peso
Government: Federal republic

MICRONESIA

Capital: Palikir
Population: 105,000
Area: 271 sq. mi. (702 sq km)
Language: English, Chuukese, Kosrean, Pohnpeian, Yapese
Money: US dollar
Government: Constitutional government in free association with the United States

MOLDOVA

Capital: Chisinau
Population: 3,510,000
Area: 13,067 sq. mi. (333,843 sq km)
Language: Moldovan, Russian, Gagauz
Money: Leu
Government: Republic

MONACO

Capital: Monaco
Population: 31,000
Area: 0.75 sq. mi. (1.95 sq km)
Language: French, English,
Italian, Monegasque
Money: Euro
Government: Constitutional
monarchy

MONGOLIA

Capital: Ulan Bator
Population: 3,031,000
Area: 603,909 sq. mi.
(1,564,116 sq km)
Language: Khalka Mongol,
Turkic, Russian
Money: Togrog/Tughrik
Government: Mixed
parliamentary/presidential

Morocco is a North African country about the size of California. Part of it is covered by the Sahara Desert, whose 3,500,000 square miles (9,064,958 sq km) make it the largest nonpolar desert in the world.

MONTENEGRO

Capital: Podgorica
Population: 645,000
Area: 5,415 sq. mi. (14,026 sq km)
Language: Montenegrin, Serbian,
Bosnian, Albanian, Croatian
Money: Euro
Government: Republic

MOROCCO

Capital: Rabat
Population: 33,656,000
Area: 172,414 sq. mi.
(446,550 sq km)
Language: Arabic, Berber
dialects, French
Money: Dirham
Government: Constitutional
monarchy

MOZAMBIQUE

Capital: Maputo
Population: 25,930,000
Area: 309,496 sq. mi.
(801,590 sq km)
Language: Portuguese,
Emakhuwa, Xichangana, Elomwe,
Cisena
Money: Metical
Government: Republic

NAMIBIA

Capital: Windhoek
Population: 2,225,000
Area: 318,696 sq. mi.
(825,418 sq km)
Language: Afrikaans, German,
English, other indigenous
languages
Money: Dollar, South African rand
Government: Republic

NAURU

Capital: Yaren
Population: 10,000
Area: 8 sq. mi. (21 sq km)
Language: Nauruan, English
Money: Australian dollar
Government: Republic

NEPAL

Capital: Kathmandu
Population: 32,111,000
Area: 56,827 sq. mi.
(147,181 sq km)
Language: Nepali, Maithili,
English
Money: Rupee
Government: Federal
democratic republic

NETHERLANDS

Capital: Amsterdam
Population: 17,017,000
Area: 16,033 sq. mi. (41,526 sq km)
Language: Dutch, Frisian
Money: Euro
Government: Constitutional
monarchy

NEW ZEALAND

Capital: Wellington
Population: 4,475,000
Area: 103,738 sq. mi.
(268,680 sq km)
Language: English, Maori, sign
language
Money: Dollar
Government: Parliamentary
democracy

NICARAGUA

Capital: Managua
Population: 5,967,000
Area: 49,998 sq. mi.
(129,494 sq km)
Language: Spanish, English,
indigenous languages on Atlantic
coast
Money: Gold cordoba
Government: Republic

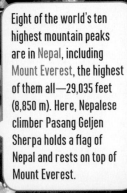

Eight of the world's ten highest mountain peaks are in Nepal, including Mount Everest, the highest of them all—29,035 feet (8,850 m). Here, Nepalese climber Pasang Geljen Sherpa holds a flag of Nepal and rests on top of Mount Everest.

NIGER

Capital: Niamey
Population: 18,639,000
Area: 489,191 sq. mi.
(1,267,000 sq km)
Language: French, Hausa,
Djerma
Money: West African CFA franc
Government: Republic

NIGERIA

Capital: Abuja
Population: 186,053,000
Area: 356,669 sq. mi.
(923,768 sq km)
Language: English, Hausa,
Yoruba, Igbo, Fulani
Money: Naira
Government: Federal republic

NORWAY

Capital: Oslo
Population: 5,265,000
Area: 125,021 sq. mi.
(323,802 sq km)
Language: Bokmal Norwegian,
Nynorsk Norwegian, Sami
Money: Krone
Government: Constitutional
monarchy

OMAN

Capital: Muscat
Population: 3,355,000
Area: 82,031 sq. mi.
(212,460 sq km)
Language: Arabic, English,
Baluchi, Urdu, Indian dialects
Money: Rial
Government: Monarchy

Moving glaciers during the
Ice Age left Norway with a
jagged coastline marked by
long strips of water-filled
fjords and thousands of
islands.

PALAU

Capital: Melekeok
Population: 21,000
Area: 177 sq. mi. (458 sq km)
Language: English, Palauan,
various Asian languages
Money: US dollar
Government: Constitutional
government in free association
with the United States

PAKISTAN

Capital: Islamabad
Population: 201,996,000
Area: 310,403 sq. mi.
(803,940 sq km)
Language: English, Urdu,
Punjabi, Sindhi, Siraiki, Pashtu
Money: Rupee
Government: Federal republic

PANAMA

Capital: Panama City
Population: 3,705,000
Area: 30,193 sq. mi. (78,200 sq km)
Language: Spanish, English
Money: Balboa
Government: Constitutional democracy

PAPUA NEW GUINEA

Capital: Port Moresby
Population: 6,791,000
Area: 178,704 sq. mi. (462,840 sq km)
Language: Melanesian Pidgin, English, 820 indigenous languages
Money: Kina
Government: Constitutional parliamentary democracy

PARAGUAY

Capital: Asuncíon
Population: 6,863,000
Area: 157,047 sq. mi. (406,750 sq km)
Language: Spanish, Guarani
Money: Guarani
Government: Constitutional republic

Spain was the first country to think of cutting a canal across the Isthmus of Panama. The French started building the 51-mile-long (82 km) canal in 1881 and the United States finished it in 1914.

PERU

Capital: Lima
Population: 30,741,000
Area: 496,226 sq. mi. (1,285,220 sq km)
Language: Spanish, Quechua, Aymara, numerous minor languages
Money: Nuevo sol
Government: Constitutional republic

PHILIPPINES

Capital: Manila
Population: 111,563,000
Area: 115,831 sq. mi. (300,000 sq km)
Language: Filipino, English, 8 major dialects
Money: Peso
Government: Republic

POLAND

Capital: Warsaw
Population: 38,250,000
Area: 120,726 sq. mi. (312,679 sq km)
Language: Polish
Money: Zloty
Government: Republic

PORTUGAL

Capital: Lisbon
Population: 10,834,000
Area: 35,672 sq. mi. (92,391 sq km)
Language: Portuguese, Mirandese
Money: Euro
Government: Republic, parliamentary democracy

QATAR

Capital: Doha
Population: 2,258,000
Area: 4,416 sq. mi. (11,437 sq km)
Language: Arabic, English
Money: Riyal
Government: Emirate

ROMANIA

Capital: Bucharest
Population: 21,600,000
Area: 91,699 sq. mi. (237,500 sq km)
Language: Romanian, Hungarian, Romany (Gypsy)
Money: New leu
Government: Republic

RUSSIA

Capital: Moscow
Population: 142,355,000
Area: 6,592,772 sq. mi. (17,075,200 sq km)
Language: Russian, many minority languages
Money: Ruble
Government: Federation

RWANDA

Capital: Kigali
Population: 12,988,000
Area: 10,169 sq. mi. (26,338 sq km)
Language: Kinyarwanda, French, English, Swahili
Money: Franc
Government: Republic, presidential-multiparty system

SAINT KITTS and NEVIS

Capital: Basseterre
Population: 52,000
Area: 101 sq. mi. (261 sq km)
Language: English
Money: Dollar
Government: Parliamentary democracy

Cruel 15th-century Romanian prince Vlad Tepes was the model for the horror novel *Dracula*. One of Vlad's homes, Bran Castle, is Romania's most popular tourist attraction.

SAINT LUCIA

Capital: Castries
Population: 164,000
Area: 238 sq. mi. (616 sq km)
Language: English, French patois
Money: Dollar
Government: Parliamentary democracy

SAINT VINCENT and the GRENADINES

Capital: Kingstown
Population: 102,000
Area: 150 sq. mi. (389 sq km)
Language: English, French patois
Money: Dollar
Government: Parliamentary democracy

SAMOA

Capital: Apia
Population: 199,000
Area: 1,137 sq. mi. (2,944 sq km)
Language: Samoan, English
Money: Tala
Government: Parliamentary democracy

SAN MARINO

Capital: San Marino
Population: 33,000
Area: 24 sq. mi. (61 sq km)
Language: Italian
Money: Euro
Government: Republic

SÃO TOMÉ and PRINCIPE

Capital: São Tomé
Population: 198,000
Area: 387 sq. mi. (1,001 sq km)
Language: Portuguese
Money: Dobra
Government: Republic

SAUDI ARABIA

Capital: Riyadh
Population: 28,160,000
Area: 830,000 sq. mi. (2,149,690 sq km)
Language: Arabic
Money: Riyal
Government: Monarchy

Muslim pilgrims from around the world pray together in Mecca, Saudi Arabia.

SENEGAL

Capital: Dakar
Population: 14,320,000
Area: 75,749 sq. mi. (196,190 sq km)
Language: French, Wolof, Pulaar, Jola, Mandinka
Money: West African CFA Franc
Government: Republic

SERBIA

Capital: Belgrade
Population: 7,144,000
Area: 29,913 sq. mi. (77,474 sq km)
Language: Serbian, Hungarian
Money: Dinar
Government: Republic

SEYCHELLES

Capital: Victoria
Population: 93,000
Area: 176 sq. mi. (455 sq km)
Language: Creole, English
Money: Rupee
Government: Republic

From the early 1500s to the 1700s, Seychelles was a popular pirate hideout. Some say the pirate Olivier Levasseur left a treasure worth over $160,000, which still remains hidden.

SIERRA LEONE

Capital: Freetown
Population: 6,019,000
Area: 27,699 sq. mi. (71,740 sq km)
Language: English, Mende and Temne vernaculars, Krio (English-based Creole)
Money: Leone
Government: Constitutional democracy

SINGAPORE

Capital: Singapore
Population: 5,782,000
Area: 269 sq. mi. (697 sq km)
Language: Mandarin, English, Malay, Hokkien, Cantonese, Tenchew
Money: Dollar
Government: Republic

SLOVAKIA

Capital: Bratislava
Population: 5,498,000
Area: 18,859 sq. mi. (48,845 sq km)
Language: Slovak, Hungarian
Money: Euro
Government: Parliamentary democracy

SLOVENIA

Capital: Ljubljana
Population: 1,978,000
Area: 7,827 sq. mi. (20,273 sq km)
Language: Slovenian, Serbo-Croatian
Money: Euro
Government: Parliamentary democracy

SOLOMON ISLANDS

Capital: Honiara
Population: 635,000
Area: 10,985 sq. mi. (28,450 sq km)
Language: English, Melanesian pidgin, 120 indigenous languages
Money: Dollar
Government: Parliamentary democracy

SOMALIA

Capital: Mogadishu
Population: 10,817,000
Area: 246,201 sq. mi. (637,657 sq km)
Language: English, Arabic, Italian
Money: Shilling
Government: In process of building a federal parliamentary republic

The area around Dyer Island, South Africa, is known as the best place in the world to see great white sharks in their natural habitat.

SOUTH AFRICA

Capital: Pretoria (administrative), Cape Town (legislative), Bloemfontein (judicial)
Population: 48,339,000
Area: 471,011 sq. mi. (1,219,912 sq km)
Language: IsiZulu, IsiXhosa, Afrikaans, English, Sepedi, Setswana, Sesotho
Money: Rand
Government: Republic

SOUTH SUDAN

Capital: Juba
Population: 12,531,000
Area: 248,777 sq. mi. (644,329 sq km)
Language: English, Arabic, Dinka, Nuer, Bari, Zande, Shilluk
Money: South Sudanese pound
Government: Republic

SPAIN

Capital: Madrid
Population: 48,563,000
Area: 194,897 sq. mi. (504,782 sq km)
Language: Castilian Spanish, Catalan, Galician, Basque
Money: Euro
Government: Parliamentary monarchy

SRI LANKA

Capital: Colombo
Population: 22,235,000
Area: 25,332 sq. mi.
(65,610 sq km)
Language: Sinhala, Tamil,
English
Money: Rupee
Government: Republic

SUDAN

Capital: Khartoum
Population: 36,730,000
Area: 718,723 sq. mi.
(1,861,484 sq km)
Language: Arabic, Nubian, Ta
Bedawie, Nilotic, Nilo-Hamitic,
Sudanic dialects, English
Money: Pound
Government: Military-backed
interim regime

SURINAME

Capital: Paramaribo
Population: 586,000
Area: 63,039 sq. mi. (163,270 sq km)
Language: Dutch, English, Sranan
Tongo, Caribbean Hindustani,
Javanese
Money: Dollar
Government: Constitutional
democracy

Sri Lanka is the third-
largest exporter of tea in
the world, behind Kenya
and China. The tea is still
called Ceylon although the
country was renamed Sri
Lanka in 1972.

SWAZILAND

Capital: Lobamba, Mbabane
Population: 1,451,000
Area: 6,704 sq. mi.
(17,363 sq km)
Language: English, siSwati
Money: Lilangeni
Government: Monarchy

SWEDEN

Capital: Stockholm
Population: 9,881,000
Area: 173,732 sq. mi.
(449,964 sq km)
Language: Swedish, Finnish,
Sami
Money: Krona
Government: Constitutional
monarchy

SWITZERLAND

Capital: Bern
Population: 8,179,000
Area: 15,942 sq. mi.
(41,290 sq km)
Language: German, French,
Italian, Romansch
Money: Franc
Government: Federal
republic—like confederation

SYRIA

Capital: Damascus
Population: 23,465,000
Area: 71,498 sq. mi.
(185,180 sq km)
Language: Arabic, Kurdish,
Armenian, Aramaic,
Circassian
Money: Pound
Government: Republic
(under military regime)

TAIWAN

Capital: Taipei
Population: 23,465,000
Area: 13,892 sq. mi. (35,980 sq km)
Language: Mandarin, Taiwanese, Hakka
Money: Dollar (yuan)
Government: Multiparty democracy

TAJIKISTAN

Capital: Dushanbe
Population: 8,331,000
Area: 55,251 sq. mi. (143,100 sq km)
Language: Tajik, Russian
Money: Somoni
Government: Republic

TANZANIA

Capital: Dodoma
Population: 52,483,000
Area: 364,900 sq. mi. (945,087 sq km)
Language: Kiswahili, English, Arabic, many local languages
Money: Shilling
Government: Republic

The rushing waters of Thailand's Mae Taeng River make it popular for white-water rafting.

THAILAND

Capital: Bangkok
Population: 68,201,000
Area: 198,457 sq. mi. (514,000 sq km)
Language: Thai, English, other ethnic languages
Money: Baht
Government: Constitutional monarchy

TIMOR-LESTE

Capital: Dili
Population: 1,261,000
Area: 5,794 sq. mi. (15,007 sq km)
Language: Tetum, Portuguese, Indonesian, English
Money: US dollar
Government: Republic

TOGO

Capital: Lomé
Population: 7,757,000
Area: 21,925 sq. mi. (56,785 sq km)
Language: French, Ewe, Mina, Kabye, Dagomba
Money: West African CFA franc
Government: Republic (under transition to multiparty democratic rule)

> Every *Star Wars* movie but one was filmed in Tunisia. So was *Indiana Jones: Raiders of the Lost Ark.*

TRINIDAD and TOBAGO

Capital: Port of Spain
Population: 1,220,000
Area: 1,980 sq. mi. (5,128 sq km)
Language: English, Caribbean Hindustani, French, Spanish, Chinese
Money: Dollar
Government: Parliamentary democracy

TONGA

Capital: Nuku'alofa
Population: 107,000
Area: 289 sq. mi. (748 sq km)
Language: Tongan, English
Money: Pa'anga
Government: Constitutional monarchy

TUNISIA

Capital: Tunis
Population: 11,135,000
Area: 63,170 sq. mi. (163,610 sq km)
Language: Arabic, French
Money: Dinar
Government: Republic

TURKEY

Capital: Ankara
Population: 83,407,000
Area: 301,384 sq. mi. (780,580 sq km)
Language: Turkish, Kurdish, Dimli
Money: New lira
Government: Republican parliamentary democracy

TURKMENISTAN

Capital: Ashgabat
Population: 5,291,000
Area: 188,456 sq. mi. (488,100 sq km)
Language: Turkmen, Russian, Uzbek
Money: Manat
Government: Republic under authoritarian presidential rule

TUVALU

Capital: Funafuti
Population: 11,000
Area: 10 sq. mi. (26 sq km)
Language: Tuvaluan, English, Samoan
Money: Australian dollar
Government: Constitutional monarchy with parliamentary democracy

In September 2014, scientists discovered monuments and other buildings buried under 4,000-year-old Stonehenge in Wiltshire, England, United Kingdom.

UGANDA

Capital: Kampala
Population: 38,319,000
Area: 91,136 sq. mi.
(236,040 sq km)
Language: English, Ganda, Luganda
Money: Shilling
Government: Republic

UKRAINE

Capital: Kyiv (Kiev)
Population: 43,724,000
Area: 233,090 sq. mi.
(603,700 sq km)
Language: Ukrainian, Russian, Romanian, Polish, Hungarian
Money: Hryvnia
Government: Republic

UNITED ARAB EMIRATES

Capital: Abu Dhabi
Population: 5,927,000
Area: 32,278 sq. mi.
(83,600 sq km)
Language: Arabic, Persian, English, Hindi, Urdu
Money: Dirham
Government: Federation of emirates

UNITED KINGDOM

Capital: London
Population: 64,430,000
Area: 94,526 sq. mi.
(244,820 sq km)
Language: English, Welsh, Scottish form of Gaelic
Money: Pound
Government: Constitutional monarchy

UNITED STATES

Capital: Washington, DC
Population: 323,849,000
Area: 3,794,083 sq. mi.
(9,826,630 sq km)
Language: English, Spanish, Hawaiian, other minority languages
Money: Dollar
Government: Federal republic with strong democratic tradition

URUGUAY

Capital: Montevideo
Population: 3,351,000
Area: 68,039 sq. mi. (176,220 sq km)
Language: Spanish, Portunol, Brazilero
Money: Peso
Government: Constitutional republic

UZBEKISTAN

Capital: Tashkent
Population: 29,474,000
Area: 172,742 sq. mi.
(447,400 sq km)
Language: Uzbek, Russian, Tajik
Money: Som
Government: Republic with authoritarian presidential rule

VANUATU

Capital: Port Vila
Population: 278,000
Area: 4,710 sq. mi. (12,200 sq km)
Language: Bislama, English, French, 100 local languages
Money: Vatu
Government: Parliamentary republic

VENEZUELA

Capital: Caracas
Population: 29,680,000
Area: 352,144 sq. mi. (912,050 sq km)
Language: Spanish, indigenous dialects
Money: Bolivar Fuerte
Government: Federal republic

VIETNAM

Capital: Hanoi
Population: 95,261,000
Area: 127,244 sq. mi. (329,560 sq km)
Language: Vietnamese, English, French, Chinese, Khmer
Money: Dong
Government: Communist state

YEMEN

Capital: Sana'a
Population: 27,393,000
Area: 203,850 sq. mi. (527,970 sq km)
Language: Arabic
Money: Rial
Government: Republic

ZAMBIA

Capital: Lusaka
Population: 15,511,000
Area: 290,586 sq. mi. (752,614 sq km)
Language: English, numerous vernaculars
Money: Kwacha
Government: Republic

ZIMBABWE

Capital: Harare
Population: 14,547,000
Area: 150,804 sq. mi. (390,580 sq km)
Language: English, Shona, Sindebele, minor tribal dialects
Money: Dollar
Government: Parliamentary democracy

According to legend, coffee was discovered by a goat herder who noticed his goats got livelier after eating berries from a certain plant. The plant was brought to Yemen, where it was developed into a drink.

Alaska became our 49th state on January 3, 1959, but the first bill for statehood went to Congress one hundred years ago, in 1916. At twice the size of Texas, it is our largest state by far. At the same time, Alaska has the third-lowest population, so there is plenty of room for people to spread out.

There's plenty of room for animals, too. Over 1,000 vertebrate species live here, including moose, black bears, and huge herds of caribou. Fourteen species of whales inhabit Alaska's waters. Millions and millions of birds either inhabit year-round or pass through during migration.

Among the birds is the largest concentration of American bald eagles in the country. Officials say there are about 30,000 bald eagles in Alaska. Thousands of pairs nest along the coastline in southeastern Alaska, where Juneau, the state capital, is located. In the 1960s, bald eagles were almost extinct from pesticides and loss of habitat. Because of laws passed to protect our national bird, the bald eagle has come back. It was removed from the Endangered Species List in 2007.

FLAGS & FACTS
STATES OF THE UNITED STATES

There are no roads into Juneau, Alaska's capital. Visitors come by boat or plane, many to admire wildlife that includes thousands of American bald eagles. The bald eagle has been a symbol of the United States since 1782. Read about Alaska and the other states starting on p. 318.

ALASKA

Mt Mckinley
(20,237 ft.)
• Fairbanks
Anchorage
Juneau

Alaska

Juneau

Olympia
Washington

Salem

Oregon

Montana
Helena

Idaho
Boise

North Dakota
Bismarck

South Dakota
Pierre

Wyoming

Cheyenne

Nebraska
Lincoln

Sacramento Carson City

Nevada

Salt Lake City

Utah

Denver

Colorado

Topeka

Kansas

California

Arizona

Phoenix

Santa Fe

New Mexico

Oklahoma
Oklahoma City

Texas

Austin

Honolulu

Hawaii

US States and Their Capital Cities

nnesota

St. Paul

Wisconsin

Madison

Iowa

Des Moines

Illinois

Springfield

Jefferson City

Missouri

Arkansas

Little Rock

Louisiana

Baton Rouge

Michigan

Lansing

Indiana

Indianapolis

Kentucky

Frankfort

Tennessee

Nashville

Mississippi

Jackson

Alabama

Montgomery

Ohio

Columbus

West Virginia

Charleston

Atlanta

Georgia

Tallahassee

Florida

New Hampshire

Vermont

Montpelier

Maine

Augusta

Concord

Massachusetts

Boston

Albany

New York

Providence

Rhode Island

Hartford

Connecticut

Pennsylvania

Harrisburg

Trenton

New Jersey

Dover

Delaware

Annapolis

Maryland

Washington, DC

Richmond

Virginia

Raleigh

North Carolina

Columbia

South Carolina

State Quarters by Release Date (and Statehood Dates)

■ Release Date   ■ Statehood Date

Delaware
January 4, 1999
December 7, 1787

Pennsylvania
March 8, 1999
December 12, 1787

New Jersey
May 17, 1999
December 18, 1787

Georgia
July 19, 1999
January 2, 1788

Connecticut
October 12, 1999
January 9, 1788

Massachusetts
January 3, 2000
February 6, 1788

Maryland
March 13, 2000
April 28, 1788

South Carolina
May 22, 2000
May 23, 1788

New Hampshire
August 7, 2000
June 21, 1788

Virginia
October 16, 2000
June 25, 1788

New York
January 2, 2001
July 26, 1788

North Carolina
March 12, 2001
November 21, 1789

Rhode Island
May 21, 2001
May 29, 1790

Vermont
August 6, 2001
March 4, 1791

Kentucky
October 15, 2001
June 1, 1792

Tennessee
January 2, 2002
June 1, 1796

Ohio
March 11, 2002
March 1, 1803

Louisiana
May 20, 2002
April 30, 1812

Indiana
August 2, 2002
December 11, 1816

Mississippi
October 15, 2002
December 10, 1817

Illinois
January 2, 2003
December 3, 1818

Alabama
March 17, 2003
December 14, 1819

Maine
June 2, 2003
March 15, 1820

Missouri
August 4, 2003
August 10, 1821

Arkansas
October 20, 2003
June 15, 1836

■ Release Date　　**■ Statehood Date**

Michigan
January 26, 2004
January 26, 1837

Florida
March 29, 2004
March 3, 1845

Texas
June 1, 2004
December 29, 1845

Iowa
August 30, 2004
December 28, 1846

Wisconsin
October 25, 2004
May 29, 1848

California
January 31, 2005
September 9, 1850

Minnesota
April 4, 2005
May 11, 1858

Oregon
June 6, 2005
February 14, 1859

Kansas
August 29, 2005
January 29, 1861

West Virginia
October 14, 2005
June 20, 1863

Nevada
January 31, 2006
October 31, 1864

Nebraska
April 3, 2006
March 1, 1867

Colorado
June 14, 2006
August 1, 1876

North Dakota
August 28, 2006
November 2, 1889

South Dakota
November 6, 2006
November 2, 1889

Montana
January 29, 2007
November 8, 1889

Washington
April 2, 2007
November 11, 1889

Idaho
June 4, 2007
July 3, 1890

Wyoming
September 3, 2007
July 10, 1890

Utah
November 5, 2007
January 4, 1896

Oklahoma
January 28, 2008
November 16, 1907

New Mexico
April 7, 2008
January 6, 1912

Arizona
June 2, 2008
February 14, 1912

Alaska
August 25, 2008
January 3, 1959

Hawaii
November 3, 2008
August 21, 1959

ALABAMA

Capital: Montgomery
Postal Code: AL
Nickname: Heart of Dixie
Flower: Camellia
Bird: Yellowhammer
Area: 52,420 sq. mi. (135,768 sq km)
Population: 4,849,377

Huntsville, Alabama, is the site where the first rocket that took people to the Moon was built.

ALASKA

Capital: Juneau
Postal Code: AK
Nickname: Last Frontier
Flower: Forget-me-not
Bird: Willow ptarmigan
Area: 664,988 sq. mi. (1,722,319 sq km)
Population: 736,732

Woolly mammoth remains have been found in the state's frozen ground.

ARIZONA

Capital: Phoenix
Postal Code: AZ
Nickname: Grand Canyon State
Flower: Saguaro cactus blossom
Bird: Cactus wren
Area: 113,990 sq. mi. (295,235 sq km)
Population: 6,731,484

There are more species of hummingbirds in Arizona than in any other state.

ARKANSAS

Capital: Little Rock
Postal Code: AR
Nickname: Land of Opportunity
Flower: Apple blossom
Bird: Mockingbird
Area: 53,178 sq. mi. (137,732 sq km)
Population: 2,966,369

Stuttgart, Arkansas, is home to the annual World's Championship Duck Calling Contest.

CALIFORNIA

Capital: Sacramento
Postal Code: CA
Nickname: Golden State
Flower: Golden poppy
Bird: California quail
Area: 163,694 sq. mi. (423,967 sq km)
Population: 38,802,500

The highest and lowest points in the continental United States are in California—Mount Whitney (14,494 ft./4,418 m) and Badwater in Death Valley (282 ft./86 m below sea level).

COLORADO

Capital: Denver
Postal Code: CO
Nickname: Centennial State
Flower: Rocky Mountain columbine
Bird: Lark bunting
Area: 104,094 sq. mi. (269,604 sq km)
Population: 5,355,866

Every May, the town of Fruita, Colorado, holds a festival to celebrate Mike the Headless Chicken. It honors a chicken that lived for four years after a local farmer chopped off its head in 1945

CONNECTICUT

Capital: Hartford
Postal Code: CT
Nickname: Constitution State
Flower: Mountain laurel
Bird: American robin
Area: 5,544 sq. mi. (14,358 sq km)
Population: 3,596,677

America's first newspaper, the
Hartford Courant, was printed in 1764
in Connecticut.

DECEMBER 7, 1787

DELAWARE

Capital: Dover
Postal Code: DE
Nickname: First State
Flower: Peach blossom
Bird: Blue hen chicken
Area: 2,489 sq. mi. (6,445 sq km)
Population: 935,614

Delaware was the first state to ratify
the US Constitution.

FLORIDA

Capital: Tallahassee
Postal Code: FL
Nickname: Sunshine State
Flower: Orange blossom
Bird: Mockingbird
Area: 65,758 sq. mi. (170,312 sq km)
Population: 19,893,297

Many people think Florida is the
southernmost state, but Hawaii
is farther south. Florida's name
comes from the Spanish word for
"flowery."

GEORGIA

Capital: Atlanta
Postal Code: GA
Nickname: Empire State of the South
Flower: Cherokee rose
Bird: Brown thrasher
Area: 59,425 sq. mi. (153,911 sq km)
Population: 10,097,343

The carving of Confederate Army leaders Stonewall Jackson, Jefferson Davis, and Robert E. Lee on Stone Mountain is the largest relief sculpture in the world—even bigger than Mount Rushmore.

HAWAII

Capital: Honolulu
Postal Code: HI
Nickname: Aloha State
Flower: Yellow hibiscus
Bird: Nene, or Hawaiian goose
Land Area: 6,468 sq. mi. (16,742 sq km)
Population: 1,419,561

Hawaii is made up of 132 islands. The 8 main ones are Niihau, Kauai, Oahu, Maui, Molokai, Lanai, Kahoolawe, and the Big Island.

IDAHO

Capital: Boise
Postal Code: ID
Nickname: Gem State
Flower: Syringa
Bird: Mountain bluebird
Area: 83,568 sq. mi. (216,442 sq km)
Population: 1,634,464

The world's largest population of nesting eagles, hawks, and falcons can be found in Idaho's Snake River Birds of Prey National Conservation Area.

ILLINOIS

ILLINOIS

Capital: Springfield
Postal Code: IL
Nickname: Land of Lincoln
Flower: Native violet
Bird: Northern cardinal
Area: 57,916 sq. mi. (150,002 sq km)
Population: 12,880,580

The world's first skyscraper was built in Chicago, in 1885. The second tallest building in America is the Willis (formerly Sears) Tower in Chicago, measuring 1,729 feet (527 m) from the ground to the tip of the antenna.

INDIANA

Capital: Indianapolis
Postal Code: IN
Nickname: Hoosier State
Flower: Peony
Bird: Northern cardinal
Area: 36,417 sq. mi. (94,321 sq km)
Population: 6,596,855

The first long-distance auto race in the United States was held May 30, 1911, at the Indianapolis Motor Speedway. The winner averaged 75 miles an hour (121 kph). Today the average speed is over 167 miles an hour (269 kph). The Indianapolis 500 is held every Memorial Day weekend.

IOWA

IOWA

Capital: Des Moines
Postal Code: IA
Nickname: Hawkeye State
Flower: Wild prairie rose
Bird: Eastern goldfinch (also called American goldfinch)
Area: 56,273 sq. mi. (145,746 sq km)
Population: 3,107,126

Iowa is the only state name in America that begins with two vowels.

KANSAS

Capital: Topeka
Postal Code: KS
Nickname: Sunflower State
Flower: Native sunflower
Bird: Western meadowlark
Area: 82,278 sq. mi. (213,101 sq km)
Population: 2,904,021

A point in Smith County, Kansas, is the geographical center of the forty eight contiguous United States.

KENTUCKY

Capital: Frankfort
Postal Code: KY
Nickname: Bluegrass State
Flower: Goldenrod
Bird: Northern cardinal
Area: 40,411 sq. mi. (104,665 sq km)
Population: 4,413,457

The Kentucky Derby, held the first Saturday in May, is the oldest annual horse race in the United States.

LOUISIANA

Capital: Baton Rouge
Postal Code: LA
Nickname: Pelican State
Flower: Magnolia
Bird: Eastern brown pelican
Area: 51,988 sq. mi. (134,649 sq km)
Population: 4,649,676

The 273-foot (82.3 m) Mercedes-Benz Superdome in New Orleans is the largest fixed-dome structure in the world. It is powered by 400 miles of electrical wiring.

MAINE

Capital: Augusta
Postal Code: ME
Nickname: Pine Tree State
Flower: White pine cone and tassel
Bird: Black-capped chickadee
Area: 35,384 sq. mi. (91,644 sq km)
Population: 1,330,089

Lubec, Maine, is the first town in America to see the sunrise because it is the town farthest east.

MARYLAND

Capital: Annapolis
Postal Code: MD
Nickname: Old Line State
Flower: Black-eyed Susan
Bird: Baltimore oriole
Area: 12,406 sq. mi. (32,131 sq km)
Population: 5,976,407

Edward Warren, a 13-year-old from Baltimore, was aboard the country's first successful manned balloon launch on June 24, 1784.

MASSACHUSETTS

Capital: Boston
Postal Code: MA
Nickname: Bay State
Flower: Mayflower
Bird: Black-capped chickadee
Area: 10,554 sq. mi. (27,336 sq km)
Population: 6,745,408

Volleyball was invented in 1895 in Holyoke, Massachusetts, by gym teacher William Morgan. The game was originally called mintonette. Basketball was invented in nearby Springfield.

MICHIGAN

Capital: Lansing
Postal Code: MI
Nickname: Wolverine State
Flower: Apple blossom
Bird: American robin
Area: 96,713 sq. mi. (250,486 sq km)
Population: 9,909,877

With more than 11,000 inland lakes and 36,000 miles (57,936 km) of rivers and streams, Michigan has the longest freshwater shoreline in the world.

MINNESOTA

Capital: St. Paul
Postal Code: MN
Nickname: Gopher State
Flower: Pink and white lady's slipper
Bird: Common loon
Area: 86,935 sq. mi. (225,163 sq km)
Population: 5,457,173

The Mall of America in Bloomington, Minnesota, is 4.87 million square feet (452,437.805 sq m)—about the size of 83 football fields!

MISSISSIPPI

Capital: Jackson
Postal Code: MS
Nickname: Magnolia State
Flower: Magnolia
Bird: Mockingbird
Area: 48,432 sq. mi. (125,438 sq km)
Population: 2,994,079

A year after the Civil War, four women in the city of Columbus decided to leave flowers on the graves of both Confederate and Union soldiers in a local cemetery. Residents say this forgiving act was one inspiration for Memorial Day, on which America honors its fallen soldiers.

MISSOURI

Capital: Jefferson City
Postal Code: MO
Nickname: Show Me State
Flower: Hawthorn
Bird: Eastern bluebird
Area: 69,702 sq. mi. (180,529 sq km)
Population: 6,063,589

Some say the St. Louis World's Fair in 1904 was so hot that Richard Blechynden decided to serve his tea over ice—and invented iced tea.

MONTANA

Capital: Helena
Postal Code: MT
Nickname: Treasure State
Flower: Bitterroot
Bird: Western meadowlark
Area: 147,039 sq. mi. (380,831 sq km)
Population: 1,023,579

The average square mile (1.6 sq km) of land in Montana contains 1.4 pronghorn antelope, 1.4 elk, and 3.3 deer. Montana has the largest number of mammal species in the United States.

NEBRASKA

Capital: Lincoln
Postal Code: NE
Nickname: Cornhusker State
Flower: Goldenrod
Bird: Western meadowlark
Area: 77,349 sq. mi. (200,334 sq km)
Population: 1,881,503

Alliance, Nebraska, is famous for Carhenge, a reproduction of England's Stonehenge made from junkyard cars painted gray.

NEVADA

Capital: Carson City
Postal Code: NV
Nickname: Silver State
Flower: Sagebrush
Bird: Mountain bluebird
Area: 110,572 sq. mi. (286,382 sq km)
Population: 2,839,099

Nevada is the driest state, receiving an average of 9.5 inches (24 cm) of precipitation a year. Native animals include the kangaroo rat, which can go for a year without a drop of water.

NEW HAMPSHIRE

Capital: Concord
Postal Code: NH
Nickname: Granite State
Flower: Purple lilac
Bird: Purple finch
Area: 9,348 sq. mi. (24,210 sq km)
Population: 1,326,813

The winds on top of New Hampshire's Mount Washington have been recorded at speeds over 231 miles (372 km) an hour—the fastest winds on Earth!

NEW JERSEY

Capital: Trenton
Postal Code: NJ
Nickname: Garden State
Flower: Purple violet
Bird: Eastern goldfinch
Area: 8,723 sq. mi. (22,592 sq km)
Population: 8,938,175

The street names in the game Monopoly come from real street names in Atlantic City, New Jersey.

NEW MEXICO

Capital: Santa Fe
Postal Code: NM
Nickname: Land of Enchantment
Flower: Yucca flower
Bird: Roadrunner (also called greater roadrunner)
Area: 121,590 sq. mi. (314,919 sq km)
Population: 2,085,572

There are more than 110 caves in Carlsbad Caverns. One cave is 22 stories high and is home to tens of thousands of bats.

NEW YORK

Capital: Albany
Postal Code: NY
Nickname: Empire State
Flower: Rose
Bird: Eastern bluebird
Area: 54,555 sq. mi. (141,298 sq km)
Population: 19,746,227

More than 100 million people have visited the top of the Empire State Building in New York City. The building is 1,454 feet (443 m) from the street to the top of the lightning rod.

NORTH CAROLINA

Capital: Raleigh
Postal Code: NC
Nickname: Tar Heel State
Flower: Dogwood
Bird: Northern cardinal
Area: 53,819 sq. mi. (139,391 sq km)
Population: 9,943,964

On March 7, 1914, in Fayetteville, North Carolina, George Herman "Babe" Ruth hit his first professional home run.

NORTH DAKOTA

Capital: Bismarck
Postal Code: ND
Nickname: Flickertail State
Flower: Wild prairie rose
Bird: Western meadowlark
Area: 70,698 sq. mi. (183,109 sq km)
Population: 739,482

Jamestown, North Dakota, is home to the World's Largest Buffalo Monument. It stands 26 feet (7.9 m) high and 46 feet (14 m) long, and weighs 60 tons (54,441 kg).

OHIO

Capital: Columbus
Postal Code: OH
Nickname: Buckeye State
Flower: Scarlet carnation
Bird: Northern cardinal
Area: 44,825 sq. mi. (116,097 sq km)
Population: 11,594,163

A total of 726 musicians have been inducted into the Rock and Roll Hall of Fame in Cleveland. Ringo Starr and Green Day were among the 2015 inductees.

OKLAHOMA

Capital: Oklahoma City
Postal Code: OK
Nickname: Sooner State
Flower: Mistletoe
Bird: Scissor-tailed flycatcher
Area: 69,899 sq. mi. (181,038 sq km)
Population: 3,878,051

Oklahoma is one of only two states whose state capital includes the name of the state. (Look through this chapter to find the other one! Answer on p. 350.)

OREGON

Capital: Salem
Postal Code: OR
Nickname: Beaver State
Flower: Oregon grape
Bird: Western meadowlark
Area: 98,379 sq. mi. (254,801 sq km)
Population: 3,970,239

Two pioneers founded Portland, Oregon. One was from Boston, Massachusetts, and the other was from Portland, Maine. They couldn't decide what to name the city, so they flipped a coin. Guess who won!

PENNSYLVANIA

Capital: Harrisburg
Postal Code: PA
Nickname: Keystone State
Flower: Mountain laurel
Bird: Ruffed grouse
Area: 46,055 sq. mi. (119,281 sq km)
Population: 12,787,209

In 1953, Dr. Jonas Salk created the polio vaccine at the University of Pittsburgh.

RHODE ISLAND

Capital: Providence
Postal Code: RI
Nickname: Ocean State
Flower: Violet
Bird: Rhode Island Red chicken
Area: 1,545 sq. mi. (4,001 sq km)
Population: 1,055,173

How small is Rhode Island? The nation's smallest state could fit into California 105 times.

SOUTH CAROLINA

Capital: Columbia
Postal Code: SC
Nickname: Palmetto State
Flower: Yellow jessamine
Bird: Great Carolina wren
Area: 32,021 sq. mi. (82,934 sq km)
Population: 4,832,482

The first battle of the Civil War was fought at Fort Sumter, South Carolina.

SOUTH DAKOTA

Capital: Pierre
Postal Code: SD
Nickname: Mount Rushmore State
Flower: Pasqueflower
Bird: Ring-necked pheasant
Area: 77,116 sq. mi. (199,730 sq km)
Population: 853,175

The faces of four presidents are sculpted into Mount Rushmore. The carvings are taller than a four-story building.

TENNESSEE

Capital: Nashville
Postal Code: TN
Nickname: Volunteer State
Flower: Iris
Bird: Mockingbird
Area: 42,144 sq. mi. (109,154 sq km)
Population: 6,549,352

Nashville's *Grand Ole Opry* is the longest continuously running live radio program in the world. It's been on every Friday and Saturday night since 1925.

TEXAS

Capital: Austin
Postal Code: TX
Nickname: Lone Star State
Flower: Bluebonnet
Bird: Mockingbird
Area: 268,597 sq. mi. (695,666 sq km)
Population: 26,956,958

The name *Texas* is actually derived from a misunderstanding of *tejas*, a Caddo Indian word meaning "friend."

UTAH

Capital: Salt Lake City
Postal Code: UT
Nickname: Beehive State
Flower: Sego lily
Bird: California gull
Area: 84,897 sq. mi. (219,883 sq km)
Population: 2,942,902

Utah's Great Salt Lake is several times saltier than seawater. It's so salty that you'd float on the surface of the water if you went swimming there!

VERMONT

Capital: Montpelier
Postal Code: VT
Nickname: Green Mountain State
Flower: Red clover
Bird: Hermit thrush
Area: 9,616 sq. mi. (24,906 sq km)
Population: 626,562

Ben & Jerry's Ice Cream, whose headquarters are in Waterbury, is urging fans to help stop global warming by using only clean energy. Their motto: "If it's melted, it's ruined."

VIRGINIA

Capital: Richmond
Postal Code: VA
Nickname: Old Dominion
Flower: American dogwood
Bird: Northern cardinal
Area: 42,775 sq. mi. (110,787 sq km)
Population: 8,326,289

More US presidents come from Virginia than from any other state—George Washington, Thomas Jefferson, James Madison, James Monroe, William Henry Harrison, John Tyler, Zachary Taylor, and Woodrow Wilson.

WASHINGTON

Capital: Olympia
Postal Code: WA
Nickname: Evergreen State
Flower: Coast rhododendron
Bird: Willow goldfinch (also called American goldfinch)
Area: 71,298 sq. mi. (184,661 sq km)
Population: 7,061,530

Washington is a hotbed of volcanic activity. There are 10 volcanoes in the state, including Mount St. Helens, which erupted in 1980.

WEST VIRGINIA

Capital: Charleston
Postal Code: WV
Nickname: Mountain State
Flower: Big rhododendron
Bird: Cardinal
Area: 24,230 sq. mi. (62,755 sq km)
Population: 1,850,326

Minnie Buckingham Harper, who was appointed to the West Virginia House of Delegates in 1928, was the first African American woman to become a member of a US lawmaking body.

WISCONSIN

1848

WISCONSIN

Capital: Madison
Postal Code: WI
Nickname: Badger State
Flower: Wood violet
Bird: American robin
Area: 65,496 sq. mi. (169,636 sq km)
Population: 5,757,564

Wisconsin produces more than 25 percent of the nation's cheese, more than any other state. Up to 90 percent of Wisconsin's milk is made into cheese.

WYOMING

Capital: Cheyenne
Postal Code: WY
Nickname: Equality State
Flower: Indian paintbrush
Bird: Western meadowlark
Area: 97,812 sq. mi. (253,334 sq km)
Population: 584,153

Devils Tower in northeastern Wyoming was the first national monument. It has been considered a sacred site by Northern Plains tribes for thousands of years.

Washington, DC Our Nation's Capital

Every state has a capital, the city where all the state's official government business takes place. Our country's capital, Washington, DC, is the center for all national, or federal, business. But our nation's capital isn't located in a state. It's part of a federal district, the District of Columbia. Congress wanted the capital to be in a district, not a state, so as not to favor any one state above the others.

The city is named after our first president, George Washington, who chose its location in 1791. It became the capital in 1800. Before that, the center of the federal government was Philadelphia, Pennsylvania.

The United States Capitol

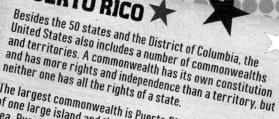

WASHINGTON, DC

Flower: American Beauty rose
Area: 68 sq. mi. (177 sq km)
Population: 658,893
Government: Federal district under the authority of Congress; mayor and city council, elected to four-year terms, run the local government

The White House, at 1600 Pennsylvania Avenue, is the official presidential residence. George Washington is the only US president who never lived there.

PUERTO RICO

Besides the 50 states and the District of Columbia, the United States also includes a number of commonwealths and territories. A commonwealth has its own constitution and has more rights and independence than a territory, but neither one has all the rights of a state.

The largest commonwealth is Puerto Rico, which is made up of one large island and three smaller ones in the Caribbean Sea. Puerto Rico was given to the United States by Spain in 1898 and became a commonwealth in 1952.

PUERTO RICO

Capital: San Juan
Land Area: 3,424 sq. mi. (8,868 sq km)
Population: 3,548,397
Language: Spanish, English
Money: US dollar
Goverment: US territory with commonwealth status

Puerto Ricans are American citizens, but they cannot vote in US presidential elections.

Other US Commonwealths and Territories

The Northern Mariana Islands in the North Pacific Ocean are the only other US commonwealth.

US territories include:

- American Samoa
- Guam
- The US Virgin Islands

The United States Minor Outlying Islands:

- Midway Islands
- Johnston Atoll
- Navassa Island
- Baker, Howland, and Jarvis Islands
- Wake Island
- Kingman Reef
- Palmyra Atoll

Index

bottom: Volt Collection/Shutterstock, Inc.; 158 top: Erwin & Peggy Bauer/U.S. Fish & Wildlife Service; 159 top left: Mike Morel/U.S. Fish & Wildlife Service; 159 top right: Adrian Pingstone/Wikimedia; 159 center left: Phyllis Cooper/U.S. Fish & Wildlife Service; 159 center right: Jeremy Richards/Thinkstock; 159 bottom: Robert Burton/U.S. Fish & Wildlife; 160 top left: Adrian Pingstone/Wikimedia; 160 top right: Courtesy Mike Bryant; 160 center: mind_killaz/iStockphoto; 160 bottom left: U.S. Fish & Wildlife Service; 160 bottom right: Bluehand/Dreamstime.com; 161 top: damnederangel/iStockphoto; 161 center: Michael Arvedlund/Wikimedia; 161 bottom: richcarey/Thinkstock; 162: photochecker/iStockphoto; 162: idreamphoto/Shutterstock, Inc.; 163 top: Adrian Pingstone/Wikimedia; 163 top right: CathyKeifer/iStockphoto; 163 bottom: arnowssr/iStockphoto; 163 center right: Ron Leighton; 163 center left: U.S. Fish and Wildlife Service; 164: davemhuntphotography/ Shutterstock, Inc.; 165 top: Ryan M. Bolton/Shutterstock, Inc.; 165 bottom: Beatrice Preve/Dreamstime; 166 top: Watje/Freeimages; 166 top right: Keith Weller/USDA; 166 bottom left: Charlie Lawrence/Freeimages; 167 right: Eric Isselée/Fotolia; 167 left & center: GlobalP/ Thinkstock; 168 top right: me/Wikimedia; 168 top left: Selvejp/Wikimedia; 168 bottom: horsemen/Shutterstock, Inc.; 169 bottom right: Ilknur Okan Erdir/ Dreamstime; 169 top left: Bethan Hazell/ Freeimages; 169 top right: Marcelo Britofilho/Freeimages; 169 bottom left: bonvivant/Freeimage; 170-171: Ammit/ Thinkstock; 172 top, 172 bottom: Ron Leighton; 174-175: Mike/Fotolia; 178 food chart: USDA; 179 right: lzf/iStockphoto; 179 center left: gbh007/iStockphoto; 179 center: ansolovei/iStockphoto; 179 left: Christopher Futcher/iStockphoto; 179 center right: Robert-Horvat/Shutterstock, Inc.; 144-145: Luis Javier Sandoval/ Getty Images; 180: Ron Leighton; 180-181: Emmanouil Pavlis/Dreamstime; 181: The OceanCleanup; 182-183 background: Andrewy Bada/Shutterstock, Inc.; 183 bottom: Scruggelgreen/Shutterstock, Inc.; 183 top: Andrewy Bada/Shutterstock, Inc.; 185 bottom: oksanaphoto/iStockphoto; 185 top center: PinkBadger/iStockphoto; 185 top left: bedo/iStockphoto; 186-187: Luis Louro/Dreamstime; 188: Liz Van Steenburgh/Shutterstock, Inc.; 190-191: MR1805/iStockphoto; 192: fotostory/ Shutterstock; 193 top: USDA/Forest Service/USGS; 193 bottom: Katerina Sysoeva/Shutterstock, Inc.; 194 bottom: U.S. Coast Guard photograph by Petty Officer 2nd Class Kyle Niemi; 194 top: Mike Trenchard, Earth Sciences & Image Analysis Laboratory, Johnson Space Center/NASA; 195 top: Library of Congress; 195 center: OAR/ERL/National Severe Storms Laboratory (NSSL)

History: 196-197: Oliver Killig/picture-alliance/dpa/AP Images; 198 center bottom: Kharbine-Tapabor /The Art Archive at Art Resource, NY; 198 center top: Ron Leighton; 198 bottom: Ahazan/ Wikimedia; 198 top: NASA; 199 bottom: Timothy McCarthy/Art Resource, NY; 199 center bottom: The Granger Collection; 199 center top: Images of Africa Photobank/Alamy Images; 200 top: Mulad/Wikimedia; 201 top: bpk, Berlin/ Staatliche Museen/Art Resource, NY; 201: GL Archive/Alamy Images; 201: maria luisa berti/Thinkstock; 201: Photos.com/ Thinkstock; 202 top: Thyssen-Bornemisza Collection, Madrid, Spain/Bridgeman Images; 202 bottom: Look and Learn/Elgar Collection/Bridgeman Images; 202 center:

Answer

Answer to question on p. 329: Indiana (Indianapolis)

HIP/Art Resource, NY; 203: DEA Picture Library/Getty Images; 203: Pictorial Press Ltd/Alamy Images; 203: Niday Picture Library/Alamy Images; 204 bottom: Leonard Zhukovsky/Shutterstock, Inc.; 204 center: Lionel Cironneau/AP Images; 204 top: Private Collection/Prismatic Pictures/ Bridgeman Images; 205 bottom: Pablo Utrilla/Dreamstime; 205 center bottom: Dinodia Photos/Getty Images; 205: Library of Congress; 205: Print Collector/Getty Images; 206 top: Northfoto/Shutterstock, Inc.; 206 bottom: Specialist 2nd Class Justin Stumberg/U.S. Navy; 207 top: giulio napolitano/Shutterstock, Inc.; 207 center: Official White House Photo by Pete Souza; 207 bottom: U.S. State Department; 208-209: f11photo/Shutterstock, Inc.; 211: Architect of the Capitol; 214 top left: Alexander Shalamov/Dreamstime; 214 bottom left: Ron Leighton; 214 top right: FineArt/Alamy Images; 215: Bill Sponn; 215: C. Bevilacquadea/Getty Images; 215 bottom right: William A. Crafts/Wikimedia; 216 bottom: Corbis Images; 216: Archive Photos/Getty Images; 216: National Archives and Records Administration; 216 center bottom: Architect of the Capitol; 217 top: Museum of the City of New York, USA/ Bridgman Images; 217: Archive Images/ Alamy Images; 217: Library of Congress; 218: Library of Congress; 218: NASA; 219: NASA; 220 top: Carol M. Highsmith/LC-DIG-highsm-12368/Library of Congress; 220 bottom: U.S. Coast Guard/USGS; 221 top: NASA/Wikimedia; 221 bottom: Americanspirit/Dreamstime; 222-223: Michael Reynolds-Pool/Getty Images; 223 inset: Manuel Balce Ceneta/AP Images; 224 center: Firo002/Wikimedia; 224 bottom: Mesut Dogan/Shutterstock, Inc.; 225: Smithsonian National Museum of American History; 226 center left: Courtesy U.S. House of Representatives/Wikimedia; 226 center right: U.S. Senate Photographic Studio/Wikimedia; 227 bottom: Neamov/ Shutterstock, Inc.; 227 top: Mesut Dogan/ Shutterstock, Inc.; 231: gustavofrazao/ Fotolia; 232 $100 bill: newmoney.gov;

232 all other bills: Bureau of Engraving and Printing, U.S. Department of the Treasury; 232 all coins: United States Mint; 241 Dwight D. Eisenhower: Dwight D. Eisenhower Presidential Library and Museum; 241 John F. Kennedy: National Archives; 241 Lyndon Johnson: LBJ Library photo by Arnold Newman; 242 Richard M Nixon: National Archives; 242 Gerald Ford: Courtesy Gerald R. Ford Library; 242 Ronald Reagan: Ronald Reagan Presidential Library and Museum; 242 George HW Bush: George Bush Presidential Library and Museum; 243 Bill Clinton: The William J. Clinton Presidential Library; 243 George W. Bush: Eric Draper, White House; 243 Barack Obama Jr.: Pete Souza/Change.gov; 233-243 all other portraits: Library of Congress

Geography: 244-245: Ben Margot/AP Images; 246, 250 background: The World Factbook 2013-14, Central Intelligence Agency; 250 top: Chin Lee Ma/iStockphoto; 250 bottom: RazSvet/Shutterstock, Inc.; 250 bottom left: Yavuz Sariyildiz/ Shutterstock, Inc.; 251: Dan Price (ishnaf)/ Freeimages; 252 background: The World Factbook 2013-14, Central Intelligence Agency; 252 top: EcoPic/iStockphoto; 252 bottom: Ron Leighton; 253 left: Zhukov Oleg/Shutterstock, Inc.; 253 right: Johncarnemolla/Dreamstime; 254 background: The World Factbook 2013-14, Central Intelligence Agency; 254 top: abey/iStockphoto; 254 bottom: Scanrail/ Dreamstime; 255: National Park Service; 256 background: The World Factbook 2013-14, Central Intelligence Agency; 256 top: A.Ricardo/Shutterstock, Inc.; 256 bottom: Roberto Caucino/Dreamstime; 257: gary yim/Shutterstock, Inc.; 258 background: The World Factbook 2013-14, Central Intelligence Agency; 258 left: Radu Razvan/Shutterstock, Inc.; 258 right: Javier Martin/Shutterstock, Inc.; 259: RazSvet/Shutterstock, Inc.; 260 background: The World Factbook 2013-14, Central Intelligence Agency;

260 top: Shchipkova Elena; 260 bottom: Jeremy Richards/Thinkstock; 261: Derek Rogers/Dreamstime; 262 top, 262 bottom: The World Factbook 2013-14, Central Intelligence Agency; 263 top: Pniesen/Dreamstime; 263 bottom left: Andras Deak//Dreamstime; 263 bottom right: Salkit Leung/Dreamstime; 266 top: JonMilnes/Shutterstock, Inc.; 266 center: Jeff Schmaltz/MODIS Rapid Response Team/NASA; 266 bottom: Julien Hautcoeur/Dreamstime; 267 top: FabioFilzi/iStockphoto; 267 bottom: Ron Chapple/Dreamstime; 268-269 background: Oscity/Shutterstock, Inc.; 268 top: HABY/iStockphoto; 268 center: Lorcel G/Dreamstime; 268 bottom: Wollertz/Dreamstime; 270 top: National Park Service; 270 bottom: National Park Service; 272-273: turtix/Shutterstock, Inc.; 276-277: Kyodo via AP Images; 280 birds: zixian/Shutterstock, Inc.; 281: Ericsmandes/Shutterstock, Inc.; 282: Dana Ward/Shutterstock, Inc.; 283: Vladgalenko/Dreamstime; 284: Davemhuntphotography/Dreamstime; 285: TrudiDesign/Fotolia; 286: Moolkum/Shutterstock, Inc.; 287: Lena Ivanova/Shutterstock, Inc.; 288: Roman Zherdytskyi/Shutterstock, Inc.; 289: Augustas Didžgalvis/Wikimedia; 290: Filmfoto/Dreamstime; 291 left: Ron Leighton; 291 right: Jenkedco/Dreamstime; 292: Nataliaderiabina/Dreamstime; 293: Mikadun/Shutterstock, Inc.; 294: Ruta Production/Shutterstock, Inc.; 295: Anjo Kan/Shutterstock, Inc.; 296-297: Kungverylucky/Dreamstime; 298: Nathan Dappen/Dreamstime; 299: Zhukov Oleg/Shutterstock, Inc.; 300: Da Dendi Sherpa/AP Images; 301: Lili Rozet/Shutterstock, Inc.; 302: Meunierd/Dreamstime; 303: Olimpiu Alexa-pop/Dreamstime; 304: Hikrcn/Dreamstime; 305: Filip Fuxa/Dreamstime; 306: kbrowne41/Shutterstock, Inc.; 307: Denis Filatov/Shutterstock, Inc.; 308: TPm13thx/Shutterstock, Inc.; 309: Lukasz Janyst/Shutterstock, Inc.; 310: Emanuele Leoni/Dreamstime; 311 main: Member/Shutterstock, Inc.; 311 inset: bodu9/Thinkstock; 312 inset: FloridaStock/Shutterstock, Inc.; 312-313: orangecrush/Shutterstock, Inc.; 316-317 Quarter-dollar coin images: United States Mint; 318 top: Lavinia Marin/Freeimages; 318 bottom: Birdiegal717/Dreamstime; 320: Sherry Young/Dreamstime; 321 top: KyleAndMelissa22/Wikimedia; 321 bottom left: Michelle Dennix/Freeimages; 322: Giorces/Wikimedia; 323 top: winhorse/iStockphoto; 323 bottom: Kenneth Keifer/Shutterstock, Inc.; 324 top: Kobby Dagan/Dreamstime; 324 bottom: Valerie Cantone/Dreamstime; 325: boboling/iStockphoto; 326 top: Pavel Losevsky/Dreamstime; 326 bottom: B Creavis/Freeimages; 327: AppalachianViews/iStockphotos; 328 top left: Galyna Andrushko; 328 top right: Marc Venema/Shutterstock, Inc.; 328 bottom: Library of Congress; 329: Daniel M. Silva/Shutterstock, Inc.; 330: BMJ/Shutterstock, Inc.; 331 bottom: Lee Karney/U.S. Fish & Wildlife Service; 332 top: Belozorova Elena/Shutterstock, Inc.; 332 bottom: Jorg Hackemann/Dreamstime; 333: Library of Congress; 334 top: Svetlana Foote/Dreamstime; 334 bottom: Wildnerspix/Shutterstock, Inc.